ANXIETY DISORDERS OF CHILDHOOD

Edited by
RACHEL GITTELMAN
New York State Psychiatric Institute and
College of Physicians and Surgeons, Columbia University

THE GUILFORD PRESS
New York London

© 1986 The Guilford Press
A Division of Guilford Publications, Inc.
200 Park Avenue South, New York, N.Y. 10003

Library of Congress Cataloging in Publication Data

Main entry under title:

Anxiety disorders of childhood.

  Includes bibliographies and indexes.
  1. Anxiety in children. I. Gittelman, Rachel.
[DNLM: 1. Anxiety Disorders—in infancy & childhood.
WS 350.6 A637]
RJ506.A58A59 1986   618.92'8522   85–30538
ISBN 0-89862-658-7

CONTRIBUTORS

David Behar, MD, Department of Psychiatry, Medical College of Pennsylvania, Philadelphia, Pennsylvania

Carol J. Berg, MA, Child Psychiatry Branch, National Institute of Mental Health, Bethesda, Maryland

Susan B. Campbell, PhD, Department of Psychology, University of Pittsburgh, Pittsburgh, Pennsylvania

Caryn L. Carlson, PhD, Department of Psychology, Indiana University, Bloomington, Indiana

Rolando G. Figueroa, PhD, Chief of Psychology, Georgia Retardation Center, Athens, Georgia

Rachel Gittelman, PhD, New York State Psychiatric Institute, and College of Physicians and Surgeons, Columbia University, New York, New York

Harold S. Koplewicz, MD, New York State Psychiatric Institute, and College of Physicians and Surgeons, Columbia University, New York, New York

Benjamin B. Lahey, MD, Department of Psychology, University of Georgia, Athens, Georgia

Melvin Lewis, MD, Child Study Center, Yale University, New Haven, Connecticut

Helen Orvaschel, PhD, University of Pittsburgh School of Medicine, Western Psychiatric Institute and Clinic, Pittsburgh, Pennsylvania

Joaquim Puig-Antich, MD, Department of Psychiatry, University of Pittsburgh School of Medicine, Western Psychiatric Institute and Clinic, Pittsburgh, Pennsylvania

Harris Rabinovich, MD, New York State Psychiatric Institute, and College of Physicians and Surgeons, Columbia University, New York, New York

Judith L. Rapoport, MD, Child Psychiatry Branch, National Institute of Mental Health, Bethesda, Maryland

David Shaffer, MB, BS, MRCP, FRCPsych, Division of Child Psychiatry, New York State Psychiatric Institute, and Departments of Clinical Psychiatry and Pediatrics, College of Physicians and Surgeons, Columbia University, New York, New York

Stephen J. Suomi, PhD, Laboratory of Comparative Ethology, National Institute of Child Health and Human Development, National Institutes of Health, Bethesda, Maryland

Paul D. Trautman, MD, New York State Psychiatric Institute, and College of Physicians and Surgeons, Columbia University, New York, New York

Myrna M. Weissman, PhD, Department of Psychiatry, Depression Research Unit, Yale University School of Medicine, New Haven, Connecticut

John S. Werry, MD, Department of Psychiatry, University of Auckland, Auckland, New Zealand

Theodore P. Zahn, PhD, Laboratory of Psychology and Psychopathology, National Institute of Mental Health, Bethesda, Maryland

PREFACE

Childhood anxiety disorders have recently attracted a great deal of attention. This interest has been sparked, in part, by the advances made in the study of adult anxiety disorders. Understandably, the hopeful expectation has been generated that similar developments may be possible in the evaluation and treatment of children. Renewed interest in childhood anxiety disorders results not only from the progress made in the treatment of adult anxiety disorders, and in the investigation of their biological characteristics, but also from accumulating evidence from varying approaches that adult anxiety states are often likely to be already manifest in childhood. Therefore, it makes sense to examine the early forms of what may later on become an adult anxiety disorder. The experience of pathological anxiety may prove to be a model of the old adage that the child is father to the man (or, perhaps more accurately, mother to the woman).

In the context of current clinical and research activities, this volume is very timely, bringing together experts in the evaluation and treatment of childhood disorders.

Because anxiety has played such a pivotal role in theories of personality development and psychopathology, a summary of the major views are included in this text. David Shaffer presents a critical overview of learning theories, with a pointed discussion of the problems associated with applying them to the clinical situation, while Paul Trautman reviews the historical changes in theories of anxiety, and in psychoanalytic concepts of development, and reports how these have affected notions of childhood anxiety.

Theoretical models of psychopathology are not mere intellectual exercises; they have direct influence on therapeutic practices. The treatment approaches that the behavioral and psychodynamic models have spurred are discussed by experts in the field: Benjamin Lahey and associates on behavior therapy, and Melvin Lewis on psychoanalytic psychotherapy. They are not only experienced practitioners, but also influential teachers of their respective forms of therapy.

The study of anxiety is at a distinct advantage in having excellent animal models. Stephen Suomi provides a rich, interesting summary of the findings from animal studies. In addition, he offers a lucid discussion of the potential usefulness of animal models, as well as their possible limitations, that will enable the untutored reader to appreciate the contribution that researchers with primates have made to our study of anxiety in children. In the related area of developmental aspects of anxiety, Susan Campbell provides a comprehensive, critical review of how anxiety manifests itself at different stages of development, how these patterns have been understood, and how concepts of child development are relevant to the understanding of pathological childhood anxiety.

My review chapter on the correlates, origins, and outcome of childhood anxiety disorders allows a glimpse of where the field stands. A key to furthering knowledge about important aspects of anxiety disorders in children is the study of anxiety in the population at large, not only in the clinic. Helen Orvaschel and Myrna Weissman summarize the epidemiologic studies and allow for an appreciation of the prevalence of fears in children, and their stability.

Anxiety, in children as well as adults, is a ubiquitous clinical phenomenon in mental disorders. Yet, two conditions, obsessive-compulsive and depressive disorders, stand out as having long been believed to be related to anxiety disorders. Judith Rapoport and her associates present data that raise doubts concerning this tenacious notion. Joaquim Puig-Antich and Harris Rabinovich discuss the overlap between depression and anxiety, and document that although the two states often coexist in children, their joint presence does not appear to have different clinical implications.

The use of medication to treat emotional disorders is a growing endeavor that has been extremely fruitful in providing efficacious interventions. However, pharmacotherapy in childhood anxiety disorders has received very limited attention. Our current state of knowledge is summarized in the chapter by myself and Harold Koplewicz.

No modern text on psychopathology would be complete without a review of assessment techniques. John Werry's chapter on the topic has the virtue of providing useful guidelines for the evaluation of anxiety in children, as well as giving pointed criticisms of the existing measures.

This book is ambitious in trying to report on diverse aspects of childhood anxiety. At the same time, its perusal will enable an appreciation of how much we still need to learn.

Rachel Gittelman

CONTENTS

‡ 1 ‡

ANXIETY-LIKE DISORDERS IN YOUNG NONHUMAN PRIMATES

STEPHEN J. SUOMI

INTRODUCTION

This chapter is about the development of anxiety-like disorders in nonhuman primate infants, juveniles, and adolescents. Our knowledge of such disorders is largely of quite recent origin. Indeed, it was once commonly thought that anxiety was an exclusive property of *Homo sapiens*. According to the classical orthodox view, all other animal species, including nonhuman primates, were seen as lacking the cognitive capacity and emotional richness deemed necessary to develop and sustain anxiety-based syndromes of psychopathology (e.g., Kubie, 1953). Such beliefs have changed considerably during the past two decades, due in part to new interests among clinicians regarding the origins and expression of human anxiety, and partly as the result of major advances in what we know about cognitive, emotional, social, and physiological development in nonhuman primates.

There is currently little serious argument about the existence of compelling nonhuman primate analogues to human anxiety disorders. The evidence to date indicates that expressions of anxiety are ubiquitous among virtually all advanced primate species, especially in certain individuals of particular ages under specific environmental conditions. The real questions relevant to this volume concern to what extent the careful study of such anxious-like phenomena in nonhuman

Stephen J. Suomi. Laboratory of Comparative Ethology, National Institute of Child Health and Human Development, National Institutes of Health, Bethesda, Maryland.

1

primates can add meaningfully to our ability to identify, understand, and ultimately treat anxiety disorders in young humans. This chapter addresses such questions.

The chapter begins with some background considerations about the nature of developmental approaches to the study of psychopathology and the issue of cross-species generality between human and nonhuman primate data. There follows a description of the major behavior patterns and concomitant physiological changes that characterize anxiety reactions in macaque monkeys. In these primate species the behavioral expressions of anxiety change throughout development and generally differ somewhat among subjects of contrasting early rearing histories. Nevertheless, certain physiological concomitants of these different behavioral expressions of axiety seem strikingly similar across different ages and species. Moreover, it is clear that certain physical and social environmental settings or events are especially likely to elicit particular displays of anxiety, and one particular class of anxiety-eliciting events—separations from family and/or friends—is discussed. An examination of individual differences in the frequency and intensity of anxiety reactions then is presented. Finally, some implications of the results of research carried out with macaque monkeys for understanding and treating anxiety disorders in human children and adolescents are addressed.

DEVELOPMENTAL ISSUES IN THE STUDY OF CHILDHOOD PSYCHOPATHOLOGY

It can be persuasively argued that few areas of scientific inquiry pose more formidable challenges—theoretical, empirical, or applied—than the study of developmental anomalies, especially in organisms whose nervous systems remain relatively "plastic" throughout most of their respective life spans. Those who study anxiety disorders in children must routinely deal with biologic systems that often express themselves in quite independent fashion at different levels of analysis. Researchers and clinical workers in this area are frequently faced with decisions as to whether the phenomenon under investigation truly represents a pathology rather than merely being "unusual" or extreme in the statistical sense alone. Moreover, there are profound complications that accompany rigorous study of any developing systems or individuals, relative to those that are already mature and/or stable, whether normal or anomalous. As stated by Sackett, Sameroff, Cairns, and Suomi:

> The study of development poses a major paradox for students of behavior. The problem arises from the fact that change is an essential property of development. Virtually all features of the organism undergo modification durings its life span. On the other hand, continuity over time seems essential for individual uniqueness, organization and the maintenance of integrated patterns of behavior. The paradox is simply this: How can continuity and persistence be achieved in an organismic system that necessarily undergoes maturational, interactional, and social–cultural change? (1981, p. 23)

To illustrate some of the problems for research and clinical application inherent in this basic paradox of development, consider the case of an individual who, as a young child, exhibits an apparently intense fear of strange small furry animals. The fear might seem irrational to a knowledgeable adult, especially if most other children of similar age not only were unafraid of the same small animals but actually were attracted to them through curious interest, for example, typically expressing a desire to pet or pick them up. This child's fear might also seem irrational if similarly intense reactions were not elicited by familiar small (or even large) furry animals such as the family dog, or even toward new arrivals, such as a litter of kittens. Why should this child have such a phobia when others do not, and why should the fear be elicited by some small furry animals but not by others?

What might be the origin of this particular childhood phobia? There exist several possible etiologies. Perhaps the child was once bitten by a rat or, more likely, was surprised by a small wild animal on a walk home alone in the dark. Alternatively, this child might possess a biologically based predisposition to be unusually fearful of such stimuli, ultimately traceable to specific genetic material not present in the DNA of his or her peers. A psychoanalytic interpretation might postulate the origin of the fear to lie in symbolic representation of the genital region of the child's mother. On the other hand the child might have once witnessed his or her mother's screaming reaction to the sight of a mouse running across the kitchen floor and thereafter be affected by that specific observational learning experience. This list of possible etiologies is clearly not exhaustive, nor are the alternatives necessarily mutually exclusive to one another. Sorting them out is usually no easy matter for even the most competent researchers and therapists.

Once it has been ascertained that the child's extreme fear of strange small furry animals is abnormal, what should be done? Is some form of intervention, perhaps even pharmacologic treatment, the appropriate course of action, or will the child simply "outgrow" the phobia without any formal treatment as he or she passes through childhood? Finally, what will be the long-term prognosis for this individual, and will it make any difference in the long run whether or not he or she received some form of treatment for the phobia as a child? For example, should an individual who had a small animal phobia as a child be at greater than normal risk for developing other types of phobias (or other forms of psychopathology) later in life, relative to individuals with no history of childhood phobias, and what might be the implications for treatment of these adult disorder(s)?

Most of these questions could be posed in similar form for practically any childhood anxiety disorder or, for that matter, any other psychopathology displayed early in life. These questions address very basic issues in the scientific study and clinical treatment of developmental disorders. Unfortunately, these questions are also usually very difficult to investigate directly in rigorous scientific fashion in most child clinical populations. The ethical and practical problems typically encountered in characterizing symptoms, iden-tifying etiologies, and fashioning effective treatments for developing young humans are trying enough without even considering the study of long-term consequences, which ideally should be examined in prospective longitudinal fashion over at least a generation's time (cf. Sackett *et al.*, 1981), but for which the bulk of our current knowledge comes from retrospective reports.

ANIMAL MODELS AND CROSS-SPECIES GENERALITY

Faced with the difficulties outlined above, some developmental and clinical researchers have turned to *animal models* for answers to basic questions about developmental psychopathologies. Animal models, broadly defined, are experimental efforts to reproduce in nonhuman subjects the essential features of various human disorders or conditions

(Suomi, 1982). Historically, animal models have been widely utilized throughout the biomedical sciences, and few major medical advances during the past century have been achieved without employing some form of animal model in at least some phase of the relevant research. Nevertheless, one might reasonably ask why any researcher interested in learning more about a particular human disorder would choose to study its attempted reproduction in a different species, when presumably plenty of affected human cases exist for possible study.

Perhaps the most powerful motivation for developing animal models stems from the many problems inherent in almost all developmental studies involving human subjects or patients, as noted above. Research with animals is not subject to the same limitations and restrictions that clearly characterize most human clinical research. Although there presently exist numerous regulations and ethical standards governing animal research—and they recently have become far more rigorous than they were only a decade ago—such regulations and standards nevertheless allow manipulations and measurements with animals that simply are not ethically permissible or practically possible with human subjects. For example, animals can be placed in prospective studies specifically designed to induce pathology. They can be reared, maintained, and observed in well-controlled laboratory environments literally every day of their lives. A variety of measures of behavioral and physiological functioning too obtrusive to be gathered from humans can routinely be collected in animal subjects. Various therapeutic treatments can be administered and their effects determined with certainty in animal subjects via careful comparison with scientifically appropriate controls. Finally, and perhaps most significantly from a developmental perspective, because most laboratory animals develop more rapidly and have shorter natural life spans than humans, long-term consequences of pathology or effectiveness of treatment can be assessed in a fraction of the time it would take to obtain comparable longitudinal human developmental data.

Animal models, of course, are empirically meaningful and clinically useful only to the extent that they *generalize* to the human disorder or condition being modeled. In recent years a number of investigators have offered relatively objective criteria by which animal models can be judged with respect to such generality (e.g., McKinney & Bunney, 1969; Harlow & Suomi, 1974; Abramson & Seligman, 1977; Kornetsky, 1977; Suomi & Immelmann, 1983). These criteria include commonality between animal model and human phenomenon with

respect to etiology, behavioral symptomatology, concomitant physiological characteristics, effective therapeutic treatments, and parallel or
identical ultimate and proximate factors. We now know that there
exist different degrees of cross-species generality, with correspondingly different implications for the validity and utility of the specific
animal model under consideration.

Some animal models bear only superficial similarity to human
phenomena in terms of their basic features and essential characteristics, yet clearly share some common principles with the human
case. For example, numerous authors (e.g., Bowlby, 1969; Hoffman &
Ratner, 1973) have pointed out similarities between the phenomenon
of filial imprinting in newly hatched ducklings and the development of
mother-directed attachment by human infants. In both cases the
ducklings and the human infants must be exposed to their mothers (or
appropriate surrogates) during sensitive phases early in life in order
for species-typical social relationships to emerge and be maintained
later in life (cf. Lorenz, 1935; Bowlby, 1969; Immelmann & Suomi,
1981). These phenomena are clearly not homologous, however; the
parameters of the respective sensitive phases differ dramatically, and
the actual physiological mechanisms involved in forming and
maintaining the social bonds with mother are obviously not equivalent
in the two species (Harlow, Gluck, & Suomi, 1972). On the other hand,
these two phenomena clearly have some common features; for
example, both involve sensitive phases that may have life-long
consequences for the behavioral repertoires of the infants involved,
and both illustrate the principle that socialization and species
recognition begins with the early formation of a one-to-one bond.
Nevertheless, it is difficult to simulate realistically most complex
aspects of human mother–infant attachment within the framework of
filial imprinting, at least as it occurs in ducklings.

Meaningful applications of these types of animal models have
been limited. In some cases they have been employed as screening
devices for new pharmacologic compounds designed to treat various
human disorders, even though the drug effects in the animal subjects
may bear only superficial resemblance to the human disorder (cf.
Kornetsky, 1977, for the relevant example of Conditioned Avoidance
Responding [CAR] paradigms as screening devices for anxiolytic
compounds). These kinds of animal models can also provide important
heuristic insights or help integrate disparate sets of cross-species data
(cf. McKinney & Bunney, 1969), even if their immediate practical

applications are more restricted than those of animal models based on more compelling generalizations.

A more useful class of models can be found in those that are *simulative* in nature. Here, some features of the animal model are essentially identical to corresponding components of the human disorder or phenomenon, although the generalization may be incomplete in other aspects. For example, consider the comparison between "amphetamine psychosis" in humans and in rhesus monkeys. Chronic amphetamine abuse invariably results in excessive stereotypic activities, visual hallucinations, and displays of obvious paranoia in human patients (Angrist & Gershon, 1970). Chronic administration of amphetamine to rhesus monkeys living in social groups results in the appearance of stereotypic activity, displays of inappropriate social "signals" in the absence of obvious social stimulation, and excessive monitoring of familiar group members largely ignored prior to drug treatment (Haber, Barchas, & Barchas, 1977). It seems reasonable to conclude that many basic symptoms characteristic of human amphetamine psychosis can be simulated in these rhesus monkeys. There are also some behavioral differences between the drug-treated monkeys and human "speed freaks," however; verbal expressions of paranoia by the latter but not the former provide one example. Here, as in other simulative animal models, the generalization between human and animal data is not entirely complete.

Because simulative animal models involve cross-species comparisons that are not identical in all respects, direct application of data from these animal models to human cases or situations carries some risk, and the risk increases, the less complete the generalization becomes. These models can be used effectively, however, to simulate different etiologies proposed for the human disorder being modeled, and parametric studies of different treatment regimes can be carried out. In addition, relationships between behavioral changes and alternation of physiological processes can be readily explored in these models.

Finally, the most scientifically valid and practically useful forms of animal models are those that are *substitutive* in nature. Substitutive animal models are those in which the phenomena or characteristics in question for the human case are in virtually all respects identical to those in the animal model; that is, the cross-species generalization is complete. An example of such complete generalization can be found in the visual system of humans and chimpanzees. The basic components of the system (e.g., cornea, iris, lens, rods, cones, fovea, bipolar cells, horizontal cells, optic nerve, etc.) are the same in humans and chimpanzees in both their respective structure and their respective functions. Moreover, the basic operating characteristics of the human visual system (e.g., relatively poor night vision, range of visual acuity, structural and functional changes during early development and advanced age, etc.) are matched by those in chimpanzees, suggesting parallel evolutionary selection pressures for the visual system in both species. Perhaps most importantly from the standpoint of modeling, the kinds of *disorders* of the visual system that routinely occur in human populations (e.g., myopia, astigmatism, glaucoma, etc.) are also seen in chimpanzee subjects. Indeed, if it were not for ethical and moral reasons one could envision a chimpanzee "eye bank" for humans and *vice versa*. In truly substitutive animal models, a system in the nonhuman subject can be literally substituted for the comparable system in a human patient.

The scientific potential and the possible practical applications of substitutive animal models are enormous. They permit researchers to substitute directly animal subjects for human patients or clients in developing, practicing, and assessing diagnostic and treatment procedures. The use of these models permits far more carefully controlled and rigorous experimentation than is almost ever possible with human subjects, and the results of these different studies can then be directly applied to knowledge and treatment of the human disorder. Unfortunately, animal models that are truly substitutive in all respects are relatively rare, because such complete generalization is seldom found between *any* two species.

In sum, animal models provide investigators with research tools that can be used to surmount, if not bypass completely, many of the methodological and practical obstacles facing researchers working with human subjects and patients. However, the actual usefulness of any animal model for either human research or clinical practice is ultimately a function of the degree to which the animal model generalizes to the human case in question. For the specific human case of childhood anxiety, this means that the promise that any animal model may carry—in terms of clarifying symptoms, specifying physiological concomitants and/or mechanisms, identifying actual etiologies, demonstrating treatment efficacy, and providing for long-term prognosis—depends in large part on how convincing are the parallels between the development of anxious-like behavior in animal subjects and the appearance of anxiety disorders in human children. In this area the most convincing animal data clearly come from studies of advanced nonhuman primate species.

EXPRESSIONS OF ANXIOUS-LIKE BEHAVIOR IN YOUNG RHESUS MONKEYS AND OTHER NONHUMAN PRIMATES

Anxiety at the human level is often characterized or conceptualized as a basic feeling or an emotional state. Feelings and emotional states, strictly speaking, are merely constructs, not really "existing" in the empirical sense. The "construct" anxiety, however, is thought to encompass physiological, cognitive, and behavioral components, and each of these can be measured empirically. Current definitions of human anxiety therefore tend to focus on such measurements, even though the phenomena they measure often represent quite different levels of analysis.

Even the most sophisticated nonhuman primate models of human anxiety are likewise forced to rely on measures of behavior, cognitive performance, and physiological change to define and assess "anxiety" in their nonhuman primate subjects. Furthermore, verbal verification by human subjects or patients of their current feeling or mood state cannot be modeled in any nonhuman primate subject, so primate investigators must necessarily infer such states from their subjects' activities (both external and internal) in particular situations or environmental conditions. Most studies of anxious behavior in captive rhesus monkeys, as in other nonhuman primate species, have also relied heavily on the common characterization of human anxiety as involving fearful behavior in the apparent absence of any obvious fear stimulus (e.g., Bowlby, 1969; Zuckerman & Spielberger, 1976).

Thus, the most frequent descriptions of monkey anxiety have centered on the exhibition of behavior patterns and physiological changes normally associated with fear reactions but which are displayed in the absence of any obvious and immediate fear stimulus. Because monkeys of different ages react to fear-producing stimuli with quite different characteristic behavior patterns, it is not surprising that subjects of different ages likewise differ in how they display anxiety, at least at the behavior level.

For example, a rhesus monkey infant reared by its biological mother typically displays anxiety by sharply increasing the incidence and intensity of contact-seeking and maintaining behavior (attachment) directed toward her. Concomitant displays of facial grimaces and increases in nonnutritive nipple contact are also common. Correspondingly, social play, exploration, and locomotion away from the mother all but disappear. Such behavior characterizes an infant's reaction to the presentation of fear stimuli. Thus, when similar patterns are displayed in the absence of any apparent fear-producing stimulus (i.e., in situations where other infants readily locomote, explore, and play), inferences concerning anxiety can be made according to the previous definition.

Anxiety in juvenile (1- to 3-year-old) and adolescent (4- to 5-year-old) rhesus monkeys is often characterized by behavioral regression, in that patterns of behavior previously displayed only during infancy reappear in the monkeys' repertoires. For example, socially competent juveniles of both sexes may try to cling to their mothers or to a peer partner when anxious, even though normally they would rarely seek such contact after their 1st year of life. Anxious juveniles also exhibit agitated behavior typified by idiosyncratic stereotypes; they appear to be "on edge." Adolescents continue to express anxious behavior primarily through increases in agitated and stereotypic activity, often displaying regressive motor behavior. However, they do not regress all the way to infantile behavior patterns; for example, 5-year-old adolescent males do not attempt to cling to their mothers. Anxious juveniles and adolescents typically cease most exploratory, play, sexual, or grooming patterns of behavior more characteristic of normal juvenile and adolescent rhesus monkey activity.

Behavioral agitation is perhaps most characteristic of anxiety in young adult rhesus monkeys (6- to 8-year-olds). Anxious agitation in older monkeys can also appear in various forms, such as the repetitive pacing displayed by some "middle-aged" adults. Additionally, regressive behavior is often displayed. Monkeys who earlier in life developed individualized patterns of stereotypic activity are highly likely to return to such patterns when faced with situations thought to induce anxiety. In most cases "anxious" behavior in adult monkeys also interrupts their previously stable patterns of social and/or exploratory activity, as in younger rhesus monkey subjects. These behavioral forms of emotional expression are not unique to rhesus monkeys but instead appear to have widespread representation among other advanced nonhuman primate species, especially the great apes.

During the past few years a number of investigators have begun to study physiological correlates of behavioral patterns thought to denote anxiety in nonhuman primate subjects. Such work has encompassed subjects of different species, ages, and rearing histories; nevertheless, a general picture of substantial physiological activation concomitant with behavioral expressions of anxiety now seems to be emerging. Such activation is characterized by elevations in heart rate and body temperature (Reite, Short, Seiler, & Panley, 1981) and by immediate activation of the adrenocortical system (Coe & Levine, 1981; Levine, 1983). Any extreme elevation, however, is usually short-lived in nature for many of the above measures. Indeed, available evidence suggests that adrenocortical recovery generally precedes behavioral recovery following exposure to anxiety-inducing stimuli. On the other hand recent findings indicate that "anxious" subjects consistently have higher levels of neurohormonal and sympathetic arousal following challenge, and this tendency appears to be quite stable throughout development, at least under certain environmental conditions, as will be discussed subsequently.

To summarize, although monkeys of different ages have some-what different characteristic ways of displaying anxiety, certain common features do exist. First, the displays closely resemble those exhibited in the presence of fear-eliciting stimuli, yet they often occur in situations with no obvious external precipitating events. Second, the displays frequently involve specific patterns of behavior that may have been common earlier in the subject's life but currently have all but disappeared from the monkey's basic behavioral repertoire. In other words, anxious monkey behavior is often regressive in nature. Finally, anxiety in these subjects is usually characterized by general physiological activation, at least over the short term.

SITUATIONAL SPECIFICITY OF ANXIOUS-LIKE BEHAVIOR: SOCIAL SEPARATION

Over the past two decades a large number of researchers studying a variety of nonhuman species in a wide range of environmental settings have been particularly consistent in one conclusion: Young primates involuntarily separated from their mothers or other attachment objects almost always react at least initially as if they were greatly frightened or highly anxious. Indeed, in many cases the immediate separation reaction resembles that of human-like panic, although such behavior quickly disappears when the monkeys are returned to their familiar group and surroundings. However, in the days, weeks, and sometimes even months after such separation (and subsequent reunion), these subjects frequently display much higher levels of anxious-like behavior than they did prior to the separation; they appear to be "jumpy" and on edge. Stimuli that immediately preceded a given subject's separation thereafter may be able to trigger an extreme, albeit brief, "anxiety attack" in that subject by themselves (Suomi, Kraemer, Baysinger, & Delizio, 1981).

Evidence to date also suggests that there exists a variety of experiential factors that can not only increase a monkey's likelihood of displaying anxious behavior in response to social separation later in life but also affect the relative severity of such reactions when they are displayed. These factors include early or frequent separation from mother, rearing by a neglectful or abusive mother, frequent changes in the subject's social group composition, and lack of stability in that group's dominance hierarchy (Suomi et al., 1981). Compelling parallels to these monkey data can be found in the human anxiety literature.

Nevertheless, as rhesus monkey infants grow older, their behavioral reactions to separation from family or friends change dramatically in both form and apparent intensity (Higley, Suomi, & Delizio, 1984). This developmental change in behavioral reaction to separation appears to parallel the developmental changes in anxious-like behavior elicited in other environmental contexts (e.g., Suomi & Harlow, 1976; Suomi et al., 1981; Suomi, 1982). For example, most adolescent rhesus monkeys react to separation from familiar others not so much with panic or protest but instead with ever-increasing agitated activity, often of a highly stereotypic nature. In contrast to the truly dramatic increases in level of "coo" vocalizations typically displayed by separated infants, most adolescent monkeys react to separation with relative silence (Mineka, Suomi, & Delizio, 1981). Thus, the same basic experimental manipulation—separation of a subject from its closest conspecifics—yields qualitatively different (but nevertheless predictable) behavioral reactions from monkeys at different ages or stages of development.

In contrast the same separation manipulation produces qualitatively *similar* changes in some measures of physiological activation in infant, juvenile, adolescent, and middle-age monkeys alike. It is now well-established that rhesus monkey infants consistently react to short-term (e.g., 1–4 hours') separation from their social group with dramatic increases in output of plasma cortisol directly attributable to activation of the hypothalamic–pituitary–adrenal (HPA) axis (e.g., Mendoza, Smotherman, Miner, Kaplan, & Levine, 1978; Coe & Levine, 1981; Levine, 1983; Suomi, 1983). More recently, Scanlan (1984) has demonstrated similar increases over baseline levels of cortisol during the first 2 hours of separation from social group among adolescent (2–5 years), young adult (5–7 years), and middle-age adult (13–16 years) rhesus monkeys, although absolute levels of cortisol following separation appear to decline monotonically with increasing age.

Thus, the basic pattern of adrenocortical response to a standardized separation episode is roughly the same in infants, adolescents, and middle-age adults, even though the behavioral concomitants of these episodes change substantially as the subjects grow older. Whether other physiological changes accompanying separation (e.g., increases in heart rate), are likewise qualitatively similar for monkeys of vastly different ages is a question currently under investigation in my laboratory. At any rate, existing data regarding specific behavior patterns (e.g., high levels of coo vocalizations) and adrenocortical response to separation strongly suggest that the relationship between behavioral responses and physiological changes following separation is not the same in adolescence and adulthood as in infancy and childhood.

INDIVIDUAL DIFFERENCES IN EXPRESSION OF ANXIOUS-LIKE BEHAVIOR

Research that my colleagues and I have carried out in my laboratory over the past 6 years has revealed substantial individual differences among young rhesus monkeys in the extent and intensity of their expression of anxious-like behavior. We have found that some rhesus monkey infants, juveniles, and adolescents consistently display behavioral and physiological signs of fearfulness and anxiety in standardized situations where other rhesus monkeys of comparable age and social-rearing background consistently initiate exploratory behavior and/or playful social interactions. The standardized situations that elicit differential reactions in these monkeys typically involve exposure to moderately novel stimuli, or they present the subject with a mild challenge, such as brief separation from familiar conspecifics. Once a novel stimulus becomes familiar or the subject is returned to its social group, behavioral differences between these "anxiety-prone" or "timid" individuals and their more outgoing (and less cautious) peers generally disappear over time (Suomi, 1981). Nevertheless, longitudinal studies (e.g., Higley *et al.,* 1984) have demonstrated that infants who display fearful or anxious reactions to the standardized stimuli tend to remain likely to show anxious reactions to comparable stimuli or situations when they become juveniles, adolescents, and (among females, at least) young adults. Individuals who as infants reacted to these moderate environmental manipulations with exploration or play rather than with anxious-like behavior are unlikely to display anxious behavior in the face of equivalent manipulations later in life. In other words individual differences in response to challenge that appear in infancy remain remarkably stable across major periods of physical, physiological, neuroendocrine, and behavioral development, even though (1) the characteristic mode of behavioral reaction changes dramatically during this time and (2) these individual differences in reactivity are masked during periods of uninterrupted group living.

Other research (e.g., Suomi, 1981) has revealed that monkey infants who are highly reactive behaviorally to mild challenge or stress also tend to be highly reactive physiologically, relative to their less (behaviorally) reactive peers. Once again, these individual differences in physiological reaction to challenge generally are masked during nonstressful baseline periods but nevertheless appear to be quite stable from infancy to at least adolescence. Thus, for example, infants who are high-reactive (behaviorally) display more dramatic and prolonged elevations over baseline in levels of plasma cortisol, and these differences observed early in life can be used to predict relative rank order of cortisol elevation following a comparable challenge later in life; such long-term predictive accuracy for cortisol values is not obtained when samples obtained during baseline periods are compared.

When young rhesus monkeys who differ in their behavioral and physiological reactions to mild challenge are subjected to more extreme environmental manipulations, the individual differences become exaggerated. For example, if social separation from mother or peers is prolonged for more than a few hours, many of those infants or juveniles who previously displayed the most extreme reactions to mild challenges begin to show symptoms of depression; that is, they become socially withdrawn and lethargic, and they frequently exhibit disruption of established patterns of eating and sleeping. In contrast, monkeys who typically do not display any evidence of anxiety in the face of novelty or mild challenge almost never develop depressive symptomology during extended periods of social separation. Instead, their physiological and neuroendocrine activity falls back within normal preseparation circadian ranges, and they typically initiate behavioral efforts to cope actively with their new environmental situation.

Thus, young rhesus monkeys who appear to be unusually fearful or anxious when faced with everyday changes in their physical and social environment are prone to display depressive reactions to social separations of more than a few hours' duration, while their "nonanxious" cohorts seem relatively immune to depression following separation. Such individual differences in separation reaction are remarkably stable in the face of repeated separations, whether the separations occur weekly or are interspersed between several months of uninterrupted group living. Indeed, behavior differences in relative intensity of both behavioral and physiological reactions to separation appear to be at least as stable developmentally as are the previously described individual differences in response to milder challenges or briefer separations.

It is worth noting that the data regarding individual differences in the nature and relative intensity of reactions to social separation manipulations are not without a few apparent paradoxes. Perhaps the most glaring paradox concerns the immediate response to separation from mother and/or peers displayed by "low-reactive" rhesus monkey infants. These infants typically do not respond to novelty or mild challenge with obvious displays of anxiety, they almost never exhibit depressive symptomatology in the face of extended social separations, and they are relatively unresponsive physiologically to such environmental manipulations. Yet, their *immediate behavioral* response to involuntary physical separation from rearing partners (mothers or peers) often involves far greater physical and vocal activity than the comparable response of infants who under conditions of "milder" challenge are judged to be highly reactive and who are at risk for depressive reactions to the separation, should it be extended. These otherwise low-reactive infants emit *higher* levels of coo vocalizations immediately following physical separation than do either their high-reactive cohorts or individuals whose relative reactivity is generally moderate. The tendency for low-reactive infants to be the most vocal is especially evident when the infants are able to see their mother or familiar peers during periods of physical separation. Indeed, for these infants, levels of coo vocalizations and increases in levels of plasma cortisol shortly after the onset of separation are significantly *negatively* correlated (Suomi, 1983; Levine, Franklin, & Gonzalez, 1984).

Given that many previous authors have used frequency of distress vocalizations as an index of intensity of disturbance and emotional upset (as well as relative strength of attachment to the separated other; cf. Bowlby, 1969), the inverse relationship between apparent vocal distress and measured adrenocorticoid response appears paradoxical. How can it be that those infants who display the most obvious "panic" upon separation are the least aroused physiologically at the time and in other challenge situations seem to be the least anxious? One way to account for this apparent inconsistency is to consider coo or "distress" vocalizations as representing activation of a species-normative *coping reaction,* rather than as an index of emotional distress. Levine *et al.* (1984), in particular, have argued convincingly that these vocalizations are the product of natural selection and, for monkey infants living in the wild, they serve to alert the attention of caretakers when the infants lose visual contact with them, such as during an extended period of foraging for food. Thus, according to this point of view, monkey infants who react to experimental separation with high levels of coo vocalization are actually summoning a prepotent behavioral reaction that in the wild would represent an effective coping response. A similar argument has been put forward by Kaufman (Kaufman, 1977; Kaufman & Rosenblum, 1967).

If one accepts the argument that coo vocalizations represent adaptive rather than debilitating responses to brief separation, then the apparent paradox disappears: monkeys who in other situations seem least anxious respond to potentially life-threatening (at least in the wild) separation with active, adaptive coping behavior and with relatively low physiological arousal. In contrast, monkey infants who routinely display anxious behavior and heightened physiological arousal in less threatening situations display relatively poor coping responses, and very great physiological arousal, in reaction to separation. Furthermore, as mentioned earlier, these high-reactive infants are at considerable risk to develop depressive patterns of behavior if the separation is prolonged—again, in contrast to their less reactive cohorts.

Longitudinal data gathered on high- and low-reactive rhesus monkeys when subjected to social separations during infancy and/or childhood can be used to predict individual differences in reaction to separations performed when these monkeys grow to adolescence and young adulthood, as was previously discussed. However, neither behavioral nor physiological data collected on high- and low-reactive infants and juveniles under normative conditions (i.e., those not involving any obvious challenge or stress) appear to be useful in predicting relative stress reactivity in these monkeys later in life. In fact, data collected from normative situations early in life generally do not even provide accurate predictions of individual differences in either behavior or physiology in normative settings later in life. In other words individual differences in stress reactivity tend to be masked or otherwise obscured when subjects are not under conditions of stress or challenge, whether they are infants, juveniles, adolescents, or young adults at the time of the assessment.

Thus, individual differences in response to stress and challenge can be detected early in life, and these differences are remarkably stable throughout development, even though the actual behavior patterns characterizing stress reactivity change substantially from infancy to adulthood and even though these differences tend to disappear under nonstressful conditions. What might be the origin of these individual differences in relative stress reactivity? It is apparent that a variety of environmental factors can influence how often any given individual is likely to display evidence of anxiety; these factors include early or repeated separation from mother, prolonged experience with a neglectful or abusive caretaker, and living in a chronically unstable social environment, among others (Suomi et al., 1981; Suomi, 1983). However, it also appears that observed individual differences in rhesus monkey stress reactivity may carry a substantial genetic component.

We now know that rhesus monkey infants reared under identical circumstances are more likely to share the same relative stress reactivity the more closely they are related genetically, even if they are not reared by their biologic mothers and do not interact with each other while they are growing up. More specifically, among siblings and half-siblings separated from their mothers at birth and reared apart but in identical laboratory environments, there is significantly less variability in cortisol levels and behavioral scores following stress than there is between identically reared but genetically unrelated individuals (Suomi, 1981; Scanlan, Suomi, Higley, Scallet, & Kraemer, 1982).

Similar results have been obtained using a measure of psycho-physiological reactivity (Suomi *et al.*, 1981). These findings, of course, provide only indirect evidence of any so-called genetic component for relative stress reactivity in populations of rhesus monkeys, and more direct evidence of heritability (e.g., that obtained from analyses of cellular or chromosomal material) has yet to be obtained. Nevertheless, an increasing body of pedigree data from my laboratory's rhesus colony is consistent with the hypothesis that high stress reactivity involves a highly heritable trait characteristic.

Whether or not one accepts the premise that individual differences in stress reactivity are at least in part reflective of genomic differences within rhesus monkey populations, the fact remains that high stress reactivity is a relatively stable characteristic of individual monkeys throughout major periods of development, even if masked under stress-free conditions. How early in life can such a characteristic be detected or predicted? Recent studies (e.g., Suomi, 1983, 1984) have suggested that individual differences in behavioral expressions of "anxiety" do not begin to stabilize until the 2nd month of life in rhesus monkey infants (a roughly comparable developmental age for human infants would be 4–8 months), while individual differences in cortisol levels following a standard challenge are predictively useless prior to 30 days of age. Nevertheless, Schneider (1984) has developed a standardized battery of neonatal reflex and state assessment tests (based in large part on current human pediatric neonatal exam protocols) that differentiate infants in terms of muscle tone and predominant state as early as 1–2 weeks of age, and these measures appear to be predictive of both behavioral and physiological stress reactivity later in development. It is worth noting that characteristics that appear to differentiate future high reactors from low reactors essentially disappear from the young monkeys' behavioral repertoires after 6 weeks or so (Suomi, 1984), but by that time individual differences in actual stress reactivity have already begun to stabilize developmentally.

FUTURE RESEARCH DIRECTIONS AND POSSIBLE HUMAN APPLICATIONS FOR STUDIES OF ANXIOUS-LIKE DISORDERS IN MONKEYS

The results of studies summarized in this chapter reveal that rhesus monkeys are clearly capable of displaying behavioral and physiological reactions that provide compelling analogues, if not homologues, to at least some forms of human anxiety. These reactions can be reliably elicted (at least in some individuals) under certain laboratory conditions, but they also can be observed among free-ranging groups of monkeys growing up in naturalistic environments. Although the characteristic forms of behavioral reaction typically undergo dramatic developmental change, at least some physiological concomitants are developmentally stable. While certain environmental events, in both laboratory and field settings, consistently result in some display of fearfulness or anxiety by virtually all subjects, there are developmentally stable individual differences in both the intensity and duration of these reactions, as well as in the range of other environmental events or situations that will elicit comparable reactions. These individual differences may be in part genetically determined; at the very least, they can be prediced quite early in life, even though they are apparently masked in the absence of precipitating environmental stimulation.

The capability to characterize individuals very early in life in terms of their likely reactivity status later in development makes it possible to carry out prospective longitudinal studies that systematically manipulate the frequency, intensity, and timing, as well as the source, of stressful or challenging events and situations for monkeys of known stress reactivity predisposition. In this way researchers can identify possible genetic–environmental interactions in the etiology of anxious-like behavior for specific individuals. For example, in an ongoing study in our laboratory, neonates of known pedigree who have been identified as potential high reactors or potential low reactors are being cross-fostered with multiparous females who have a history of either unusually nurturant or unusually punitive maternal treatment of previous offspring. Thus, these high and low reactive monkeys are being reared under circumstances in which their respective foster mothers are likely to buffer them from environmental stresses or challenges (in the case of nurturant foster mothers), as opposed to actually contributing and perhaps exaggerating such stress (in the case of punitive foster mothers). Research of this sort can be used to model various proposed etiologies for different forms of human anxiety.

Identification of monkeys who differ in relative reactivity also permits research efforts that focus on physiological and/or biochemical pathways or mechanisms that might underlie the observed differences in reactivity. Such studies can encompass whole physiological systems, such as the HPA axis, or they can be restricted to more molecular levels of analysis, such as specific neurotransmitter–receptor binding sites. Pharmacologically based investigations can be directed not only toward elucidation of mode of action of various anxiolytic compounds (and whether such modes differ either qualitatively or quantitatively in high- vs. low-reactive subjects), but also toward the development of more "efficient" screening techniques for new compounds, such as by using only high-reactive subjects in screening tests. Finally, one can conduct prospective longitudinal studies in which therapeutic or preventive interventions are initiated for high-reactive monkeys at various points in development, and not only short-term efficacy but also long-term consequences regarding subsequent risk status can be assessed in broad-ranging systematic fashion. Some of these possible studies are currently in progress or in planning in my laboratory.

To what extent can research utilizing nonhuman primate models of childhood anxiety disorders add meaningfully to diagnosis, treatment, and understanding of the human disorders themselves? Many of the studies summarized in this chapter have involved monkey models that are at least simulative in nature, and some might actually be substitutive at certain levels of analysis. For example, Kagan (1982) has reported that human toddlers and preschool children display developmentally stable individual differences in a personality or behavioral characteristic that Kagan terms "timidity" or "vigilance." Not only do some of these children consistently display fearfulness, anxiety, and cautious withdrawal in the face of novelty or challenge (but *not* in the absence of stress), but they also show individual differences in psychophysiological and adrenocorticoid reactivity that appear to closely parallel the rhesus monkey data previously described. To date, no investigator has prospectively studied possible developmental antecedents of relative timidity or vigilance among human neonates, nor has differential risk for development of childhood anxiety disorders or various forms of subsequent adult psychopathology been demonstrated for timid or vigilant children. However, given the monkey data, it is not surprising that such human studies are currently being planned by several investigators.

Regardless of whether there exists substitutive generality between any monkey model and actual clinical cases of human childhood anxiety disorders, two general principles that emerge from the monkey data seem relevant to human concerns. First, there are clearly some situations in which displays of fear and/or anxiety represent perfectly normal, developmentally appropriate reactions that most likely have been shaped by natural selection. Indeed, when a particular individual fails to display fear or anxiety in these situations, something is probably amiss. On the other hand, a reaction that is appropriate in one situation or at a given stage of development might be quite abnormal in a different context or if displayed by a chronologically older individual. It appears unwise to focus exclusively on particular behavioral patterns or physiological responses without considering situational and developmental factors.

A second principle concerns individual differences and possible etiological roots of childhood anxiety disorders. Even if there is, in fact, a clear-cut genetic difference between high-reacting and low-reacting rhesus monkey infants, and even if such hypothesized genetically determined individual differences generalize to human infants and children, it is wise to remember that a mere predisposition does not a full-blown syndrome make. There is no reason to believe that high-reactive infants will inevitably develop childhood anxiety disorders or other forms of psychopathology when they grow up. We already know that high-reactive monkeys are indistinguishable from their low-reactive counterparts when they are observed in benign physical and social settings. It certainly is possible that various coping strategies or styles could be acquired by high-reactive individuals during development that would minimize their apparent susceptibility if and when novelty or stress is actually encountered. Such a possibility holds considerable promise for high-reactive monkey infants and juveniles, and there is every reason to believe that it could hold at least as much promise for at-risk human children as well.

REFERENCES

Abramson, L. Y., & Seligman, M. E. P. Modeling psychopathology in the laboratory: History and rationale. In J. D. Maser & M. E. P. Seligman (Eds.), *Psychopathology: Experimental models.* San Francisco: Freeman, 1977.

Angrist, B., & Gershon, S. The phenomenology of experimentally induced amphetamine psychosis—Preliminary observations. *Biological Psychiatry,* 1970, *2,* 95–107.

Bowlby, J. *Attachment and loss* (Vol. 1: *Attachment*). New York: Basic Books, 1969.

Coe, C. L., & Levine, S. Normal responses to mother–infant separation in nonhuman primates. In D. Klein & J. Rabkin (Eds.), *Anxiety: New research and changing concepts.* New York: Raven Press, 1981.

Haber, S., Barchas, P. R., & Barchas, J. D. Effects of amphetamine on social behavior of rhesus macaques: An animal model of paranoia. In I. Hanin & E. Usdin (Eds.), *Animal models in psychiatry and neurology.* New York: Pergamon Press, 1977.

Harlow, H. F., Gluck, J. P., & Suomi, S. J. Generalization of behavioral data between nonhuman and human animals. *American Psychologist,* 1972, *27,* 709–716.

Harlow, H. F., & Suomi, S. J. Induced depression in monkeys. *Behavioral Biology,* 1974, *12,* 273–296.

Higley, J. D., Suomi, S. J., & Delizio, R. D. *Continuity of social separation behaviors from infancy to adolescence.* Paper presented at the 7th meeting of the American Society of Primatologists, Arcata, Calif., 1984.

Hoffman, H. S., & Ratner, A. M. A reinforcement model of imprinting: Implications for socialization in monkeys and men. *Psychological Review,* 1973, *80,* 527–544.

Immelmann, K., & Suomi, S. J. Sensitive phases in development. In K. Immelmann, G. Barlow, P. Petrinovich, & M. Main (Eds.), *Behavioral development: The Bielefeld interdisciplinary project.* New York: Cambridge University Press, 1981.

Kagan, J. Heart rate and heart rate variability as signs of a temperamental dimension. In C. E. Izard (Ed.), *Measuring emotions in infants and children.* New York: Cambridge University Press, 1982.

Kaufman, I. C. Developmental considerations of anxiety and depression: Psychobiological studies in monkeys. In T. Shapiro (Ed.), *Psychoanalysis and contemporary science.* New York: International Universities Press, 1977.

Kaufman, I. C., & Rosenblum, L. A. The reaction to separation in infant monkeys: Anaclitic depression and conservation-withdrawal. *Psychosomatic Medicine,* 1967, *29,* 648–675.

Kornetsky, C. Animal models: Promises and problems. In I. Hanin & E. Usdin (Eds.), *Animal models in psychiatry and neurology.* New York: Pergamon Press, 1977.

Kubie, L. S. The concept of normality and neurosis. In M. Heiman (Ed.), *Psychoanalysis and social work.* International Universities Press, 1953.

Levine, S. A psychobiological approach to the ontogeny of coping. In N. Garmezy & M. Rutter (Eds.), *Stress, coping, and development in children.* New York: McGraw-Hill, 1983.

Levine, S., Franklin, D., & Gonzalez, C. A. Influence of social variables on the biobehavioral response to separation in rhesus monkey infants. *Child Development,* 1984, *55,* 1386–1393.

Lorenz, K. Der Kumpan in der Umwelt des Vogels. *Journal für Ornithologie,* 1935, *83,* 137–213.

McKinney, W. T., & Bunney, W. E. Animal model of depression. *Archives of General Psychiatry,* 1969, *21,* 240–248.

Mendoza, S. P., Smotherman, W. P., Miner, M., Kaplan, J., & Levine, S. Pituitary–adrenal response to separation in mother and infant squirrel monkeys. *Developmental Psychobiology,* 1978, *11,* 169–175.

Mineka, S., Suomi, S. J., & Delizio, R. D. Multiple separations in adolescent monkeys: An opponent-process interpretation. *Journal of Experimental Psychology: General,* 1981, *110,* 56–85.

Reite, M., Short, R., Seiler, C., & Pauley, J. D. Attachment, loss, and depression. *Journal of Child Psychology and Psychiatry,* 1981, *22,* 141–169.

Sackett, G. P., Sameroff, A. S., Cairns, R. B., & Suomi, S. J. Continuity and change in behavioral development. In K. Immelmann, G. Barlow, L. Petrinovich, & M. Main (Eds.), *Behavioral development: The Bielefeld interdisciplinary project.* New York: Cambridge University Press, 1981.

Scanlan, J. M. *Adrenocortical and behavioral responses to acute novel and stressful conditions: The influence of gonadal status, timecourse of response, age, and motor activity.* Unpublished master's thesis, University of Wisconsin at Madison, 1984.

Scanlan, J. M., Suomi, S. J., Higley, J. D., Scallet, A. S., & Kraemer, G. W. Stress and heredity in adrenocortical response in rhesus monkeys *(Macaca mulatta). Society for Neuroscience Abstracts,* 1982, *8,* 461.

Schneider, M. L. *Neonatal assessment in rhesus monkeys.* Unpublished master's thesis, University of Wisconsin at Madison, 1984.

Suomi, S. J. Genetic, maternal, and environmental influences on social development in rhesus monkeys. In B. Chiarelli & R. Corruccini (Eds.), *Primate behavior and sociobiology.* Berlin: Springer-Verlag, 1981.

Suomi, S. J. Animal models of human psychopathology: Relevance for clinical psychology. In P. Kendall & J. Butcher (Eds.), *Handbook of research methods in clinical psychology.* New York: Wiley, 1982.

Suomi, S. J. Social development in rhesus monkeys: Consideration of individual differences. In A. Oliverio & M. Zappella (Eds.), *The behavior of human infants.* New York: Plenum Press, 1983.

Suomi, S. J. The development of affect in rhesus monkeys. In N. Fox & R. Davidson (Eds.), *The psychobiology of affective development.* Hillsdale, N.J.: Erlbaum, 1984.

Suomi, S. J., & Harlow, H. F. The facts and functions of fear. In M. Zuckerman & C. D. Spielberger (Eds.), *Emotions and anxiety.* Hillsdale, N.J.: Erlbaum, 1976.

Suomi, S. J., & Immelmann, K. On the process and product of cross-species generalization. In D. W. Rajecki (Ed.), *Studying man studying animals.* Hillsdale, N.J.: Erlbaum, 1983.

Suomi, S. J., Kraemer, G. U., Baysinger, C. M., & Delizio, R. D. Inherited and experiential factors associated with individual differences in anxious behavior displayed by rhesus monkeys. In D. Klein & J. Rabkin (Eds.), *Anxiety: New research and changing concepts.* New York: Raven Press, 1981.

Zuckerman, M., & Spielberger, C. D. (Eds.). *Emotions and anxiety.* Hillsdale, N.J.: Erlbaum, 1976.

‡ 2 ‡

DEVELOPMENTAL ISSUES
IN CHILDHOOD ANXIETY

SUSAN B. CAMPBELL

INTRODUCTION

Although anxiety and fear appear to be universal and permanent features of the human condition, their nature and development remain poorly understood. There is relatively wide agreement that fear and anxiety may be adaptive or maladaptive (e.g., Bowlby, 1973; Lewis & Brooks, 1974), either protecting the child from harm or interfering with exploration and environmental mastery.

Distinctions are often made between fear, which is focused on a specific object or situation, and anxiety, which is conceptualized as nonspecific, diffuse, and anticipatory (Johnson & Melamed, 1977; Miller, Barrett, & Hampe, 1974). However, as noted in DSM-III (American Psychiatric Association, 1980), both anxiety and fear are reflected in the same cognitive, affective, and physiological patterns including thoughts of imminent danger, feelings of apprehension, and autonomic reactions such as sweating, trembling, and gastrointestinal distress. Bowlby (1973) also recognizes that fear and anxiety evoke the same cluster of reactions and suggests that alarm and anxiety are two variants of the overall emotion of fear. He conceptualizes alarm as avoidance of the feared object and anxiety as stemming from the unavailability of an attachment figure, both serving the biologic function of protection. In the developmental literature, most attention has been paid to specific fears (Bronson, 1972; Jersild & Holmes, 1935; Scarr & Salapatek, 1970), with little mention of anxiety as a separate construct. These terms, therefore, will be used interchangeably.

Susan B. Campbell. Department of Psychology, University of Pittsburgh, Pittsburgh, Pennsylvania.

It is widely recognized that the behavioral manifestations of fear change, becoming more differentiated with development. Infants in the first weeks of life respond to fear-provoking stimuli with startle reactions and crying, relatively general signs of distress. With physical maturation and cognitive development, responses become more differentiated to include sobering and gaze aversion. Once the infant becomes mobile, more overt avoidance behavior becomes possible, such as moving away from the frightening stimulus and seeking contact with and comfort from the mother. However, as Lewis (1980) notes, these behaviors are not all necessarily indicative of fear. Gaze aversion may denote lack of interest; seeking contact with the mother may signal fatigue, hunger, or irritability. In children of preschool age and older, fear may or may not be directly or even overtly expressed, particularly as the nature of children's fears changes to include imaginary and anticipated events in addition to concrete stimuli (Jersild, Telford, & Sawrey, 1975). Thus, the child who is afraid of monsters may express bedtime fears or fear of the dark or may show apprehension indirectly through nightmares, bed-wetting, temper tantrums, social withdrawal, or aggressive behavior with peers. Wide individual differences exist in the way children express fears, and these are influenced by temperamental characteristics, contextual factors, and past experiences, as well as the child's age and developmental level. Thus, behavioral responses are a relatively poor index of fear, making empirical investigation of children's fears a difficult undertaking.

Despite these problems, studies have been conducted using behavioral observations of children's reactions to potentially fear-provoking stimuli (Scarr & Salapatek, 1970), parents as observers of their children's fears (Jersild & Holmes, 1935), parent reports on interviews (Lapouse & Monk, 1959) and questionnaires (Miller, Barrett, Hampe, & Noble, 1972), and the reports of the children themselves (Bauer, 1976). Some studies have catalogued the nature of children's fears across the age range (Angelino, Dollins, & Mech, 1956; Bauer, 1976; Jersild & Holmes, 1935; Maurer, 1965) and have noted that with development, children's fears undergo qualitative changes. Others have explored specific age-related fears such as fear of strangers (Morgan & Riccuiti, 1969; Lewis & Brooks, 1974) and test anxiety (Hill & Sarason, 1966). This chapter will focus on the development of children's fears and anxieties by attempting to integrate these descriptive studies with theoretical models.

Behavioral and psychoanalytic models are most commonly employed in the clinical literature, but neither adequately explains the origins of children's fears nor the nature of developmental changes. Since these theoretical models are reviewed elsewhere in this volume (see Chapters 8 and 9) they will not be dealt with here. Rather, cognitive–developmental and ethological constructs will be employed in an attempt to explain the origins and vicissitudes of children's fears.

THEORETICAL ISSUES

ETHOLOGICAL CONSTRUCTS

The ethological view of development rests on the assumption that much of behavior is biologically based and that species-specific response patterns are preprogrammed in meaningful ways. The focus is on the evolutionary adaptedness of species-typical behavior, studied within the ecological niche of the organism. Behavior is seen as being organized into systems that are adaptive and ultimately maximize the survival of the individual and the species (Bowlby, 1969, 1973; Blurton Jones, 1972; Charlesworth, 1974; Hess, 1970). Genetically programmed behaviors are necessary for the survival of the individual and are particularly important in early infancy, when the organism is helpless and dependent.

Within this framework, preprogrammed infant behaviors such as crying and clinging are assumed to promote and maintain proximity to caretakers, thereby protecting the infant from exposure or harm and ensuring sustenance (Ainsworth, 1973; Bowlby, 1969). Normal, healthy infants initially possess a small repertoire of genetically programmed social behaviors (clinging, sucking, visual following, orientation to the human voice, crying, and somewhat later, smiling), which are directed indiscriminately toward members of the species and serve to elicit caretaking behavior (Bowlby, 1969). Although the infant is entirely helpless and dependent on adults for protection and nurturance during the early months of life, these basic social capacities permit the infant to initiate interaction; for example, the crying of a distressed infant is likely to alert the mother, who will approach her infant and attend to the infant's needs. Further, infant behaviors such as clinging, smiling, and visual contact are highly rewarding to adults and serve not only to initiate, but to prolong sequences of social interaction between young infants and adults (Stern, 1974). It has also been suggested that the appeal of an infant's facial characteristics, which Hess (1970) terms "babyishness," plays a role in stimulating adult behaviors, including caretaking and social interaction. Thus, according to the ethological view, both infants and adults have a built-in behavioral bias to become attached to members of the species and a repertoire of behaviors to facilitate this process, thereby promoting survival of the individual infant and, ultimately, the species as a whole.

Over the course of the 1st year, as the infant's cognitive and affective capacities develop, social and attachment behaviors are directed more selectively to familiar people, usually the primary caretakers, and specific attachment relationships develop with parental figures. With the development of focused attachment, the infant begins to withdraw from unfamiliar people and to seek and obtain comfort only from attachment figures. Thus, some time during the second half of the 1st year, fear of strangers and separation distress begin to emerge; these will be discussed more fully later.

Bowlby (1973) has cogently discussed the development of fears from his ethological perspective. He argues that the human organism is genetically programmed to fear certain types of situations and stimuli. These innately determined fears are both natural and adaptive in an evolutionary sense in that they serve to protect man from predators and other harmful situations. Thus, natural fears are typical features of the human condition across the life span and have obvious survival value.

Bowlby contends that the human infant is innately programmed to fear loud noises, objects that approach rapidly or expand, heights, loss of support, darkness, strangeness, and being alone. While several of these fears (e.g., loud noises, loss of support, and looming objects) appear in early infancy with little or no apparent learning necessary, others (strangeness, being alone) depend upon a certain level of cognitive development. Bowlby argues that these feared objects and events are not inherently dangerous, but that they are associated with an increased risk of danger; they may signal the approach of predators, the occurrence of a natural disaster, or the appearance of other environmental hazards.

Central to this view is the role the attachment figure plays in the infant's development. When the attachment figure is available and responsive, the infant develops a sense of security and trust. Unavailability and/or unresponsiveness on the part of attachment figures results in heightened levels of anxiety and distress. While anxiety about loss, isolation, and abandonment persists in varying degrees across the life span, Bowlby conceptualizes this anxiety as stemming from early experiences with attachment figures and deriving from a biologically based need for protection and nurturance.

Humans, therefore, have evolved with basic biologic equipment that leads them to respond with fear and avoidance to naturally occurring cues to danger. Thus, children's anxieties and fears may be conceptualized as developing normally out of biologically determined, species-specific response tendencies that lead to the avoidance of possible hazards in the environment and to the approach toward protective figures. While the specific nature of potential dangers may vary from primitive societies living in the wild to more technological and urban ones, most of these innately organized fears appear to have continuing survival value.

COGNITIVE-DEVELOPMENTAL CONSTRUCTS

While certain fears appear to be largely innate, others depend upon the development of certain cognitive prerequisites. Two-month-old infants are not likely to become upset when held by a stranger, nor do they routinely show fear of animals or the dark, fears that are relatively common in slightly older children. These are fears that require some experience with the world and are dependent to some extent on learning. Learned fears may reflect fear of the familiar, based on the recall of a painful or unpleasant experience such as a visit to the pediatrician or separation from the mother (Lewis & Rosenblum, 1974). Such fears have been explained on the basis of simple association or conditioning (Jones & Jones, 1928). It is likely, however, that such fears require some degree of memory capacity and the ability to anticipate future events. Still other learned fears appear to be responses to the novel or unfamiliar, such as strange people or new situations.

Much research on the development of children's fears has focused on fear of the strange (Bronson, 1972; Scarr & Salapatek, 1970; Sroufe, 1977). Early formulations of fear in man and other animals (Hebb, 1946; Bronson, 1968) and the almost universal phenomenon of stranger anxiety in infants (Spitz, 1950) have led to an interest in fear of the unfamiliar. Current notions derive from Hebb's (1946) early observations of fear of novelty in chimpanzees and from Berlyne's (1960) theorizing on the role that novelty plays in increasing arousal and directing exploration, as well as from Piagetian views of cognitive development (Flavell, 1963). Several variations of Hebb's violation of expectancy model have been proposed (Bronson, 1968; Kagan, 1971, 1974; Lewis & Brooks, 1974; Schaffer, 1966; Sroufe, 1977). These models have in common the assumption that once a certain level of cognitive development is attained, including the development of object permanence and basic memory capacity, some time around the age of 8 months, infants are able to discriminate the familiar from the strange. In certain instances stimuli differing from the familiar will elicit either a mild negative reaction, termed wariness, or a more full-blown distress reaction, fear (Bretherton & Ainsworth, 1974; Sroufe, 1977).

Kagan (1971, 1974) suggests that a discrepant event or an unexpected environmental change will cause the infant to cease an ongoing activity and become alert. This alerting or orienting is followed by an attempt by the infant to assimilate the novel event into an already existing cognitive structure or schema. If the event is successfully assimilated, the infant may vocalize or smile and return to the previous activity. In any case no negative affect is aroused. If the event is too discrepant from established schemas to be readily assimilated, the infant may merely lose interest or become distressed. The specifics of the infant's response will depend upon the context of the event, immediately preceding events, and the infant's developmental level and temperamental characteristics. Thus, for instance, the appearance of mother wearing a mask may elicit crying in one infant and laughter in another, depending on contextual and other variables.

Sroufe, Waters, and Matas (1974) have suggested that the recognition of discrepancy is only the first step in the process. Once the infant recognizes that an event is unfamiliar or discrepant, the infant must then appraise or evaluate its threat potential. Contextual factors such as the presence or absence of the mother, familiarity of setting, past experience, arousal level, the response options available to the infant, and the infant's characteristic reaction to heightened arousal will influence whether or not the discrepancy is interpreted as threatening, neutral, or even amusing.

The discrepancy hypothesis has been used primarily to explain fear of the unfamiliar in infants. It is obvious, however, that as children develop and their experiences widen, their interpretations of the world change. What seems strange and potentially threatening to the 1-year-old may appear interesting, amusing, or irrelevant to the 3- or 4-year-old. With cognitive development, children begin to evaluate quite different objects and events as novel or as possibly fear provoking. Furthermore, differential experiences paired with a shift in cognitive functioning from the concrete to the more abstract and from the diffuse to the more specific would be expected to lead to wider individual differences in the nature of children's fears; variability would be expected to increase with age and cognitive development. Studies of children's fears, however, also suggest that some clear developmental patterns emerge.

DEVELOPMENTAL CHANGES IN THE NATURE OF CHILDREN'S FEARS

As noted earlier, fears and anxieties appear to be a permanent feature of the human condition and are relatively common in childhood. Studies find that most children experience some specific fears and worries over the course of development. For example, MacFarlane, Allen, and Honzik (1954) reported that 90% of the children in their longitudinal sample were described by their mothers as showing at least one specific fear at some time between the ages of 2 and 14 years. In their classic study Jersild and Holmes (1935) found that parents recorded some instances of fear in most of the 136 infants, preschoolers, and school-age children who were observed at home over a 3-week period. A mean of 4.64 instances of fear was recorded per child. Lapouse and Monk (1959) found that 43% of the representative sample of 6- to 12-year-old children they studied were described by mothers as suffering from seven or more fears and worries. Thus, these studies, which relied on parental reports, consistently found that fears are a relatively common feature of childhood. It is worth noting, however, that these fears were not disabling and that excessive fears are relatively rare (Miller et al.,1972; Rutter, Tizard, & Whitmore, 1970).

Findings also converge in showing qualitative changes with age in the nature of children's fears. Studies are almost exclusively cross-sectional in design, with few longitudinal studies addressed to this issue. Studies also vary widely in sample size and methodological rigor. Nevertheless, a number of studies using observational measures, interviews, questionnaires, and sampling children across the age range from infancy to adolescence indicate relatively consistent age changes in children's fears.

Observational and parent-report data clearly indicate that young infants fear sudden, loud, and unpredictable stimuli, loss of support, and heights (Ball & Tronick, 1971; Bronson, 1972; Jersild & Holmes, 1935). Toward the end of the 1st year, infants are likely to fear strange people and novel objects (Bronson, 1972; Scarr & Salapatek, 1970) and to begin to evidence distress at separation from their mother or other primary caretaker (Bowlby, 1969). These fears all reflect concrete and immediate events that are directly tied to the infant's daily experience.

As children's cognitive abilities develop to permit means–end thinking, the rudiments of language, and the capacity to operate at a symbolic level, typical fears change as well. In the early preschool years fear of animals, the dark, and imaginary creatures begin to emerge, as children are able to anticipate harmful or frightening events and to worry about things that are not in their immediate environment or that they have not directly experienced (Jersild & Holmes, 1935). Fear of animals and the dark are widespread in preschoolers and younger school-age children and tend to decrease as children mature (Bauer, 1976; Jersild & Holmes, 1935; Lapouse & Monk, 1959; Maurer, 1965). Similarly, younger children fear frightening dreams and imaginary creatures such as ghosts and monsters, and these fears tend to decrease systematically with increasing age in elementary school-age samples (Angelino et al., 1956; Bauer, 1976; Maurer, 1965).

For example, Bauer (1976) interviewed kindergarten, second, and sixth graders about their fears. Kindergarteners and second graders were more likely to spontaneously report fear of monsters, ghosts, and animals, fears that were rarely mentioned by sixth graders. Second- and sixth-grade children also reported fears of bodily injury and physical danger. When asked specifically about bedtime fears and frightening dreams, over half the kindergarten and second-grade children acknowledged bedtime fears, while 75% reported bad dreams. Reports of these fears declined drastically among the sixth graders, a finding that may reflect reluctance to admit such fears or a real developmental difference due in part to the increasing ability to differentiate reality from fantasy.

Maurer (1965) likewise interviewed children between the ages of 5 and 14 about their fears. Her sample consisted of children who had been referred to the school psychologist for a psychological assessment. Nevertheless, her results are consistent with those from studies of nonreferred samples. Fear of animals, the dark, and monsters were common among younger children. Eighty percent of 5- to 6-year-olds named animals as fear provoking, but only 23% of 13- to 14-year-olds reported fear of animals. Children's reports of fear of the dark and of nonexistent entities such as "spooks" had dropped to zero by age 10.

As Bauer (1976) notes, children's self-reported fears change with development. Initially, their fears reflect the formless and imaginary. With wider experience, greater understanding, and increased control over their environment, children's fears become more realistic. Fear of bodily injury, physical danger, loss, and natural hazards as well as concerns about school achievement and social relations increase with age in the middle school years and into adolescence (Bauer, 1976; Angelino et al., 1956; Maurer, 1965; Miller et al., 1974).

Miller et al. (1972) obtained parents' ratings of specific fears in a sample of 179 children, ages 6–16. Of these 78 had been referred to a psychology clinic and had been diagnosed as phobic; the remaining 101 subjects were nonreferred and essentially normal. A factor analysis revealed that children's fears, as perceived by their parents, fell into three main categories: physical injury, natural and supernatural events, and psychic stress. The physical injury category reflected societal dangers and included fear of harm to self and family members, as well as fear of loss or abandonment. The natural events factor included fear of natural phenomena such as storms, the dark, animals, and enclosed places and supernatural phenomena such as ghosts. Finally, the psychic stress factor reflected fear of school, criticism, social interaction, separation, and medical procedures. Miller et al. note that factor analytic studies of the fears reported by adults are not dissimilar. Psychic anxiety around achievement and social acceptance, fear of physical danger, and fear of being alone are among the more common concerns expressed by adults (Bernstein & Allen, 1969).

The question of whether children's fears persist has received minimal attention. While Jersild and Holmes (1935) reported that children's fears tended to be transient, they followed only a small sample (n = 15) of 2- to 5-year-olds who were observed on two occasions by their parents over a 1-year interval. However, these authors' data are often used to support the view that fears do not persist. Similarly, in the clinical literature, it is generally assumed that phobic symptoms tend to remit, although treatment speeds recovery (Hampe, Noble, Miller, & Barrett, 1973). These investigators followed a sample of 67 phobic children and found that 80% were symptom free 2 years later, while only 7% continued to evidence a severe phobic disorder. Agras, Chapin, and Oliveau (1972) followed 10 phobic children and adolescents (age range unspecified) over a 5-year period and found that symptoms had disappeared completely. Symptoms were more likely to remit in children and adolescents than in adults. While studies of phobic children may indicate that symptom remission is relatively common when children are followed over several years, few studies have examined children's reports of their fears over time, using a longitudinal design or nonclinical samples.

Eme and Schmidt (1978) specifically explored the stability of children's reports of their fears in a small sample of fourth graders who were followed up 1 year later. Both the number and types of fears reported remained remarkably stable. Fear of bodily harm, disaster, and animals were most frequently noted, and these fears were more stable among girls than boys. The paucity of data on the stability of children's fears is surprising. What little data exist are based on small numbers of children studied over short periods. Further, the persistence of fears may vary with the nature of the fear and the age of the child; particular fears may also show some stability at particular stages of development. There is some evidence on the short-term stability of fear of the unfamiliar in infants (Bronson, 1972) as well as suggestive evidence that separation distress may be more maladaptive and persistent in infants whose mothers are unresponsive to their signals (Ainsworth, Blehar, Waters, & Wall, 1978). In older children, anxiety proneness appears to show some short-term stability (Sarason, Davidson, Lighthall, Waite, & Ruebush, 1960; Spielberger, 1973).

Furthermore, particular types of fears appear to develop in middle to late childhood and to be in evidence throughout the life span, for example, fear of loss and bodily injury. Similarly, social anxiety and fear of failure are common across a wide age range and may persist within individuals. Thus, while stranger anxiety or fear of monsters may be expected to change as a function of cognitive and social development, realistic fears that develop in later childhood and reflect typical social pressures may be less transient. It appears that the appropriate studies on the persistence of children's fears have not yet been conducted.

SPECIFIC AGE-RELATED FEARS

Few studies have explored the developmental course of children's fears or systematically assessed their determinants, onset, duration, intensity, or impact on development. Indeed, the limited data available on children's fears belie the ubiquitous nature of fears over the course of normal development. However, particular age-related fears have been studied in some depth. These include stranger fear and separation anxiety in infants and test anxiety in school-age children. Each of these is examined here in some detail. Further, since separation anxiety has particular manifestations in infancy, but remains an issue throughout the life span, separation anxiety is considered in preschoolers and school-age children as well. Social change in the form of increased rates of maternal employment and divorce has also broadened the nature of typical separation experiences. These issues are touched on briefly.

FEAR OF STRANGERS

As noted earlier, infants initially respond similarly to any adult who engages in caretaking or social interaction with them. In the early months, infants will look at, vocalize to, and smile at an approaching stranger. By 4 or 5 months of age infants begin to discriminate familiar caretakers from new people and, at about 8 months, they may actively avoid contact with unfamiliar people. Fear of strangers or "8th-month anxiety" has been the subject of considerable research (Bronson, 1972; Lewis & Brooks, 1974; Morgan & Riccuiti, 1969; Schaffer & Emerson, 1964) and heated debate (Batter & Davidson, 1979; Rheingold & Eckerman, 1973; Sroufe, 1977).

Although a wealth of data confirm that most infants will show some signs of avoidance of strange adults at some time during the second half of the 1st year, this phenomenon is not as developmentally fixed as was once supposed (Sroufe, 1977). While most infants show some reaction to the presence of a stranger, the persistence of the response and its developmental course appear to vary. Some infants show a sudden reaction to strangers that quickly wanes; others have more persistent though relatively mild reactions; still others evidence more persistent, prolonged, and intense reactions. The time of onset of stranger reactions also varies. In some studies negative reactions have been observed as early as 5 months (Bronson, 1972; Tennes & Lampl, 1964); however, the majority of studies find wary responses are apparent in most infants by 8 months, with almost all infants showing stranger reactions by the end of the 1st year. Sobering, staring, or gaze aversion are more common reactions than full-blown crying and outright distress; that is, wariness is a more typical response than fear (Bretherton & Ainsworth, 1974; Sroufe, 1977). Cross-cultural differences in the age of onset and the intensity of typical stranger reactions suggest the importance of experiential factors in accounting for some of these variations (Ainsworth *et al.*, 1978).

Stranger reactions are complexly determined and many variables influence whether or not the presence of a strange adult will in fact elicit a wary or fearful reaction. The methodological problems inherent in studies of stranger anxiety have been discussed in detail by Rheingold and Eckerman (1973) and by Sroufe (1977). Despite variations in methodology, there is some consistency in findings. Strangers who approach rapidly and/or try to engage the infant physically by touching or holding are likely to elicit negative reactions in a majority of infants in the 8- to 18-month age range. Strangers who approach slowly, engage in toy-mediated interaction, or initiate social interaction across a distance are less likely to evoke negative affect; indeed, they are likely to elicit interest and social behavior (Rheingold & Eckerman, 1973).

Other factors are also relevant, most importantly the presence and proximity of mother or other familiar people, the familiarity of the setting, and the response options available to the infant. Thus, an infant sitting on his or her mother's lap is less likely to be distressed by the approach of a stranger than is an infant whose mother is in view, but not within arm's reach. However, if that infant is mobile and can approach mother for contact should he or she wish, the approach of the stranger will be less distressing, since the infant has some control over the situation. Characteristics of the stranger, including age and sex, also influence infants' reactions. Female strangers tend to be less fear-provoking than males, and children elicit less fear than adults (Brooks & Lewis, 1976).

These findings have been interpreted in terms of the discrepancy hypothesis outlined above (Lewis & Brooks, 1974; Schaffer, 1966, 1974). Schaffer (1974) suggests that stranger anxiety appears at about 8 months because of the major transformations in cognitive and affective development that occur at that time. At 8 months a specific attachment relationship is established, as indicated by differential responsiveness and the use of the mother as a source of comfort and as a secure base for environmental exploration (Ainsworth *et al.,* 1978; Bowlby, 1969). At 8 months the infant also begins to inhibit impulsive responding in order to evaluate the situation and compare the stranger to an internal representation of familiar people, primarily mother (Schaffer, 1974). This ability develops once object permanence is established and people and objects are perceived as existing independent of their appearance in the infant's immediate environment. In addition, at this time the infant's memory capacity has advanced to permit recall rather than mere recognition of the familiar. However, this explanation does not entirely account for the marked variations observed in infants' reactions to strangers (Sroufe *et al.,* 1974). Furthermore, fear of all strangers would hardly be adaptive. As Bronson (1972) has noted, it is necessary for the infant to approach the strange in order to learn more about the world, while avoiding environmental hazards.

Stranger reactions have been viewed by others in ethological terms by considering the balance among the behavioral systems of fear-wariness, attachment, affiliation, and exploration (Bretherton & Ainsworth, 1974; Sroufe, 1977). Infants do show fear of strangers in certain circumstances; fear leads to the activation of attachment behaviors, since infants will signal to, approach, and seek protection and comfort from mother when frightened or distressed. On the other hand fear and attachment are incompatible with exploration of novel objects and friendly interactions with other people. When infants are in novel environments with interesting toys, they tend to leave their mother's side and explore, returning briefly to check in or interacting with her across a distance (Ainsworth *et al.,* 1978; Rheingold & Eckerman, 1973). However, should the mother get up to leave, a stranger enter, or some other disturbing element be introduced into the situation, the balance will shift away from exploration to wariness and attachment. The infant will stop playing, study the situation, and either approach, cry, or otherwise signal to mother. The quiet and gradual approach of a stranger, when the infant is comfortably playing at mother's feet may elicit a brief period of wariness, followed by interest and friendly overtures from a distance—smiling, vocalizing, showing a toy to the stranger. After initial appraisal of the situation as not threatening, since mother is nearby and the stranger is behaving in a way that does not seem frightening, the balance will shift from wariness to affiliation. Should the stranger proceed to try to pick up the infant, however, the balance would be expected to shift away from affiliative, friendly responses to wariness of the stranger and comfort seeking from mother. The situation would be appraised as threatening (Bowlby, 1973). Thus, in ethological terms, the characteristics of the situation, particularly the availability of the attachment figure, will determine which behavioral system is activated, that is, whether the stranger will elicit wariness and avoidance or interest and social approach.

Wariness of strangers may persist throughout the preschool years where it may manifest as shyness (Bronson, 1970) or reluctance to enter new situations. Overtly fearful reactions tend to disappear sometime during the toddler period, as the child has a greater range of response options available that permit him or her to avoid contact with strangers. With more advanced cognitive development and wider experience, the older child has more resources to draw on that can be used to evaluate new situations as less novel and less threatening.

SEPARATION ANXIETY

As infants develop a focused attachment relationship, they begin to avoid strangers and seek comfort and protection from their primary attachment figure. At the same time they begin to show distress at separation and apprehension in the face of anticipated separation from their mothers. The term "separation anxiety" has been used in this context to refer to protest at the mother's departure, distress caused by her absence, and anxiety about her anticipated absence (Bowlby, 1973; Stayton, Ainsworth, & Main, 1973; Weinraub & Lewis, 1977).

Like stranger anxiety, separation anxiety is a universal phenomenon, but it is complexly determined. Behavioral manifestations, duration, and intensity of reactions vary with the age of the child (Stayton et al., 1973), the quality of the mother–infant attachment (Ainsworth et al., 1978; Stayton & Ainsworth, 1973), the nature of the situation (Weinraub & Lewis, 1977), and previous experiences with separation (Bowlby, 1973; Kagan, 1974; Schaffer & Emerson, 1964). Sex differences in the intensity of separation protest have been noted in some studies (Goldberg & Lewis, 1969), but not others (Corter, 1976; Stayton et al., 1973). A variety of events involving separation of infant from mother have been studied under this rubric, including normal, brief everyday separations in the home (Stayton et al., 1973); brief but atypical separations in the laboratory (Ainsworth & Wittig, 1969; Spelke, Zelazo, Kagan, & Kotelchuck, 1973); and longer separations such as hospitalization (Schaffer & Callender, 1959). Clearly, these very different separation experiences should elicit very different reactions in children, and responses should vary as a function of age, past experience, and a range of other factors.

Separation reactions have been conceptualized most often from an ethological perspective (Bowlby, 1973; Stayton et al., 1973; Weinraub & Lewis, 1977). Bowlby (1973) has suggested that the infant's distress at separation, either actual or anticipated, and the behavioral systems activated by this distress (fear–wariness and attachment) can be seen as adaptive, since being alone carries an increased risk of danger for the infant. He argues that fear of being alone is a basic feature of human biologic and behavioral make-up that has developed over the course of evolution because of the role it plays in species survival. The infant alone in the wild was at risk from predators, exposure, and starving to death. Within this framework, then, separation protest and distress when alone are both normal and adaptive responses to potential danger. Further, Bowlby argues that the quality of early experiences with attachment figures, their availability and ability to protect the young infant from danger and excessive distress, sets the stage for later close relationships, influencing the degree of trust and confidence children and adults place in relationships with parents, lovers, and friends.

Over the course of the 1st year, as infants develop a focused attachment, they also build up a "working model" of the attachment figure and her accessibility and responsiveness (Bowlby, 1973). Infants who have experienced responsive and available mothering develop a sense of security and trust. They have learned that when their mother leaves, she will return and that their signals of distress or discomfort will be acknowledged and responded to. Secure infants are less likely to become upset by typical brief separations than are insecure infants who have experienced a relationship with an unpredictable, unavailable, rejecting, or unresponsive attachment figure. The latter infants will be prone to more intense upset at separation and/or experience chronic anxiety about the whereabouts, responsiveness, and eventual return of the attachment figure, who has failed to serve as an adequate protector or source of comfort. Infants may manifest these distress reactions in attempts to seek and maintain proximity to mother by crying, clinging, or searching; or, the infant may become disorganized by anxiety and freeze or avoid contact (Ainsworth *et al.*, 1978). It should be noted that predictions from ethological theory are the reverse of those derived from both learning theory and psychoanalytic formulations of separation anxiety, since both predict that infants would be more likely to protest separation from more reinforcing or need-gratifying figures (Ainsworth, 1969; Bowlby, 1973; Weinraub & Lewis, 1977).

Of particular interest, given the focus on normal development, are infants' reactions to typical separations that occur naturally in the course of daily living: being left in the playpen while mother prepares dinner, being left with a babysitter while mother goes out, being left at a day-care center or at grandmother's while mother goes to work. While all these typical situations involve separation of the infant from mother in the sense that mother is not physically present, they vary enormously in terms of frequency, familiarity of the setting, presence of strange people, and accessibility of mother. Unfortunately, research has not dealt systematically with many different forms of separation experiences, and many of the situations noted above involve more than separation per se. However, studies of separation responses in the natural environment (Schaffer & Emerson, 1964; Stayton & Ainsworth, 1973; Stayton *et al.*, 1973) and in the laboratory (Ainsworth *et al.*, 1978; Spelke *et al.*, 1973) shed some light on the natural course of separation reactions and their determinants.

Few studies have examined infants' reactions to typical everyday separations. Schaffer and Emerson (1964) in one of the pioneering studies in the field, interviewed 60 working-class Scottish mothers about the onset and course of separation protest over the first 18 months using a short-term longitudinal design. In the first few months infants became distressed when put down after being held, suggesting that separation involved the loss of close bodily contact. Over the course of the 1st year, being left alone was most likely to evoke protest, and this situation continued to be especially stressful. Despite wide individual differences in the age of onset and intensity of separation reactions, infants through the age of 18 months continued to protest when left. Furthermore, once a focused attachment had developed, departure of other familiar people, especially fathers, grandparents, and siblings also elicited some protest in over half the sample.

Ainsworth and colleagues (Ainsworth *et al.,* 1978; Stayton *et al.,* 1973) studied the onset and course of separation protest longitudinally in a sample of 26 middle-class infants who were observed at home at 3-week intervals from 15 to 54 weeks of age. Some infants as young as 15 weeks were observed to cry when mother left the room, with peaks at roughly 33 weeks and again at 45 weeks. Distress reactions occurred earlier when infants were left alone than when they were left in the company of others. While Stayton *et al.* found that separation protest was differential to mother from its onset, they also found that infants under 6 months of age clearly protested the departure of others as well; being alone elicited more intense distress than did maternal departure. These findings are consistent with the ethological view of attachment noted above. Infants 6 months and younger respond relatively indiscriminately to other members of the species, and the experience of being alone elicits anxiety in some situations as a natural cue to danger (Bowlby, 1973). By 8 months or so, as the attachment relationship becomes focused and comfort is sought primarily from the attachment figure, separation protest becomes almost exclusively directed to the departure of the mother.

By the end of the 1st year, when most of the infants in the sample were mobile, Stayton *et al.* (1973) reported that infants were much more likely to follow their mother than to cry when she left the room. The authors concluded that in the familiar home environment, infants were more likely to display positive behaviors such as greeting and following than to cry and were active in seeking to regain contact with mother. However, infant behaviors even in familiar situations are influenced by the quality of the mother–infant relationship.

Additional research by Stayton and Ainsworth (1973) indicates that maternal responsiveness and accessibility are associated with a secure attachment relationship and that securely attached infants are less upset by separation in the home. Conversely, infants who are anxious about the availability of a mother who has been unresponsive or unpredictable in her responses are more likely to become distressed even when left alone briefly in a familiar environment. They are also less likely than securely attached infants to respond actively and positively, for example, by greeting mother on reunion. These data support Bowlby's (1973) model, which posits that anxiety can be aroused by the possibility that the attachment figure will be unavailable when needed.

Many studies of infants' separation reactions have been conducted in laboratory settings, which are unfamiliar to the infant and which may involve sequences of familiar and unfamiliar people coming and going at predetermined intervals (Ainsworth *et al.*, 1978: Spelke *et al.*, 1973). These are obviously not pure assessments of separation behavior, because they are confounded by reactions to unfamiliar people behaving in unpredictable ways in a strange environment. While early researchers interpreted the intensity of separation protest to be one index of the quality of the infant–mother bond (Schaffer & Emerson, 1964; Tennes & Lampl, 1964), there is general agreement that this is not the case, particularly when the infant is observed in an artificial and unfamiliar setting (Ainsworth *et al.*, 1978; Bowlby, 1973; Spelke *et al.*, 1973; Weinraub & Lewis, 1977).

Nevertheless, these laboratory studies produce some consistent findings. Not surprisingly, most 12- to 24-month-old infants become distressed when left alone or alone with a stranger in a strange environment (Ainsworth *et al.*, 1978; Rheingold, 1969; Spelke *et al.*, 1973; Tennes & Lampl, 1964; Weinraub & Lewis, 1977). The intensity of infants' reactions varies with age, past experience with parental departures, maternal behavior immediately preceding the separation, the amount of control the infant has over the situation, the infant's level of cognitive development, and temperamental characteristics. Indeed, when the infant has initiated the separation in order to explore interesting toys in an adjoining room, but mother is accessible, separation will not engender distress (Rheingold & Eckerman, 1970). On the other hand enforced separation, even when mother is in view, may elicit crying and attempts to regain contact (Goldberg & Lewis, 1969). Results from laboratory studies have been interpreted in terms of the discrepancy hypothesis, since the situations encountered by the infant may be quite unlike the infant's typical experiences with brief separations. Further, mother's behavior in the laboratory may also be quite discrepant, since she may act in uncharacteristic ways that the infant cannot readily assimilate into existing schemas of maternal behavior (Kagan, 1974). From an ethological perspective, the unavailability of mother in a strange environment may be interpreted as a sign of potential danger, leading the infant to become distressed and to seek to regain contact with mother.

Weinraub and Lewis (1977) distinguished between the responses of 2-year-olds to mother's actual departure and their responses to her absence in a laboratory situation. Infants who were most distressed by departure were not necessarily the ones who showed the most upset during separation. Some infants, for example, who cried when mother left settled down to play once she was gone; others who let her go quietly cried, called, or searched for her during her absence. Findings also indicated individual differences in maternal departure style that were associated with infants' responses to maternal absence. Some mothers merely left the room without a word; others told the infant they were leaving; still others explained to the infant that they were leaving and gave the infant explicit instructions about what to do during their absence. Not surprisingly, infants whose mothers left without warning evidenced the most distress during separation; infants whose mothers provided explicit instructions showed the least distress. While cause-and-effect relationships cannot be determined from these data, they are consistent with both ethological and cognitive–developmental formulations of separation distress.

Weinraub and Lewis (1977) suggest that protest at mother's departure may be adaptive, because it prevents the mother from leaving the child alone and vulnerable. Distress during maternal absence may or may not be adaptive, depending on the situation. Distress calls when the infant is alone may lead to mother's return or may alert predators. A more adaptive response in the latter situation would be for the infant to play quietly and wait for mother to return. Infants whose mothers gave them explicit instructions tended to do just that. This finding is compatible with the notion that maternal sensitivity to the infant is reflected in less anxiety during separation. That is, mothers who explained their departure to their infant were more in tune with their infant's developmental needs, and their infants were more secure in the knowledge that maternal departure would be followed by return. From a cognitive–developmental perspective, too, mothers who gave their infants an explanation and told them what to do during their absence were facilitating the child's ability to integrate the separation into past experiences with similar situations in which the child played quietly and mother eventually returned.

Real-life separation experiences have received less attention in empirical studies, because of the methodological difficulties they present. However, a number of complex situations that involve separation of a child from one or both parents are pertinent to a discussion of relatively common events in the lives of young children. These events include hospitalization, entry into preschool or day care, maternal employment, and parental divorce. Although each of these experiences results in parent–child separation, either for a regular portion of each week or for a more concentrated and/or prolonged period of time, none is a "pure" example of separation. Each of these situations may be conceptualized as a stressful life event (Rutter, 1981b) that confronts the child with some combination of anxiety-arousing experiences such as physical discomfort, significant changes in caretakers, daily environment, and routine, and the decreased accessibility of one or both parents. Further, these events are often interrelated. For example, divorce may mean that altered financial circumstances force the mother to return to work and to place the child in day care.

Studies of the effects of hospitalization clearly document the profound social withdrawal that often results, especially in infants and young children who are in the process of forming or have recently formed a focused attachment relationship. At this age children have not yet achieved a level of cognitive development sufficient for them to understand the reasons for their hospitalization or to anticipate what is going to happen to them (Bowlby, 1973; Rutter, 1974; Schaffer & Callender, 1959). Rutter (1974, 1981b) notes that children between the ages of 6 months and 4 years are more vulnerable to stress from the separation inherent in hospitalization, partly because at this age relationships are especially difficult to maintain over time in the absence of regular contact with the attachment figure. Bowlby (1969, 1973) has described the typical grief reaction displayed by young children separated from parents for several weeks in the hospital. The initial stage of separation protest is followed by sadness and withdrawal (despair) and ultimately by detachment and emotional withdrawal from and avoidance of parents. Obviously, other factors also contribute to the distress that accompanies hospitalization including the strange environment; separation from other familiar figures, environment, and routine; and the unpleasant procedures that are inherent in hospitalization. In young children, however, the distress is greatly reduced with frequent maternal visiting, and some pediatric hospitals encourage parents of young children to remain overnight through part or all of the child's hospital stay. Negative effects tend to dissipate with time, except in cases of extreme stress, additional environmental adversity, or repeated admissions (Rutter, 1981b).

Entry into preschool is likewise a common event in the lives of young children, and there appear to be wide individual differences in the ease or difficulty with which children adapt (Hughes, Pinkerton, &

Plewis, 1979; McGrew, 1972; Schwarz & Wynn, 1971). McGrew (1972) observed the behavior of 12 3-year-olds as they entered a preschool for the first time. Generally, children were found to avoid contact with the teacher and to cling to their mothers upon first entering the classroom; four children cried when their mothers left, and two had to be restrained from following their mothers. Within 5–10 minutes after the mothers' departure, however, most children were involved in a play activity. Only one child in the sample exhibited prolonged separation distress. Not surprisingly, children with older siblings in the classroom adapted to the preschool more readily and showed less initial distress. Blurton Jones and Leach (1972) also observed separations of young children (ages 2–4) from their mothers as they entered a familiar play group. Children under the age of 2½ years were much more likely to cry than children 2½ years old and older. Within the younger group, children with older siblings also attending the play group were significantly less likely to cry than were younger children attending alone. These findings support other observations of children that indicate that the effects of separation from mother are attenuated by the presence of other familiar people (Bowlby, 1973; Rutter, 1981b). Also, in both these studies crying appeared to be associated with mother leaving unannounced, consistent with the laboratory findings of Weinraub and Lewis (1977).

Studies of slightly older preschoolers suggest that previous peer group experience is associated with less separation distress on the first day of nursery school and that children are integrated into the group relatively quickly (Feldbaum, Christenson, & O'Neal, 1980; Schwarz & Wynn, 1971). Schwarz and Wynn (1971) observed a sample of 100 3½- to 5-year-olds on their 1st day of preschool; only six children actually cried, albeit briefly; none of these children had had a prior peer group experience. While Schwarz and Wynn systematically examined the effects of a previsit to the nursery school and of maternal presence in ameliorating separation distress, what was noteworthy in their study was the relatively low level of distress that emerged and the rapid adaptation made by all but a few children.

Despite the limited data available on the separation distress associated with entry into preschool, it appears that this too is a complex phenomenon. Separation reactions in this context appear to be influenced by previous experience with peer group activities, past separation experiences, the presence of familiar peers or siblings, familiarity with the setting, the child's general social competence, the quality of the mother–child relationship, and specific maternal behaviors during separation. In addition, specific characteristics of the preschool setting appear to influence the nature of preschool play behavior and social interactions among peers (Carpenter & Huston-Stein, 1980) and these factors may well influence the child's adaptation to the nursery school environment. However, it appears that for most children the initial anxiety accompanying preschool entry quickly dissipates as children become involved in play activities and social interaction.

Children usually attend preschool for only a few hours each week, while day care usually involves relatively prolonged daily separations of the child from the mother and the familiar environment. Numerous studies have been conducted over the past 10 years in an attempt to examine the effects of day care on the development of infants and preschoolers. Two reviews have documented the limitations of much of this research (Belsky & Steinberg, 1978; Rutter, 1981a). In particular, studies have been confined primarily to high-quality day care centers, which are not representative of the facilities in which most children are placed. These studies tend to use rather restricted outcome measures that may lack ecological validity and to examine relatively short-term effects. Moreover, appropriate control groups are difficult to obtain, since family attitudes appear to differentiate day-care users from nonusers. Studies also include children varying widely in age, ranging from infancy to the preschool years; the age of entry in day care; the length of the day-care experience; and the reason they are attending day care—all factors that might influence the child's adjustment, as well as subsequent social and emotional development. Despite the many problems with the day-care studies, however, there are few data to support the contention that regular and daily separations from mother have negative effects on the quality of the infant–mother attachment or that children in day care are excessively anxious or insecure (Doyle, 1975; Kagan, Kearsley, & Zelazo, 1978; Roopnarine & Lamb, 1979).

Studies of maternal employment may also be viewed in this context. These studies suggest that the increased financial resources, self-esteem, and social stimulation that result when women work outside the home may have beneficial effects on the family (Hoffman, 1979). The few studies that have compared mother–infant interaction in working and nonworking mothers (e.g., Hock, 1980) have failed to find systematic differences in the quality of the attachment relationship or in the infant's social behavior toward the mother. Hock suggests that the congruence between a woman's views on exclusive maternal care and her employment status may be more relevant to the quality of her relationship with her infant than the fact of her working or not working. Studies of preschoolers and school-age youngsters with working mothers indicate that maternal employment may foster greater independence in children and less over-involvement on the part of mothers (Gold & Andres, 1978a, 1978b). Further, the working mother becomes a model for competence and, in two-parent families, the father tends to be more involved in the day-to-day management of the household, with less sex-stereotyped division of labor (Hoffman, 1979). While only limited data are available on the relation between separation distress and maternal employment, findings do not indicate deleterious effects from the separation experiences that result when mothers work. Obviously, the impact of maternal employment on the family as a whole and on the marital relationship will influence maternal behavior (Belsky, 1981). In addition, a woman's attitudes toward and satisfaction with her job, her views of the maternal role, the amount and quality of her caretaking and social behavior with her infant, and the quality and accessibility of alternative child care arrangements are among the many factors that must be considered before any conclusions can be drawn about the influence of maternal employment and the attendant separation experiences on the development of infants and young children.

While day care and maternal employment may not have obvious negative effects on the child's emotional bonds with parents, studies of divorce indicate profound effects on children (Hess & Camara, 1979; Hetherington, 1979; Wallerstein & Kelly, 1980). Most studies of divorce have examined the effect of separation from the father, though this is clearly not an example of pure separation. As noted in the growing literature on the effects of marital separation and divorce, the rupture itself occurs in the context of predivorce tension, shifts in living arrangements and financial status, a potential move, and the possibility that the mother may begin to work—all at a time when both parents are in a state of emotional turmoil, rage, and/or depression. In this complicated and emotionally charged context, it is not surprising that children across the age range from toddlerhood to adolescence experience profound sadness, loss, anger, guilt, and concern about current nurturance and future living and visiting arrangements. These feelings may be expressed in a variety of symptoms, depending upon the age and sex of the child, predivorce adjustment, and the nature of the family break-up. In addition, follow-up studies indicate that many children continue to have adjustment problems for several years following the marital separation (Hetherington, 1979; Wallerstein & Kelly, 1980), although positive and consistent relationships with both parents can mitigate the negative effects of family break-up (Hess & Camara, 1979).

Taken together it appears that in the context of sensitive and responsive caretaking, most infants learn to separate from their mothers and to meet the new developmental challenges of environmental mastery, preschool entry, and the establishment of peer relationships. Most infants and young children also cope with the separation experiences inherent in more disrupting events such as hospitalization or mother's return to work, although they are likely to experience some transient distress that does not have long-term sequelae. Of the common separation experiences brought about by recent social change, divorce appears to have the most negative effects on the child's psychosocial adjustment. However, the complex life changes that accompany parental divorce make it impossible to determine which specific factors contribute to the anxiety, depression, and anger that children initially experience and that tend to persist beyond the postdivorce period in a substantial number of children.

TEST ANXIETY

Test anxiety may be conceptualized as a specific instance of anxiety about personal adequacy and achievement. Many studies of anxiety in school-age children have focused on test anxiety, since it is reasonably specific, can be measured with relative ease, and has been examined within a theoretical framework (Hill, 1972; Hill & Sarason, 1966; Sarason et al., 1960). Most early work in this area was conducted by Sarason and his associates from a psychoanalytic perspective. More recent formulations have emphasized social learning, motivation, and attentional factors (Hill, 1972; Nottelman & Hill, 1977; Wine, 1971).

Sarason (Sarason et al., 1960) first conceptualized test anxiety as having its origins in the preschool years and stemming from fear of rejection by parents whose unrealistically high standards for achievement could not be met. Fear of abandonment by parents and the resulting hostile and aggressive impulses were repressed. Instead, children became dependent, anxious, and low in self-esteem. Mothers of anxious children were seen as defensive and unsure of themselves. They tended to be critical and punitive, especially when confronted with the child's anger or the child's failure to meet their high standards of achievement. As a consequence of negative parental evaluations, fear of rejection, and the need to repress angry and hostile feelings, these youngsters developed a passive, nonaggressive personality style and high levels of anxiety in situations involving evaluations of competence.

Empirical studies have found that mothers of anxious children are more punitive and less supportive in achievement situations (Hermans, ter Laak, & Maes, 1972). Further, highly anxious subjects perform more poorly on intelligence and achievement tests (Hill & Sarason, 1966; Sarason et al., 1960). Longitudinal data indicate that anxiety has an interfering effect on performance, which shows a linear increase with increasing age from grade one through grade five (Hill & Sarason, 1966). That is, the debilitating effect of anxiety becomes more severe as children move from the primary to the middle school grades. Anxious children also receive poorer school grades and are more likely to repeat a grade than their less anxious peers.

These data may be interpreted as suggesting that anxiety interferes with intellectual functioning and academic achievement, that poor academic achievement leads to high levels of anxiety, or that poor intellectual potential leads to both poorer academic performance and high levels of anxiety. While data do not unequivocally support any of these interpretations of the complex relationships among ability, performance, and anxiety about failure, Hill and Sarason (1966) favor the notion that anxiety is causal. They cite data demonstrating that anxious children do more poorly on some types of tasks, but not others. For instance, anxious children evidence poorer performance than their less anxious peers on complex tasks, on tasks requiring new learning, and on measures that are administered in an evaluative manner. In addition, a decrease in anxiety over time is associated with improved performance on intelligence tests, providing some support for the etiological view of anxiety. In a more recent review, Hill (1972) suggests that high anxiety and lower performance have a reciprocal and cumulative effect over time; anxiety leads to poor performance, which in turn increases anxiety in cyclical fashion.

Hill (1972) has also modified his position on the development of test anxiety to incorporate a social learning perspective as well as attentional and motivational factors. He suggests that parental criticism in the preschool years paired with unrealistic standards of performance make children especially sensitive to negative evaluations and motivate them to avoid criticism, which is often associated with failure. Fear of criticism and efforts to avoid it lead to anxiety, particularly in achievement situations. One strategy that anxious children use to avoid criticism from adults is to become dependent on them for feedback and approval. Some studies do confirm that highly test-anxious children are more sensitive than their less anxious peers to social cues and social reinforcement from adults in test-like situations (Hill, 1967; Nottelman & Hill, 1977), although findings on this point have been equivocal (Silverman & Waite, 1969).

Hill (1972) and others (Sarason, 1975; Wine, 1971) have also suggested that performance anxiety in evaluative situations may interfere with efficient attention deployment and lead to other cognitive changes. Thus, studies have examined attentional and memory strategies in children selected as high and low in test anxiety. Results suggest that anxious children are more often off-task (Nottelman & Hill, 1977), are more distracted by irrelevant stimuli (Dusek, Mergler, & Kermis, 1976), and are helped by training in problem-solving strategies that aid in recall (Stevenson & Odom, 1965) or focus their attention on relevant stimulus attributes (Dusek *et al.,* 1976). Messer (1970) has also found that anxious children take a slower, more cautious approach to problem solving when faced with unclear response options. These findings have been interpreted to suggest that anxiety over possible failure causes the test-anxious individual to worry about performance and to engage in distracting, negative self-evaluations that interfere with successful problem solving (Sarason, 1975). In the context of attribution theory, test-anxious subjects make internal, global, and stable attributions for failure in test taking or other evaluative situations (Weiner & Kukla, 1970).

In summary, these theoretical viewpoints and empirical findings indicate that child-rearing practices, parental expectations, and negative experiences in evaluative contexts contribute to the development of test anxiety. Studies suggest that anxiety over test performance is related to low self-esteem, negative attributions for success, and a general personality style characterized by dependency and passivity. In addition, test anxiety interferes with the child's ability to cope with one of the major development tasks of middle childhood:

succeeding in school. The relationship between test anxiety and specific factors in the school environment such as the quality of the teacher–child relationship, the amount of positive feedback given by the teacher, and the particular academic demands of the child's grade level remain to be examined. It is likely that a number of school-related variables influence the course and intensity of school anxiety from grade to grade (Hill & Sarason, 1966). Further, the relationship between test anxiety and general anxiety has received little attention (Sarason, 1975), and the long-term stability of test anxiety beyond the middle school years has not been assessed. Children who are anxious about school success, especially when they feel they are being evaluated, may be more generally anxious about their competence in a number of areas. This anxiety may interfere with cognitive development, achievement motivation, and social relationships through adolescence and into early adulthood with profound implications for adaptation across the life span. These are among the many important issues that remain to be systematically explored.

SUMMARY AND DIRECTIONS FOR FUTURE RESEARCH

A combination of developmental and ethological approaches appears to provide a promising avenue for understanding the origins and developmental changes in children's fears. Species-specific, biologically determined tendencies appear to interact with universal learning experiences and the specific learning history of the individual child to determine the nature of fears at different ages. Despite individual differences in the age of onset, duration, and intensity of fears, most infants react with negative affect to sudden stimulus change, heights, and loss of support; somewhat later, strange people and separation from the mother evoke distress. Separation from the mother and entry into a new environment such as preschool may elicit upset in some young children, but by the early preschool years, wide individual differences in the frequency, intensity, and nature of children's fears and anxieties are apparent. With more advanced cognitive development and a wider range of experiences, children's fears become more individualized; the things children fear also broaden to include imaginary events and creatures as well as anticipated events and happenings beyond the child's own realm of experience. As pressures for social conformity in the peer group and for school success become dominant factors in the child's life, performance anxiety and social anxiety become potent sources of stress. By early adolescence, children's major concerns become quite realistic and similar to the fears of adults, with anxieties about loss, achievement, social acceptance, and natural disasters prominent.

Although a number of studies have charted the course of children's fears using cross-sectional methodology, surprisingly little longitudinal research is available on the natural history of children's fears, anxieties, and worries in nonclinical samples. For example, does an insecure and anxiously attached infant develop into an insecure and fearful preschooler, as Bowlby's (1973) theory predicts, and how is this insecurity manifest at different ages? Data beginning to emerge on patterns of attachment and later social adaptation suggest that anxious attachment is associated with less competent social functioning in preschool (Sroufe, 1983), which Sroufe refers to as "coherence in developmental organization." Does the timid and anxious preschooler who experiences severe separation difficulties at nursery school entry grow into a test-anxious or socially withdrawn fourth grader? The appropriate studies have not yet been conducted to answer questions such as this; in the absence of theoretical guidelines, researchers are unsure which behaviors to study at different points in development. Definitional and measurement problems abound, and little is known about individual behavioral manifestations or developmental shifts in children's fears. Thus, longitudinal studies on these questions have not been undertaken.

The impact of family factors on children's fears is, likewise, a neglected area. The major exception to this is the extensive work on patterns of attachment, maternal behavior, and separation distress in infants (Ainsworth et al., 1978) and on mother–infant attachment and later competence (Sroufe, 1983). However, very few studies have examined the effects of child-rearing practices, parental anxieties, or family structure on the development or amelioration of children's worries and fears. Longitudinal studies using carefully defined groups and multimethod, cross-situational assessment are clearly needed. Sroufe's work on continuity of. adaptation (Sroufe, 1983) and Hetherington's work on the effects of divorce on children (Hetherington, 1979) are models of the types of detailed studies that must be conducted, if we are to begin to understand the determinants of and transitions in children's fears and anxieties from a developmental perspective.

Finally, research on children's fears is not likely to proceed beyond its current "prescientific" state (Miller *et al.*, 1974) until some of the major methodological and measurement problems that plague it can be solved. We are dealing with a vague and poorly defined construct with unclear and variable behavioral referents that change over the course of development in unknown ways. Further, wide individual differences in specific fears and their behavioral expression, determinants, severity, and developmental course complicate research efforts. Even when recent work has focused on relatively clearly defined groups such as phobic children (e.g., Miller *et al.*, 1974) or on supposedly clear-cut and developmentally specific fears, such as stranger fear (e.g., Sroufe, 1977), the complexity of definitional, measurement, and contextual issues has become apparent. Further, since it is generally assumed that children's fears are evanescent (e.g., Miller *et al.*, 1974), researchers are not likely to invest the time and commitment required to conduct large-scale, longitudinal studies of a phenomenon that is difficult to define or measure and that may disappear with developmental change. In this context it is not surprising, then, that so little empirical research is available on children's fears across the life span.

REFERENCES

Agras, W. S., Chapin, H. N., & Oliveau, D. C. The natural history of phobias: Course and prognosis. *Archives of General Psychiatry*, 1972, *26*, 315–317.

Ainsworth, M. D. S. Object relations, dependency, and attachment: A theoretical review of the infant–mother relationship. *Child Development*, 1969, *40*, 969–1025.

Ainsworth, M. D. S. The development of infant–mother attachment. In B. Caldwell & H. Ricciuti (Eds.), *Review of child development research* (Vol. 3). Chicago: University of Chicago Press, 1973.

Ainsworth, M. D. S. Blehar, M., Waters, E., & Wall, S. *Patterns of attachment.* Hillsdale, N.J.: Erlbaum, 1978.

Ainsworth, M. D. S., & Wittig, B. A. Attachment and exploratory behaviour of one-year-olds in a strange situation. In B. M. Foss (Ed.), *Determinants of infant behavior* (Vol. 4). London: Methuen, 1969.

American Psychiatric Association. *Diagnostic and statistical manual of mental disorders* (3rd ed.). Washington, D.C.: Author, 1980.

Angelino, H., Dollins, J., & Mech, E. V. Trends in the fears and worries of school children as related to socioeconomic status and age. *Journal of Genetic Psychology*, 1956, *89*, 263–276.

Ball, W., & Tronick, E. Infant responses to impending collision: Optical and real. *Science*, 1971, *171*, 818–820.

Batter, B. S., & Davidson, C. V. Wariness of strangers: Reality or artifact? *Journal of Child Psychology and Psychiatry*, 1979, *20*, 93–110.

Bauer, D. H. An exploratory study of developmental changes in children's fears. *Journal of Child Psychology and Psychiatry*, 1976, *17*, 69–74.

Belsky, J. Early human experience: A family perspective. *Developmental Psychology*, 1981, *17*, 3–21.

Belsky, J., & Steinberg, L. D. The effects of day care: A critical review. *Child Development*, 1978, *49*, 929–949.

Berlyne, D. E. *Conflict, arousal, and curiosity*. New York: McGraw-Hill, 1960.

Bernstein, D. A., & Allen, G. J. Fear Survey Schedule. II. Normative data and factor analyses based upon a large college sample. *Behaviour Research and Therapy*, 1969, *7*, 403–407.

Blurton Jones, N. Characteristics of ethological studies of human behaviour. In N. Blurton Jones (Ed.), *Ethological studies of child behaviour*. Cambridge, England: Cambridge University Press, 1972.

Blurton Jones, N., & Leach, G. M. Behaviour of children and their mothers at separation and greeting. In N. Blurton Jones (Ed.), *Ethological studies of child behaviour*. Cambridge, England: Cambridge University Press, 1972.

Bowlby, J. *Attachment and loss* (Vol. 1: *Attachment*). New York: Basic Books, 1969.

Bowlby, J. *Attachment and loss* (Vol. 2: *Separation*). New York: Basic Books, 1973.

Bretherton, I., & Ainsworth, M. D. S. Responses of one-year-olds to a stranger in a strange situation. In M. Lewis & L. A. Rosenblum (Eds.), *The origins of fear*. New York: Wiley, 1974.

Bronson, G. W. The development of fear in man and other animals. *Child Development*, 1968, *39*, 409–432.

Bronson, G. W. Fear of visual novelty: Developmental patterns in males and females. *Developmental Psychology*, 1970, *2*, 33–40.

Bronson, G. W. Infants' reactions to unfamiliar persons and novel objects. *Monographs of the Society for Research in Child Development*, 1972, *37* (3, Serial No. 148).

Brooks, J., & Lewis, M. Infants' responses to strangers: Midget, adult, and child. *Child Development*, 1976, *47*, 323–332.

Carpenter, C. J., & Huston-Stein, A. Activity structure and sex-typed behavior in preschool children. *Child Development*, 1980, *51*, 862–872.

Charlesworth, W. R. General issues in the study of fear. In M. Lewis & L. A. Rosenblum (Eds.), *The origins of fear*. New York: Wiley, 1974.

Corter, C. M. The nature of the mother's absence and the infant's response to brief separations. *Developmental Psychology*, 1976, *12*, 428–434.

Doyle, A. B. Infant development in day care. *Developmental Psychology*, 1975, *4*, 655–656.

Dusek, J. B., Mergler, N. L., & Kermis, M. D. Attention, encoding, and information processing in low and high test anxious children. *Child Development*, 1976, *47*, 201–207.

Eme, R., & Schmidt, D. The stability of children's fears. *Child Development*, 1978, *49*, 1277–1279.

Feldbaum, C. L., Christenson, T. E., & O'Neal, E. C. An observational study of the assimilation of the newcomer to the preschool. *Child Development*, 1980, *51*, 497–507.

Flavell, J. *The developmental psychology of Jean Piaget*. Princeton, N.J.: Van Nostrand Rheinhold, 1963.

Gold, D., & Andres, D. Developmental comparisons between 10-year-old children with employed and non-employed mothers. *Child Development*, 1978, *49*, 75–84. (a)

Gold, D., & Andres, D. Relations between maternal employment and development of nursery school children. *Canadian Journal of Behavioural Science*, 1978, *10*, 116–129. (b)

Goldberg, S., & Lewis, M. Play behavior in the year-old infant: Early sex differences. *Child Development*, 1969, *40*, 21–33.

Hampe, E., Noble, H., Miller, L. C., & Barrett, C. L. Phobic children one and two years posttreatment. *Journal of Abnormal Psychology*, 1973, *82*, 446–453.

Hebb, D. O. On the nature of fear. *Psychological Review*, 1946, *53*, 259–275.

Hermans, H. J. M., ter Laak, J. J. F., & Maes, P. C. Achievement motivation and fear of failure in family and school. *Developmental Psychology*, 1972, *6*, 520–528.

Hess, E. H. Ethology and developmental psychology. In P. H. Mussen (Ed.), *Carmichael's manual of child psychology*. New York: Wiley, 1970.

Hess, R. D., & Camara, K. A. Post-divorce family relationships as mediating factors in the consequences of divorce for children. *Journal of Social Issues*, 1979, *35*, 79–96.

Hetherington, E. M. Divorce: A child's perspective. *American Psychologist*, 1979, *34*, 851–858.

Hill, K. T. Social reinforcement as a function of test anxiety and success–failure experiences. *Child Development*, 1967, *38*, 723–737.

Hill, K. T. Anxiety in the evaluative context. In W. W. Hartup (Ed.), *The young child: Reviews of research* (Vol. 2). Washington, D.C.: National Association for the Education of Young Children, 1972.

Hill, K. T., & Sarason, S. B. The relation of test anxiety and defensiveness to test and school performance over the elementary school years. *Monographs of the Society for Research in Child Development*, 1966, *31* (2, Serial No. 104).

Hock, E. Working and non-working mothers and their infants: A comparative study of maternal caregiving characteristics and infant social behavior. *Merrill-Palmer Quarterly*, 1980, *26*, 79–102.

Hoffman, L. W. Maternal employment: 1979. *American Psychologist*, 1979, *34*, 859–865.

Hughes, M., Pinkerton, G., & Plewis, I. Children's difficulties in starting infant school. *Journal of Child Psychology and Psychiatry*, 1979, *20*, 187–196.

Jersild, A. T., & Holmes, F. B. *Children's fears*. New York: Teachers College, Columbia University, 1935.

Jersild, A. T., Telford, C. W., & Sawrey, J. M. *Child psychology* (7th ed.). Englewood Cliffs, N.J.: Prentice-Hall, 1975.

Johnson, S. B., & Melamed, B. G. The assessment and treatment of children's fears. In
  B. B. Lahey & A. E. Kazdin (Eds.), *Advances in clinical child psychology* (Vol.
  4). New York: Plenum Press, 1977.

Jones, H. E., & Jones, M. C. Fear. *Childhood Education,* 1928, *5,* 136–145.

Kagan, J. *Change and continuity in infancy.* New York: Wiley, 1971.

Kagan, J. Discrepancy, temperament, and infant distress. In M. Lewis & L. A.
  Rosenblum (Eds.), *The origins of fear.* New York: Wiley, 1974.

Kagan, J., Kearsley, R., & Zelazo, P. *Infancy: Its place in human development.*
  Cambridge, Mass.: Harvard University Press, 1978.

Lapouse, R., & Monk, M. A. Fears and worries of a representative sample of children.
  American Journal of Orthopsychiatry, 1959, *29,* 803–818.

Lewis, M. Developmental theories. In I. L. Kutash & L. B. Schlesinger (Eds.),
  Handbook on stress and anxiety. San Francisco: Jossey-Bass, 1980.

Lewis, M., & Brooks, J. Self, other, and fear: Infants' reactions to people. In M. Lewis
  & L. A. Rosenblum (Eds.), *The origins of fear.* New York: Wiley, 1974.

Lewis, M., & Rosenblum, L. A. (Eds.). *The origins of fear.* New York: Wiley, 1974.

MacFarlane, J. W., Allen, L., & Honzik, M. P. *A developmental study of the behavior
  problems of normal children between twenty-one months and fourteen years.*
  Berkeley, Calif.: University of California Press, 1954.

Maurer, A. What children fear. *Journal of Genetic Psychology,* 1965, *106,* 265–277.

McGrew, W. C. Aspects of social development in nursery school children with
  emphasis on introduction to the group. In N. Blurton Jones (Ed.), *Ethological
  studies of child behaviour.* Cambridge, England: Cambridge University Press,
  1972.

Messer, S. The effect of anxiety over intellectual performance on reflection-
  impulsivity in children. *Child Development,* 1970, *41,* 723–735.

Miller, L. C., Barrett, C. L., & Hampe, E. Phobias of childhood in a prescientific era.
  In A. Davids (Ed.), *Child personality and psychopathology: Current topics*
  (Vol. 1). New York: Wiley, 1974.

Miller, L. C., Barrett, C. L., Hampe, E., & Noble, H. Factor structure of childhood fears.
  Journal of Consulting and Clinical Psychology, 1972, *39,* 264–268.

Morgan, G., & Riccuiti, H. Infants' response to strangers during the first year. In
  B. M. Foss (Ed.), *Determinants of infant behavior* (Vol. 4). London: Methuen,
  1969.

Nottelman, E. D., & Hill, K. T. Text anxiety and off-task behavior in evaluative
  situations. *Child Development,* 1977, *48,* 225–231.

Rheingold, H. L. The effect of a strange environment on the behavior of infants. In
  B. M. Foss (Ed.), *Determinants of infant behaviour* (Vol. 4). London: Methuen,
  1969.

Rheingold, H. L., & Eckerman, C. O. The infant separates himself from his mother.
  Science, 1970, *168,* 78–83.

Rheingold, H. L., & Eckerman, C. O. Fear of the stranger: A critical examination. In
  H. W. Reese (Ed.), *Advances in child development and behavior* (Vol. 8). New
  York: Academic Press, 1973.

Roopnarine, J., & Lamb, M. The effects of day care on attachment and exploratory
  behavior in a strange situation. *Merrill-Palmer Quarterly,* 1979, *24,* 85–95.

Rutter, M. *Maternal deprivation reassessed.* Baltimore: Penquin, 1974.

Rutter, M. Social-emotional consequences of day care for pre-school children. *American Journal of Orthopsychiatry,* 1981, *51,* 4-28. (a)

Rutter, M. Stress, coping, and development: Some issues and some questions. *Journal of Child Psychology and Psychiatry,* 1981, *22,* 323-356. (b)

Rutter, M., Tizard, J., & Whitmore, K. *Education, health and behaviour.* London: Longman, 1970.

Sarason, I. G. Test anxiety, attention, and the general problem of anxiety. In C. D. Spielberger & I. G. Sarason (Eds.), *Stress and anxiety* (Vol. 1). Washington, D.C.: Hemisphere, 1975.

Sarason, S. B., Davidson, K. S., Lighthall, F. F., Waite, R. R., & Ruebush, B. K. *Anxiety in elementary school children.* New York: Wiley, 1960.

Scarr, S., & Salapatek, P. Patterns of fear development during infancy. *Merrill-Palmer Quarterly,* 1970, *16,* 53-90.

Schaffer, H. R. Cognitive components of the infant's response to strangeness. In M. Lewis & L. A. Rosenblum (Eds), *The origins of fear.* New York: Wiley, 1974.

Schaffer, H. R. The onset of fear of strangers and the incongruity hypothesis. *Journal of Child Psychology and Psychiatry,* 1966, *7,* 95-106.

Schaffer, H. R. & Callender, W. M. Psychological effects of hospitalization in infancy. *Pediatrics,* 1959, *24,* 528-539.

Schaffer, H. R., & Emerson, P. E. The development of social attachments in infancy. *Monographs of the Society for Research in Child Development,* 1964, *29* (3, Serial No. 94).

Schwarz, J. C., & Wynn, R. The effects of mothers' presence and previsits on children's emotional reactions to starting nursery school. *Child Development,* 1971, *42,* 871-882.

Silverman, I. W., & Waite, S. V. Test anxiety and the effectiveness of social and nonsocial reinforcement in children. *Child Development,* 1969, *40,* 307-314.

Spelke, E., Zelazo, P., Kagan, J., & Kotelchuck, M. Father interaction and separation protest. *Developmental Psychology,* 1973, *9,* 83-90.

Spielberger, C. D. *Manual for the State-Trait Anxiety Inventory for Children.* Palo Alto, Calif.: Consulting Psychologists Press, 1973.

Spitz, R. Anxiety in infancy: A study of its manifestation in the first year of life. *International Journal of Psychoanalysis,* 1950, *31,* 537-544.

Sroufe, L. A. Wariness of strangers and the study of infant development. *Child Development,* 1977, *48,* 731-746.

Sroufe, L. A. Infant-caregiver attachment and patterns of adaptation in preschool: The roots of maladaptation and competence. In M. Perlmutter (Ed.), *Minnesota symposium on child psychology* (Vol. 16). Minneapolis: University of Minnesota Press, 1983.

Sroufe, L. A., Waters, E., & Matas, L. Contextual determinants of infant affective response. In M. Lewis & L. A. Rosenblum (Eds.), *The origins of fear.* New York: Wiley, 1974.

Stayton, D. J., & Ainsworth, M. D. S. Individual differences in infant responses to brief everyday separations as related to other infant and maternal behaviors. *Developmental Psychology,* 1973, *9,* 226-235.

Stayton, D. J., Ainsworth, M. D. S., & Main, M. B. Development of separation behavior in the first year of life: Protest, following, and greeting, *Developmental Psychology*, 1973, *9*, 213–225.

Stern, D. Mother and infant at play: The dyadic interaction involving facial, vocal, and gaze behaviors. In M. Lewis & L. Rosenblum (Eds.), *The effect of the infant on its caregiver*. New York: Wiley, 1974.

Stevenson, H. W., & Odom, R. D. The relation of anxiety to children's performance on learning and problem-solving tasks. *Child Development*, 1965, *36*, 1003–1012.

Tennes, K. H., & Lampl, E. E. Stranger and separation anxiety in infancy. *Journal of Nervous and Mental Diseases*, 1964, *139*, 247–254.

Wallerstein, J. S., & Kelly, J. B. *Surviving the breakup—How children and parents cope with divorce*. New York: Basic Books, 1980.

Weiner, B., & Kukla, A. An attributional analysis of achievement motivation. *Journal of Personality and Social Psychology*, 1970, *15*, 1–20.

Weinraub, M., & Lewis, M. The determinants of children's responses to separation. *Monographs of the Society for Research in Child Development*, 1977, *42* (4, Serial No. 172).

Wine, J. Test anxiety and direction of attention. *Psychological Bulletin*, 1971, *76*, 92–104.

‡ 3 ‡

EPIDEMIOLOGY OF ANXIETY DISORDERS IN CHILDREN: A REVIEW

HELEN ORVASCHEL
MYRNA M. WEISSMAN

INTRODUCTION

Epidemiology is a science dealing with the distribution and determinants of health states in a population (Gould, Wunsch-Hitzig, & Dohrenwend, 1981; MacMahon & Pugh, 1970). On the one hand it is a descriptive science, in that it seeks to record the occurrence of diseases and disorders. On the other hand it is a predictive science, concerning itself with the determinants of and risk factors for disorders, as well as the control, management, and prevention of disease states. Epidemiologic data also provide the information necessary for the planning and evaluation of service and treatment programs by obtaining estimates of the prevalence and incidence of disorders.

Incidence is a measure of the new occurrence of a disorder while prevalence is a measure of the number of individuals who have a particular disorder. Prevalence therefore is a function of incidence and duration. Estimates of prevalence are useful for those concerned with the extent to which a disorder is present in the population at a given time, but incidence data are more valuable for identifying causal factors.

Helen Orvaschel. University of Pittsburgh School of Medicine, Western Psychiatric Institute and Clinic, Pittsburgh, Pennsylvania.

Myrna M. Weissman. Department of Psychiatry, Depression Research Unit, Yale University School of Medicine, New Haven, Connecticut.

58

ISSUES OF SAMPLING BIAS

True estimates of the prevalence of a disorder can only be obtained by measuring the extent to which the disorder is present in the total population at risk for the disorder. Sampling from the population at risk is important, since many investigators attempt to measure prevalence from treated populations alone. Measures based on treated cases are biased for several reasons. For a variety of disorders the majority of individuals affected never seek treatment. Those who do seek treatment are often of higher socioeconomic status or may represent the most severe or disabled cases. For cases involving child psychiatric disorders, the initiation of a treatment referral is almost never the child. Therefore, biases in treated child samples often involve the degree to which the child's behavior is an irritant to those around him or her. Children who act out in school are far more likely to be referred by a teacher for treatment or evaluation than are children who are quiet or withdrawn.

Not only is the prevalence estimate of a disorder likely to be biased and inaccurate if based on treated cases, but the investigator's perspective of the expression of a disorder may also be affected. For example, most observations about the differing ages of onset for various anxiety disorders are drawn from clinical samples. These observations may be expressions of when parents become alarmed enough to seek treatment for children rather than when the disorder first appeared. Frequent observations of researchers of childhood depression provide another example. Reports indicate that for childhood depression the diagnosis is more prevalent in boys than girls; acting-out behavior is found in about half the sample; for children under the age of 8, about 75% also manifest separation anxiety as a concomitant symptom of the depressive disorder. These observations have been based on clinically referred cases of childhood depression, but they have not yet been substantiated by epidemiologic investigation. In fact, it is highly likely that selection biases are determining treatment referral. Boys may be more likely to act out when emotionally distressed than girls. This acting out behavior precipitates a rereferral, which then increases the likelihood that the underlying depression is detected. Similarly, symptoms of separation anxiety are likely to be an irritant to parents, who are then more likely to seek treatment for their child. Children (and adults) with two disorders are more likely to become a treated case than are those with one disorder (Berkson, 1946). All of these factors may lead to biased views on the expression of a disorder in the population when these views are based on an examination of treated cases alone.

PROBLEMS OF CASE DEFINITION

Given that the study of treated populations alone result in biased estimates of the prevalence of psychiatric disorders as well as distorted views of their expression, epidemiologic data must be derived from both treated and untreated samples of the population. Estimating the population prevalence of a disorder also necessitates a clear delineation of the criteria used to define a case. In adult psychiatry early epidemiologic studies concentrated on measures of overall emotional distress (Langner, 1962; Leighton, Harding, & Macklin, 1963; Srole, Langner, & Michael, 1962). This practice avoided the problem of unreliability of psychiatric diagnoses and case definition while reflecting the unitary concept of mental health at the time (Weissman & Klerman, 1978). Subsequently, advances in the field of adult psychopathology began to emerge. These achievements included improved concepts, definitions, and criteria for adult psychiatric disorders such as the Feighner Criteria (Feighner et al., 1972), the Research Diagnostic Criteria (RDC) (Spitzer, Endicott, & Robins, 1978), and more recently the DSM-III criteria (American Psychiatric Association, 1980). Improvements were also made in the techniques used for symptomatic, behavioral, and diagnostic assessments. These structured and semistructured assessment tools include the Present State Exam (PSE) (Wing, Cooper, & Sartorius, 1974), the Schedule for Affective Disorders and Schizophrenia (SADS) (Spitzer & Endicott, 1978), and the Diagnostic Interview Schedule (DIS) (Robins, Helzer, Croughan, & Ratcliff, 1981). Such advances in case definition and assessment have accelerated research in adult psychiatric epidemiology by reducing the problems of criteria and information variance in assessment and improving the reliability of psychiatric diagnosis (Endicott & Spitzer, 1978).

In child psychiatry, case definition has been particularly problematic because of the lack of consensus on the classification of childhood psychiatric disorders, as well as the unavailability of reliable instrumentation to assess these disorders. However, the advent of the DSM-III criteria and recent development in assessment techniques for use with children are beginning to provide the tools necessary for obtaining epidemiologic data (Orvaschel, Sholomskas, & Weissman, 1980a, 1980b). To date, knowledge about the rates and distribution of specific child psychiatric disorders based on probability samples of children in the general population is extremely limited. This chapter provides an overview of the epidemiology of anxiety disorders in children. We review the available literature on these disorders and discuss the methodologic differences that make comparability across studies difficult.

ESTIMATES OF PREVALENCE

DSM-III (American Psychiatric Association, 1980) refers to anxiety disorders as a group of disorders in which anxiety is the most prominent disturbance. For children, the disorders included in this category are separation anxiety, avoidant disorder, overanxious disorder, phobic disorder, panic disorder, and obsessive–compulsive disorder. Each of these diagnostic categories is defined with a specific set of criteria and, for many, a specification of impaired functioning. The availability of these prespecified criteria now provide an essential element for the implementation of studies of community children. Such epidemiologic research would provide estimates of the population prevalence of specific anxiety disorders in children. However, because of the recency of the DSM-III, no such population studies have as yet been undertaken. Our knowledge of the prevalence of anxiety disorders in children therefore is based on studies that preceded DSM-III.

Studies that provide data on the epidemiology of childhood anxiety disorders vary in almost all aspects of methodology and design. These variations include the assessment measures used, the source of information about the child, the sampling frame, the age of children studied, and the definition and criteria of caseness. The studies do, however, provide an overview of the nature of the problem in the population at risk and demonstrate the importance of classification issues in epidemiologic research. For example, the now-classic epidemiologic study by Lapouse and Monk (1958) examined the frequency and intensity of a wide range of child behaviors and characteristics. They randomly selected 482 households in which children between the ages of 6–12 years were living. Children were selected by the Kish grid method, and mothers were used as the informants. The child sample consisted of 49% boys and 51% girls, with 50% aged 6–8 years and 50% aged 9–12 years. Interviews of approximately 1½ hours in length covered areas of interpersonal, social, and intellectual behaviors, as well as general adjustment and functioning and questions on fears, worries, and a variety of additional symptoms. Behaviors were rated for their presence or absence, frequency, and intensity.

Lapouse and Monk (1958) reported that the children in their study had a 43% prevalence rate of "many fears and worries" (defined as seven or more fears and worries). Fifty percent of the girls had seven or more fears and worries compared with 36% of the boys and 48% of the 6- to 8-year-olds had "many fears and worries" compared to 37% of the 9- to 12-year-olds. Black children had more fears and worries (63%) than white children (44%), and low socioeconomic children had more fears and worries (50%) than higher socioeconomic children (36%). Forty-one percent of the children had a fear of "anyone in the family getting sick, having an accident or dying" (Lapouse & Monk, 1959, p. 808), which may be viewed as an item related to separation anxiety.

Test–retest reliability of mothers' ratings ranged from 52% to 98% and was best for behaviors that were concrete, observable, and high in nuisance value. An additional clinical sample of 193 children were interviewed directly, and their responses were compared with those of their mothers. Agreement between mothers and children varied according to the items involved, averaging about 54% for fears and worries. However, the instance of fears and worries for which the mother said "yes" and the child said "no" was 5%, while the instance for which the child said "yes" and the mother said "no" was 40%. Lapouse and Monk (1958) suggested that ". . . mothers underestimate these concerns in their children and that very likely the mother is a poor source of information regarding this area of the child's experience" (p. 1143).

Lapouse and Monk (1959) also attempted to evaluate the relationship between the children's symptoms and other characteristics of their adjustment. They did not find the presence of fears and worries in children to be related to other forms of pathological behavior and stated that they ". . . do not know if the fears and worries are indicative of maladjustment, personality deviation or emotional disturbance or if they are a concomitant of the wide range of developmental phenomena in essentially normal children" (Lapouse & Monk, 1959, p. 817).

Based on the Lapouse and Monk study (1958, 1959), it would appear that "fears and worries" are common in children and are not necessarily prognostic or indicative of psychopathology. The prevalence rates decreased as the child got older, and the symptoms were not correlated with alternative indicators of psychopathology.

Additional information of the prevalence of fears or phobias and their relationship to age was provided by Agras, Sylvester, and Oliveau (1969). They conducted a two-stage epidemiologic study of fears and phobias in a random sample of 325 adults and children. They interviewed directly respondents aged 14 and over and obtained information from mothers for respondents under the age of 14. Unfortunately, data were not presented separately for the children in the sample, but estimates of prevalence, course, and treatment of common fears provided interesting insights into the development and expression of phobias across the life span. Information was obtained by an interview that listed 40 common fears and ascertained their presence, absence, intensity, duration, treatment, and any resultant avoidant behavior. A separate questionnaire including 21 items was used for children under the age of 14. A psychiatrist examined the information obtained on the questionnaire and identified those respondents believed to be phobic or possibly phobic. Another psychiatrist then conducted blind interviews with a selected number of respondents identified in cases, as well as with a number of controls.

Agras *et al.* (1969) noted three categories of fears with differing pattern of onset and chronicity. One category included fears of doctors, injections, darkness, and strangers. This category generally began in childhood, showed a sharply declining prevalence, and was often of limited duration. The second category of phobias included fears of animals, heights, storms, enclosed places, and social situations. The onset for these fears ranged from childhood to early adulthood, with a slowly declining prevalence indicative of a persistent course. The third category of fears included crowds, death, injury and illness, and separation. These fears tended to onset in adulthood, with the greatest prevalence in middle age.

The prevalence for all phobias was 7.7%. Phobias were reported to be mildly disabling in 74.7% of cases and severely disabling in 0.2% of cases. Less than 0.1% of respondents were in treatment for a phobia at the time of the interview, and only 5.7% had ever been in treatment for a phobia. The authors reported that psychiatrists were likely to see only a small proportion of individuals with a phobia, and then generally those with the most severe disabilities. Phobias were viewed as running a long-term, mildly disabling course, with a high incidence in childhood and a decline in adolescence and early adulthood, except for fears of crowds, death, injury, and illness.

A somewhat different relationship between anxiety and age was reported by Werry and Quay (1971). They studied 1753 children in kindergarten through second grade, in order to obtain prevalence data on 52 behavior problems found to be common in child guidance clinic populations. They obtained teacher ratings on a behavior problem checklist for 926 boys and 827 girls aged 5–8 years. The overall prevalence for anxiety/fearfulness was reported to be 16% for boys and 17% for girls; for tension, 23.1% for boys and 12.3% for girls; for nervousness, 21.9% for boys and 15.5% for girls. Werry and Quay found that anxiety symptoms showed a steady decline from the ages of 5 to 7 years, with an increase in frequency at the age of 8 years for boys. It is unclear, however, whether the sudden increase in symptomatology at age 8 for boys represents a true increase in the prevalence of anxiety or whether this increase is a reflection of higher rates of other behavioral disturbance, which are reported by teachers in a kind of reverse halo effect.

While the previous three studies reported on the prevalence of fears and worries and their expression across the age span, the following two studies investigated several areas of behavioral disturbance in a preschool age group and provide data suggesting a relationship between fears and worries and overall psychopathology.

Richman, Stevenson, and Graham (1975) examined the prevalence of behavior problems in 3-year-olds in a random sample of 705 children. Trained interviewers conducted a semistructured interview with mothers on their child's health, development, and behaviors such as eating, sleeping, peer relations, activity, concentration, worries and fears, and the like. They found that approximately 7% of the total population of 3-year-olds had a moderate to severe behavior problem, 15% had mild behavior problems, and boys tended to show slightly higher rates of overall problems than girls. In reporting the prevalence of several fears and worries, however, they found 2.5% of the boys and 2.6% of the girls were identified as worriers (2.6% total prevalence). The prevalence of fears in the sample was 8.0% for boys and 17.2% for girls (12.8% total prevalence).

Richman *et al.* (1975) also examined the relationship between fears and worries and children's overall scores of behavior pathology.

They found that in their problem behavior group, the prevalence of worries was 3.5% for boys and 9.5% for girls (7.1% total), and the prevalence of fears was 14.0% for boys and 85.7% for girls (44.4% total). In a subsequent study Stevenson and Richman (1978) reinterviewed part of the original sample and included a new group of language delayed (LD) children. The LD children had a higher rate of fears (20.8%) than the general population, although the rate was still lower than that of the behavior problem group. The prevalence of worries in the LD group was zero, since parents were unable to get verbalizations from their language-impaired children on these concerns.

Using assessment procedures similar to the Richman *et al.* (1975) study, Earls (1980) examined the prevalence of behavior problems in 100 3-year-old children in the United States. He, too, found approximately 7% of the children to have moderate to severe behavior problems. He reports the prevalence of several worries and fear to be 7.5% for boys and 8.6% for girls (8.0% total) for worries, and 3.7% for boys and 25.5% for girls (14.0% total) for fears. Earls also reports a higher frequency of worries in the problem behavior group than in the total sample of 3-year-olds. As a final note, however, Richman *et al.* (1975) caution against equating the findings of problem behaviors with the presence of a mental disorder in a child.

Additional information on the prevalence of anxiety symptoms in children is provided by Kastrup (1976) and Abe and Masui (1981). Kastrup reported on a cross-sectional survey of preschool children from two Danish municipalities. Using parents (mostly mothers) as informants, he obtained information on family and social background, pre- and perinatal development, disease, abilities, and behavioral and emotional symptoms for 95 boys and 80 girls between the ages of 5 and 6 years. Kastrup reported the prevalence of nightmares was 11% for boys and 5% for girls; fears, 3% for boys and 5% for girls; and fear of separation, 12% for boys and 16% for girls. About 15% of the children were reported to have "psychic disorder," which was defined as deviant behavior when the child was compared with his or her age group, and which involved distress and caused concern to parents. No information on the relationship between anxiety symptoms and other behavioral disturbances are reported.

Abe and Masui (1981) reported the results of their pilot study in Japan on sex differences in the prevalence of fears and anxiety symptoms in respondents aged 11–23 years. They administered a questionnaire to 2500 individuals (1290 boys and 1210 girls) concerning fears of lightning, going out of doors, blushing, being looked at, and talking, as well as anxiety symptoms of frequency of micturition, trembling hands, hypochondriasis, fainting spells, lump in throat, and feelings of impending death. The authors did not find persistent sex differences in anxiety symptoms, with the exception of frequency of micturition, which was more common for boys. All of the fears were found to be more prevalent in girls, with the exception of fear of talking, which was more frequently reported by boys. Fear of blushing and being looked at had their greatest prevalence in middle adolescence, as did most of the anxiety symptoms.

Specific prevalence estimates were not reported by Abe and Masui (1981). However, we extrapolated approximations of prevalence rates from the published figures provided in their paper. The prevalence of fears ranged from 2% for boys and 7% for girls for "going out of doors alone" to 38% for boys and 43% for girls for "being looked at." The frequency of anxiety symptoms ranged from 5% for boys and 4% for girls for "feeling of impending death" to 33% for boys and 31% for girls for hypochondriasis. No information is provided on the prevalence of multiple fears or combination of anxiety symptoms, and no data are reported on levels of functioning or impairment in relation to fears and anxiety.

COMPARING ACROSS STUDIES

Table 3.1 summarizes the seven studies reviewed and allows a comparison of the reported prevalence rates. Examining the studies in table format makes clear the difficulties encountered in trying to obtain a composite picture of the epidemiology of anxiety in children. Four of the seven studies were done in the United States, one in England, one in Denmark, and one in Japan. The age of the children studied ranged from 3 to 23 years; the Agras et al. (1969) study included adults but did not provide data separately for adults and children. Informants varied across studies, and all the investigators used different instruments and methods of assessment.

Compounding the problems already mentioned are the differences across studies in the types of anxiety behaviors studied, the definition of caseness used, and presentation of the data. Some studies tried to determine the relationship between anxiety symptoms and

TABLE 3.1. Studies Reporting Prevalence of Anxiety in Children

Study	Lapouse & Monk (1958)	Agras, Sylvester, & Oliveau (1969)	Werry & Quay (1971)	Richman, Stevenson, & Graham (1975)	Earls (1980)	Kastrup (1976)	Abe & Masui (1981)
				Design			
Location	US	US	US	UK	US	Denmark	Japan
Sample source	Community	Community	School	Community	Community	Community	Community
Sample size	482	325	1753	705	100	175	2500
Age of sample	6–12 years	Children and adults	5–8 years	3 years	3 years	5–6 years	11–12 years
Informants	Mother	Subject or mother	Teacher	Mother	Mother	Parent	Subject
				Results			
Fears and/or worries	43%	7.7%	16.5%	12.8% (fears) 2.6% (worries)	14.0% (fears) 8.0% (worries)	4.0%	2%–43% (fears) 4%–33% (worries)
Separation concerns	41%					13.7%	
Other anxieties			18.0% (tension) 18.0% (nerves)			8.0% (nightmares)	

alternative measures of psychiatric status while other studies did not. For the studies that did examine this relationship, one found no association and two found an association. Even these disagreements are unclear, since the studies involved included samples of very different ages and used different methods of assessment for both anxiety and other indicators of psychopathology. Interestingly, the studies by Richman *et al.* (1975) and Earls (1980) produced results most comparable to each other. These two studies also shared a common methodology and assessment procedure.

RELATIONSHIP WITH ADULT PSYCHOPATHOLOGY

According to the results of the studies reviewed thus far, the relationship between anxiety symptoms and overall psychopathology in children is unclear or, at best contradictory. Lapouse and Monk (1958, 1959) did not find a correspondence between childhood fears and alternative indicators of psychopathology. Richman *et al.* (1975) did find childhood anxiety symptoms to be associated with other measures of behavioral disturbances. These discrepant findings leave unresolved the question of whether the disturbances being measured are clinically insignificant symptoms or actual indicators of psychopathology manifested by various anxiety states.

The relationship between childhood anxiety and adult disorder is also unclear, since no prospective data on this relationship are available. Some investigators have reported that about 50% of adult patients with agoraphobia and panic disorder have childhood histories of fearfulness, dependency, separation anxiety, school adjustment difficulties, and phobia (Gittelman-Klein & Klein, 1973). Additional support for this relationship is provided from retrospective studies of age of onset in adult patients. Sheehan, Sheehan, and Minichiello (1981), in a study of 62 adult patients treated for agoraphobia, found that 31% had an onset in their first decade, and 55% had an onset by age 20. Similarly, Buglass, Clarke, Henderson, Kreitman, and Presley (1977) found a wide range of onsets downward to age 10 in a study of 30 agoraphobic housewives aged 35–53 years.

The childhood history of adult anxiety disorders has been studied more systematically to determine if childhood anxiety symptoms are specific to adult anxiety disorders or neurotic disorders, in general. The results are equivocal. Berg, Marks, McGuire, and Lipsedge (1974) used a questionnaire survey of 786 women who were members of an agoraphobia correspondence club to learn about the frequency of past school phobias. When these women were compared with 58 nonagoraphobic women who were psychiatric outpatients with a neurotic disorder, few differences were found between the groups. A history of school phobia was equally common in both groups (about 22%). The authors concluded that childhood school phobia was related to adult neurotic illness rather than specifically to agoraphobia. However, the diagnostic criteria for neurotic illness in this early study were unclear. It is also unclear how many of these nonagoraphobic women might be suffering from other anxiety or depressive disorders. In a subsequent report, Berg (1976) stated that agoraphobic women with a childhood history of school phobia have an earlier age of onset of agoraphobia, more severe symptoms, and tend to have more school phobic children than agoraphobic women without such a childhood history.

Tyrer and Tyrer (1974) interviewed 60 phobic, 60 anxious, and 120 depressed adult patients as compared with 120 age- and sex-matched orthopedic and dental patients, about problems of childhood school attendance due to refusal or truancy. They found that school refusal, but not truancy, occurred more frequently among psychiatric patients. There was a nonsignificant tendency for childhood school refusal to be higher in phobic patients. These authors concluded, in agreement with Berg, that there is a link between childhood school refusal and adult neurotic illness. Tyrer and Tyrer also stated that while epidemiologic data suggest that most school refusers become normal adults, childhood school refusers are at higher risk for adult neurotic difficulties than nonrefusers and that the risk of school refusal for adult disorder was higher in females than males.

Another study to examine the long-term implications of childhood fears was reported by Abe (1972), who compared the prevalence of a number of fears and anxiety symptoms in adult women with the retrospectively reported prevalence of the same symptoms in childhood. Abe interviewed 243 women about current symptoms and fears and obtained similar information about the presence of these symptoms when the women were children by obtaining reports from their mothers.

While the methodology of this study is somewhat error prone, some interesting findings regarding chronicity are reported. Thirty-six percent of the women had a fear of thunder, animals, or injections when they were between 6–15 years of age; 35% of these women had the fear as adults (at the time of the interview), compared with a rate of 17% in the adult sample. Seven percent had a fear of crowded places at age 6–15; 6.0% of this group had the fear as an adult compared with 0.8% of the total adult sample. Fourteen percent had the fear of going out alone as a child; 6.0% still had the fear as an adult compared with 2.1% of the adult sample. Anxiety symptoms such as headaches, insomnia over worries, indecision, and hypochondriasis were also much more common in adult women if they had the symptom as a child. The author concluded that childhood nervousness was predictive of anxiety symptoms in adulthood and that phobic adults were likely to have had some phobias in childhood. However, many childhood phobias and anxiety symptoms do disappear with age.

The studies reviewed and the available data suggest a relationship between some childhood and adult anxiety disorders. However, without truly prospective longitudinal data on children with anxiety disorders, no definitive conclusions can be drawn.

CONCLUSIONS

The review of the literature of anxiety states of childhood provides a confusing epidemiologic picture. No epidemiologic data are available regarding anxiety disorders in children. Therefore we were limited to a review of existing data on symptom prevalence. On the basis of past studies, it would appear that anxiety symptoms of all types are quite prevalent. This is true for children of all ages and for both sexes. Although a determination of risk factors from the available data would be premature and was generally not addressed, there was some suggestive information reported. On the whole, anxiety symptoms are more prevalent in girls than boys, although there is considerable variation as a function of the type of anxiety and the age of the child. Anxiety symptoms show a general decline with age, although some types of phobias have onset in early adult or later adult life. There was also some indication that anxiety symptoms were more prevalent in black children than white children and more prevalent in lower than higher socioeconomic children. Finally, the significance of these childhood anxieties is unclear. The evidence regarding the relationship between anxiety symptoms and other indicators of child psychopathology are contradictory. Even less is known about the long-term significance of anxiety symptoms of childhood. Future epidemiologic research must address these unanswered questions.

True epidemiologic data on childhood anxiety disorders can provide a more veridical picture of the expression of these disorders, the risk factors associated with their development, their distribution in the child population, their association with other forms of behavioral disturbance and functional impairment, and their implications for the prediction of adult psychiatric status.

REFERENCES

Abe, K. Phobias and nervous symptoms in childhood and maturity: Persistence and associations. *British Journal of Psychiatry*, 1972, *120*, 275–283.

Abe, K., & Masui, T. Age–sex trends of phobic and anxiety symptoms. *British Journal of Psychiatry*, 1981, *138*, 297–302.

Agras, S., Sylvester, D., & Oliveau, D. The epidemiology of common fears and phobias. *Comprehensive Psychiatry*, 1969, *10*, 151–156.

American Psychiatric Association. *Diagnostic and statistical manual of mental disorders* (3rd ed.). Washington, D.C.: Author, 1980.

Berg, I. School phobia in the children of agoraphobic women. *British Journal of Psychiatry*, 1976, *128*, 86–89.

Berg, I., Marks, I., McGuire, R., & Lipsedge, M. School phobia and agoraphobia. *Psychological Medicine*, 1974, *4*, 428–434.

Berkson, J. Limitations of the application of fourfold table analysis to hospital data. *Biometrics Bulletin*, 1946, *2*, 47–53.

Buglass, D., Clarke, J., Henderson, A. S., Kreitman, N., & Presley, A. S. A study of agoraphobic housewives. *Psychological Medicine*, 1977, *7*, 73–86.

Earls, F. The prevalence of behavior problems in three year old children. A cross-cultural replication. *Archives of General Psychiatry*, 1980, *37*, 1153–1157.

Endicott, J., & Spitzer, R. L. A diagnostic interview: The Schedule for Affective Disorders and Schizophrenia. *Archives of General Psychiatry*, 1978, *35*, 837–844.

Feighner, J. P., Robins, E., Guze, S. B., Woodruff, R. A., Winokur, G., & Muñoz, R. Diagnostic criteria for use in psychiatric research. *Archives of General Psychiatry*, 1972, *26*, 57–63.

Gittelman-Klein, R., & Klein, D. F. School phobia: Diagnostic considerations in light of imipramine effects. *Journal of Nervous and Mental Disease*, 1973, *156*, 199–210.

Gould, M. S., Wunsch-Hitzig, R., & Dohrenwend, B. Estimating the prevalence of childhood psychopathology: A critical review. *Journal of the American Academy of Child Psychiatry*, 1981, *20*, 462–476.

Kastrup, M. Psychic disorders among pre-school children in a geographically delimited area of Aarhus county, Denmark. *Acta Psychiatrica Scandinavia*, 1976, *54*, 29–42.

Langner, T. S. A 22 item screening score of psychiatric symptoms indicating impairment. *Journal of Health and Human Behavior*, 1962, *3*, 269–276.

Lapouse, R., & Monk, M. A. An epidemiologic study of behavior characteristics in children. *American Journal of Public Health*, 1958, *48*, 1134–1144.

Lapouse, R., & Monk, M. A. Fears and worries in a representative sample of children. *American Journal of Orthopsychiatry*, 1959, *29*, 803–818.

Leighton, D. C., Harding, J. S., & Macklin, D. Psychiatric findings of the Sterling County study. *American Journal of Psychiatry*, 1963, *119*, 1021–1026.

MacMahon, B., & Pugh, T. F. *Epidemiology: Principles and methods.* Boston: Little, Brown, 1970.

Orvaschel, H., Sholomskas, D., & Weissman, M. M. *The assessment of psychopathology and behavioral problems in children: A review of scales suitable for epidemiologic and clinical research (1967–1978)* (NIMH Series An No. 1, DHHS Publication No. (ADM) 80-1037). Washington, D.C.: U.S. Government Printing Office, 1980. (a)

Orvaschel, H., Sholomskas, D., & Weissman, M. M. Assessing children in psychiatric epidemiologic studies. In F. Earls (Ed.), *Monographs in psychosocial epidemiology: I. Studies in children.* New York: Prodist, 1980. (b)

Richman, N., Stevenson, J. E., & Graham, P. J. Prevalence of behavior problems in three-year old children: An epidemiologic study in a London borough. *Journal of Child Psychology and Psychiatry*, 1975, *16*, 277–287.

Robins, L. N., Helzer, J. E., Croughan, J., & Ratcliff, R. S. National Institute of Mental Health Diagnostic Interview Schedule. *Archives of General Psychiatry*, 1981, *38*, 381–389.

Sheehan, D. V., Sheehan, K. E., & Minichiello, W. E. Age of onset of phobic disorders: A reevaluation. *Comprehensive Psychiatry*, 1981, *22*, 544–553.

Spitzer, R. L., & Endicott, J. *Schedule for Affective Disorders and Schizophrenia,* NIMH Clinical Research Branch, Collaborative Program on the Psychobiology of Depression, May 1978.

Spitzer, R. L., Endicott, J., & Robins, E. Research Diagnostic Criteria: Rationale and reliability. *Archives of General Psychiatry*, 1978, *35*, 773–782.

Srole, L., Langner, T. S., & Michael, S. T. *Mental health in the metropolis: The Midtown Manhattan Study* (Vol. 1). New York: McGraw-Hill, 1962.

Stevenson, J., & Richman, N. Behavior, language, and development in three-year-old children. *Journal of Autism and Childhood Schizophrenia*, 1978, *8*, 299–313.

Tyrer, P., & Tyrer, S. School refusal, truancy, and adult neurotic illness. *Psychological Medicine*, 1974, *4*, 416–421.

Weissman, M. M., & Klerman, G. L. Epidemiology of me ital disorders. *Archives of General Psychiatry*, 1978, *35*, 705–712.

Werry, J. S., & Quay, H. C. The prevalence of behavior symptoms in younger elementary school children. *American Journal of Orthopsychiatry*, 1971, *41*, 136–143.

Wing, J. K., Cooper, J. E., & Sartorius, N. *The measurement and classification of psychiatric symptoms.* London: Cambridge University Press, 1974.

‡ 4 ‡

DIAGNOSIS AND ASSESSMENT

JOHN S. WERRY

INTRODUCTION

DEFINITION OF ANXIETY

For the purposes of this discussion, the DSM-III (American Psychiatric Association, 1980) definition of anxiety will be used: "apprehension, tension or uneasiness that stems from the anticipation of danger whether internal or external. . . . It may be focused on an object, situation or activity which is avoided (phobia) or unfocused (free floating anxiety)" (p. 354). As the DSM-III also notes, although in the past a distinction has been made between fear and anxiety, as reactions to present and anticipated danger, respectively, the manifestations of the two are identical, and the DSM-III now implicitly reject such a distinction.

SYMPTOM, DISORDER, TRAIT, AND STATE

A *symptom* is an unwanted or undesirable behavior, emotion, or physiological response that can stand alone or be one of several that collectively form a class, as in a disorder or trait.

A *disorder* is a nomothetic, primarily medical concept that adumbrates a group of symptoms into a unit that presumes abnormality and a common set of etiologic, symptomatologic, epidemiologic, historic, prognostic, and therapeutic characteristics. In

John S. Werry. Department of Psychiatry, University of Auckland, Auckland, New Zealand.

contrast to what is often believed, the etiology does not have to be physical (Gittelman-Klein, Spitzer, & Cantwell, 1978). Neither is it necessary for all five characteristics other than the symptoms defining the disorder to be known. Another important characteristic, which is often misunderstood (e.g., Achenbach, 1980), is that although a given disorder occurs within an organism and changes the organism's function in various ways, this change does not affect all and every function nor the organism in entirety. The diagnosis of a disorder thus cannot be expected to explain all the variance associated with the organism's behavior.

A *trait* or *dimension* differs from a disorder in that it is a universal characteristic by which all individuals can be measured. If there were only one or two traits, then some individuals would be predicted to have similar positions on the traits, but the larger the number of traits, the greater the probability that each individual's position in N dimensional space will be unique. Traits are also generally assumed to be stable over time, whereas no such assumption applies to a disorder.

A *state* differs from a trait only in that it is assumed to be transitory and not characteristic of the individual at all times. Otherwise it resembles a trait in conceptualization and measurement.

To a large extent, the individual concepts are bound by profession and measurement. For example, those who consult a physician expect and are likely to receive traditional medical assessment methods of history and examination—a diagnosis, a prognosis, and a course of treatment. On the other hand in nonmedical settings the procedures and parlance are likely to be different. The test of validity of each concept will ultimately depend on how useful it proves to be. None has yet been shown to have overriding validity, and differences in opinion tend to be based on territorial disputes, as much as anything.

CONCEPTS OF ABNORMALITY

In clinical settings, especially medical settings, it is difficult to escape having to define the person and his or her symptoms, traits, or state score as normal or abnormal. A disorder is by definition almost abnormal, so that the clinician who uses such a concept has only to make a binary decision—either the disease is present or it is not. This concept of abnormality is qualitative.

With traits or states the cut-off point is ordinarily decided by quantitative methods such as two standard deviations from the mean. However, unless the measure and its variance have been adjusted to some validating criterion, this is simply "beatifying" a statistical or numerical concept. The cut-off point can also be on the basis of a clinical judgment, which opens the possibility of considerable error across clinicians and across patients. Regrettably, this is still the basis upon which judgments about the symptoms of psychopathology such as anxiety are made in practice. Thus, while the diagnosis of a disorder is a dichotomous decision, the assessment of the individual symptoms leading to that judgment is often quantitative and error prone.

The behavioral judgment of abnormality seems to be defined only by nuisance value; that is, it is strictly atheoretical and pragmatic. In this respect behavioral judgment has much in common with clinical judgment about symptoms.

ANXIETY SYMPTOMS IN CHILDREN

By definition, *subjective symptoms* are not observable and depend for their identification on self-reports. The causes of anxiety in children can be classified as normative or clinical. Normative symptoms and their developmental sequence have been described in Chapter 2 of this volume, but it is important to note that 50% of children aged 2–6 years have three symptoms, while 50% of those aged 6–12 years have seven (Miller, Barrett, Hampe, & Noble, 1971, 1972). Clinical symptoms (i.e., symptoms seen in clinic samples), upon which a number of symptom checklists and other diagnostic instruments are based, reflect neither the same spectrum of symptoms nor the same relative frequency (Johnson & Melamed, 1979; Werry & Aman, 1980). For example, Miller *et al.* (1971) showed that "fear of school" occurred in only 1% of normal children, but in up to 69% of clinic children.

In general, *physiological symptoms* seem, as far as they have been studied, to be the same in children as they are in adults and are described in the next section on the DSM-III. Generally, they reflect activity in the autonomic system, especially its adrenergic divisions, but no part of the body is immune. Physical symptoms that seem to have a particular connection with anxiety in children are recurrent, non-localized abdominal pain (Kolvin & Nicol, 1979), tics (Werry, in press), and enuresis (Shaffer, 1973). It must be stressed, however, that while such symptoms may, they do not necessarily indicate anxiety. The absence of a demonstrated physical cause of these symptoms should not be taken as proof of a psychogenic origin, which must be based on demonstration of cause-and-effect relationship, associated data, or the particular characteristics of the symptom and its history.

Behavioral manifestations that are common concomitants of anxiety are motor restlessness, anxious visage, compulsions, and escape-avoidance behaviors like shyness or school refusal.

As is well known, anxiety can both elevate and disrupt *cognitive* and intellectual performance, according to the level of arousal attained and the spectrum within which optimal performance of a given function or task occurs. Inattention, distractibility, academic failure, and poor memory may all be manifestations of anxiety in children.

In summary, anxiety symptoms can be subjective and verbalized, focused or nonfocused, psychophysiological, cognitive, or behavioral. Since anxiety is a normal part of being human, however, the psychophysiological significance of these symptoms depends on their (1) severity and disabling effect, (2) persistence, (3) age appropriateness, (4) number, (5) associated symptomatology, (6) unusualness or bizarreness, and (7) family or peer group norms.

CLASSIFICATIONS

MEDICAL CLASSIFICATIONS OF ANXIETY DISORDERS

While medical or psychiatric classifications of anxiety disorders are numerous and date back over many years, only three are of sufficiently wide acceptance to merit discussion.

DSM-III

The American Psychiatric Association's (1980) DSM-III classification of anxiety disorders has been described by Gittelman-Klein *et al.* (1978) regarding application to children's disorders and criticized in some detail by Achenbach (1980), Rutter and Shaffer (1980), and Quay (in press-b), among others. The DSM-III is unique in that it provides a set of necessary and sufficient "operational" criteria for each diagnosis. The manual also summarizes the state of knowledge about the main clinical, epidemiologic, and differential diagnostic and prognostic features for each category. Some of the diagnostic criteria leave much to be desired in terms of objectivization, and the supporting data on many of the categories is painfully thin. The DSM-III, however, does provide a framework for continuing refinement and development of a truly scientific psychopathological nosology.

The system is multiaxial, providing five separate categories: (I) clinical syndrome; (II) personality, or in the case of children under 18, developmental disorders; (III) physical disorders relevant to the patient's management; (IV) a 7-point scale for assessing stress occuring within the past 12 months considered etiologic or exacerbating the disorder; and (V) a 7-point global assessment scale for the highest level of adaptive functioning in the past year.

While there is a special section for "disorders usually first evident in infancy, childhood or adolescence" (American Psychiatric Association, 1980, p. 35) the manual specifies that diagnosis in the adult section should be made in children when the clinical data suggest that this is the most appropriate type of diagnosis.

The various categories and subcategories of DSM-III anxiety disorders that, in theory, could be applied to children are described in the following paragraph. No attempt is made to list all the diagnostic criteria and descriptive data, for which the DSM-III manual should be consulted.

1. *Anxiety disorders of childhood or adolescence* are subdivided into three categories: separation anxiety disorder, avoidant disorder, and overanxious disorder. Separation anxiety is not synonymous with school phobia, as some critics appear to believe (e.g., Rutter & Shaffer, 1980); school phobia can have a variety of diagnostic causes (e.g., Kolvin & Nicol, 1979). Separation anxiety may present as school phobia, however, the key symptom in the former is an abnormal degree of difficulty in separating from key attachment figures. Avoidant disorder describes the abnormally shy child. In overanxious disorder the key problem is one of worrying about everything.

2. *Anxiety disorders* (adult forms) are described as phobic disorders (agoraphobia with and without panic, social phobia, and simple phobia), which require that the anxiety is focused, and anxiety states (panic disorder, generalized anxiety disorder,

obsessive–compulsive disorder, posttraumatic stress disorder, and atypical disorder). In anxiety states, the anxiety is more pervasive, and most of the subcategories are self-descriptive.

3. *Adjustment disorder* (with anxious mood, with mixed emotional features, and with mixed disturbance of emotions and conduct) is an acute, and presumed transitory, disorder with clear relationship to a recent (within 3 months) and clear stressor. This disorder ceases *pari passu* with the disappearance of the stressor or the achievement of a new level of adaptation.

4. In *hypochondriasis* the anxiety is focused on illness or fear of illness.

This list is by no means exhaustive, but it does reflect those conditions in which anxiety is the central and key symptomatology rather than simply one adjunctive feature.

One of the principal criticisms of the DSM-III is that it has too many subcategories, which leads to loss of reliability (Quay, in press-b; Rutter & Shaffer, 1980). One of the more attractive features of the classification of anxiety disorders is that it can be related to the four stages of development or age-specific types of anxiety (Werry & Aman, 1980). Thus, overanxious disorder can be perceived as exaggerated elemental anxiety present at birth; avoidant reaction, as persistent stranger anxiety; separation anxiety, as separation fear; and phobic anxiety, as specific conditioned anxiety (see also Chapter 2, this volume). In this context, obsessive–compulsive disorder seems to be a blend of escape–avoidance behavior (compulsions) resulting from phobic-type anxiety occurring in an overanxious individual. Panic disorder, which may or may not occur in children, is considered by Klein (1981) to be a biogenic anxiety that is related to separation anxiety.

It must be admitted, however, that developmental cogency does not substitute for the ultimate requirements of reliability and validity for etiology, therapy, epidemiology, and prognosis. Reliability data for children is, thus far, mixed (Werry, Methven, Fitzpatrick, & Dixon, 1983). As pointed out by the sharpest yet most compelling critics, Quay (in press-b) and Rutter and Shaffer (1980), the reliability data are best for the major categories, and studies producing the highest reliabilities (American Psychiatric Association, 1980, pp. 470–471; Strober, Green, & Carlson, 1981; Werry *et al.*, 1983) are those in which diagnosticians who generally work together are paired and thus, such reliabilities may be spuriously high. It is also true, however, that the study by Strober *et al.* (1981) suggests that any unreliability of the DSM-III may lie primarily in the unsatisfactory nature of the data capture methods used by most clinicians, and thus, when properly structured methods covering the domain of items needed for a DSM-III diagnosis are employed, superlative reliability can result.

Validity data are so far almost nonexistent but hopefully will be forthcoming, since this is where the final judgment must rest.

ICD 9

In contrast, the *International Classification of Diseases,* 9th Revision (ICD 9) (World Health Organization, 1980) lacks necessary and sufficient operational criteria and a well-documented supporting manual. Also, the categories for children are fewer in number than the DSM-III and are empirical–clinical rather than developmental. Although it is multiaxial, there are only three axes and they differ; in particular there is no axis for developmental disorders, which are clinical categories in their own right, and there is, instead, an axis representing intellectual level. The fourth and fifth axes of the DSM-III, stress and adaptational level, are absent.

The categories and subcategories of the ICD 9 for the anxiety disorders that might apply to children are as follows:

1. Disturbance of emotions specific to childhood and adolescence: with anxiety and fearfulness; with sensitivity, shyness, and social withdrawal; other or mixed emotional disorder
2. Anxiety states
3. Phobic state
4. Obsessive–compulsive disorder
5. Hypochondriasis
6. Anankastic personality disorder (As far as I know, unlike the DSM-III, where personality disorders require an age of 18 years or above as one of their criteria, there is no *a priori* reason why this diagnosis in the ICD 9 could not be applied to children. It is equivalent to the old obsessional personality disorder.)
7. Adjustment reaction: with predominant disturbance of other emotions; with mixed disturbance of emotions and conduct
8. Acute reaction to stress: predominant disturbance of emotions; mixed

As of yet, there are no published reliability or validity data relating to the ICD 9 in children, though Rutter and Shaffer (1980) refer to an unpublished British study that, using the case history approach, showed good reliability for the major categories among a large number of child psychiatrists who made diagnoses quite independently. There was a marked loss of reliability in subcategories, however. There is also some reliability and validity data from preparatory drafts relating to the major categories, mostly by Rutter and his associates (Rutter & Shaffer, 1980; Rutter, 1976), but this is not necessarily applicable to the ICD 9.

Isle of Wight System

The Isle of Wight System (Rutter, Tizard, Yule, Graham, & Whitmore, 1976) is mentioned only briefly here, since it has more in common with trait systems. It is popular outside the United States and has been used extensively in epidemiologic studies. There is only one category of anxiety disorder, and that is lumped together with all the dysphorias into "emotional disturbance." This system has by far the greatest proof of reliability and validity of any (see Rutter, 1976; Rutter et al., 1976; Rutter & Shaffer, 1980). It is, of course, debatable whether such a simple system is adequate for the needs of child psychiatry in the 1980s.

Summary of Medical Classifications

DSM-III and ICD 9 are similar in major categories but differ in the number and conceptualization of subcategories. Neither system has yet proven its superiority, and disputation is a poor substitute for research into their respective reliabilities and validities. The Isle of Wight system is by far the best established, but it has more in common with trait systems than either of the two main psychiatric systems.

TRAIT, DIMENSIONAL, AND EMPIRICAL–STATISTICAL CLASSIFICATIONS

Trait, dimensional, and empirical–statistical classifications differ from medical or disorder-type classifications in being derived from dimensional or trait approaches upon which some quantitative cut-off point of normality–abnormality is imposed. Unlike psychiatric classifications (with the possible exception of the Isle of Wight system), these are almost all based on empirical–statistical analyses of symptom checklists rather than on dichotomous clinical judgments derived from interview data. Although there are a number of symptom checklists for children (see section entitled "Symptom Checklists and Rating Scales"), they all produce on factor analysis similar second-order orthogonal underlying dimensions (Quay, in press-b). The first factor, accounting for the largest amount of variance, is a conduct problem or externalizing factor, and the second is an anxious–depressed–withdrawal or internalizing factor (Quay, in press-a). Other factors reflecting attention problems, hyperactivity, socialized aggression, and schizoid unresponsiveness are less robust and less important but reasonably consistent nevertheless. Although these are traits or dimensions, one of the major proponents of such methods of classification, Quay (in press-a), has described "disorders" derived from extreme scores of pure dimensional types, of which only anxious–depressed–withdrawal disorder is pertinent to this discussion.

Leaving the disorder concept aside and looking only at the dimensions of psychopathology, the same level of disagreement concerning the desire to which the primary dimensions should be subdivided seems to occur between Quay and others such as Achenbach (1978, 1980), and is similar to disagreement concerning psychiatric classifications. For example, Achenbach subdivides his orthogonal or wide-band dimension "internalizing," depending on age and sex, into three "narrow-band" syndromes of anxious–obsessive, uncommunicative, and somatic complaints. There is also a fourth mixed internalizing–externalizing syndrome, social withdrawal. Conners (see Goyette, Conners, & Ulrich, 1978) has a rather similar set of dimensions (see section in this chapter entitled "Symptom Checklists and Rating Scales"), but his are orthogonal factors and are not correlated as are those of Achenbach.

As with the simple Isle of Wight classification, Quay's (in press-a) single anxious–depressed–withdrawal category has an impressive amount of reliability and validity data to support it. Achenbach (1980) makes similar claims for his more complex system, although with less supporting evidence. The validity of dimensional systems are reviewed in detail by Quay (in press-a, in press-b).

SUMMARY OF CLASSIFICATIONS

In the end the decision about which of the competing systems is best awaits further clarification. While simple classifications, whether medical or dimensional, currently have the weight of evidence in their favor, this should not conceal the fact that they are historically older and thus, better studied; simplicity is of itself, no particular scientific virtue and, in all probability, reflects a more primitive level of knowledge than not. What is needed is less disputation among vested interests and considerably more symptomatological, cognitive, physiological, psychological, prognostic, therapeutic, and epidemiologic study. Unlike most of the other classification systems, the DSM-III offers the possibility of considerable evolution in classification, though at the moment this is only a possibility.

ASSESSMENT

GENERAL PRINCIPLES

A number of reviews and monographs devoted to assessment in children have appeared recently, so this discussion is rather cursory and directs readers to these sources.

Purposes of Assessment

As Borkovec, Weerts, and Berstein (1977), among others, point out, it is impossible to discuss assessment without first posing the question "assessment for what?" At least four such purposes can be defined as follows; in practice, however, they are not always quite so distinct:

1. *Diagnosis.* Here the term is used rather narrowly to mean the adjudgment of normality or abnormality and the affixing of a categorical label carrying with it whatever nomothetic knowledge that pertains to this disorder.
2. Formulation of a *treatment program.*
3. *Evaluation of treatment.* While this is inextricably welded to clinical practice, it is regrettably neither as well accepted nor as well researched as in physical disorders. What should be seen

as integral to good practice tends to be viewed as "research" with all the ethical, economic, and attitudinal connotations that term conjures up.

4. *Research.* The goals here are to accumulate knowledge that transcends the particulars of the case. Rules and procedures thus are different from clinical ones.

Characteristics of a Good Measure

To describe the characteristics of a good measure, only brief reiteration is in order. In general, the following features are desirable:

1. *Explication.* The measure's use, content, and interpretation are clear so as to minimize interassessor variability.

2. *Comprehensiveness.* The measure adequately samples the universe of items, populations, situations, and for children, the developmental stages applicable to the symptom, disorder, trait, state, or behavior.

3. *Practicality and ethical acceptability.* A measure that requires unusual or expensive equipment and/or is time consuming, expensive, painful, intrusive, or demeaning is of little use, even when it meets all other criteria.

4. *Reliability and validity.* Obviously, measures that are unreliable cannot be valid, but the reverse is most definitely not true.

Validity is not as simple as it might seem, since like assessment in general, it requires appending the question "valid for what?" In the clinical situation this requires some sensitivity and skill in deciding who is the consumer—child, parent, institution, society, or profession (see Mash & Terdal, 1981a; Wells, 1981; Werry, 1978). One example of this can be seen in physician rejection of parental reports about behavior in favor of the physician's own, brief, highly situation-bound observation of the child's behavior and in the clinician's shaping of interview responses into the procrustean bed of theory that he or she embraces.

The question of validity becomes particularly acute in the increasingly common situation in both research and clinical practice when the number and source of measures are numerous (Mash & Terdal, 1981a). (This is discussed further in the summary section of this chapter.)

INTERVIEWS

The interview is the stuff of clinical assessment, yet it is one of the most vilified (by researchers and behaviorists) and least researched techniques, especially as it applies to children and their parents (Mash & Terdal, 1981a). There have been several attempts to take this ordinarily rough-hewn tool and hone it into something more systematized. The best-known of such efforts are those of Rutter and Graham (1968) and Graham and Rutter (1968) for child and parent (or for examination and history, respectively). These interviews were developed for the Isle of Wight studies (Rutter et al., 1976) and are primarily for the detection of psychiatric disorder. Diagnosis is within the simplified framework previously discussed, which as far as anxiety disorders are concerned, yields only one overall category. Rutter (1976) has gone so far as to suggest that for most purposes, the interview with the child is unnecessary, since the information it yields is duplicated and more reliably obtained from the parent.

More recent efforts, of which one example is the Diagnostic Interview for Children and Adolescents (Herjanic & Campbell, 1977; Herjanic & Reich, 1982; Reich, Herjanic, Welner, & Gandhy, 1982), are specifically designed to produce the necessary data for both the actual and the DSM-III diagnosis. The Herjanic et al. interview and its NIMH derivative are long, cumbersome, and ill suited to the easygoing, free-flowing *Zeitgeist* of most clinical practice; however, in view of the poor performance of such interviews to date (Mash & Terdal, 1981; Werry, 1978), it could well be argued that the time is ripe for some structure. A more serious criticism relates to the validity and clinical utility of the diagnoses produced by this and similar instruments. Further discussion of the interview can be found in the references previously cited in this section, especially Mash and Terdal (1981a), Wells (1981), and Werry (1978). Because behavioral interviews are so closely tied to behavioral assessment concepts and methods, they are discussed in that section.

SYMPTOM CHECKLISTS AND RATING SCALES

Overview

Reviews of symptom checklists and rating scales can be found in Conners and Werry (1979), Humphries and Ciminero (1979), Mash and Terdal (1981a), Quay (in press-a), Wells (1981), and Werry (1978).

Ordinarily, such reviews consist of judgments about the presence, severity, and/or frequency of symptoms of psychopathology (much less often of normal behaviors) made by the patient or more usually, a close adult observer of his or her behavior such as teacher, nurse, or parent. The rater is required to make averagings across time and across situations, that is, ratings rather than observations.

The principal objections to rating scales discussed in the reviews listed above, are that they are rarely anchored, and thus individual raters have different criteria for presence, frequency, and severity; wording of items is often imprecise (e.g., "hyperactivity"); and the interpretation of findings is too far removed from the actual problem behavior in the situation to be helpful in treatment.

In spite of these criticisms, rating scales for children are indubitably the second-most popular assessment technique for children (after interviews), because they are cheap, acceptable, average observations across time and situations to reduce variance; in the case of teachers, are readily normed by comparison with peers; and have considerable validity diagnostically and, in some cases, as measures of change.

It is true, however, that rating scales are bedevilled by the problem of relatively low reliability between observers even when these are parents. This problem is not as serious as it first seems, in that mothers, fathers, and teachers necessarily see different runs of behavior in different situations, so that the possibility of obtaining good interobserver reliability is limited to those components of behavior that transcend situations.

Despite their low informational content, single-item or global rating scales such as the Clinical Global Impressions (see Werry, 1978) and the Stress and Adaptational Level axes of the DSM-III seem to have a high survival value. This is no doubt due in part to their simplicity and sensitivity as change measures.

Nevertheless, most of the currently accepted rating scales for children are multiitem scales, which in the main, have been subject to empirical statistical data-reduction procedures like factor analysis to make them both more easily interpretable and psychometrically more robust (see Quay, in press-a).

General Purpose Scales

General purpose scales are considerably more common than scales designed specifically for anxiety. Nevertheless, most general scales generate one or more *a priori* or empirically derived clusters of anxiety symptoms or traits that allow some normative statement about a child's anxieties to be made and, in many instances, a second-order diagnosis of disorder. As already noted, most yield a maximum of two or three anxiety-related categories at the orthogonal level. The best-known and best-studied scales are the Behavior Problem Checklist (Quay, in press-a) for parents, teachers, and other observers; the Isle of Wight parent and teacher scales (Rutter, 1976; Rutter *et al.*, 1976); Conners's teacher and parent questionnaires (Conners & Werry, 1979; Goyette *et al.*, 1978); and Achenbach's (1978, 1980) Child Behavior Checklist.

The first four scales yield a single anxiety–dysphoria category, while the last two have three similar categories of anxiety, psychosomatic complaints, and obsessionality. As noted, however, Achenbach's three categories merge into a single internalizing-externalizing factor at the orthogonal level, and Conners's psycho-somatic and obsessionality factors have few items and account for little of the variance. Achenbach also has a mixed internalizing–externalizing syndrome, withdrawing, and there is some variation in other categories as a function of age and sex.

So far, discussion has centered on adult ratings of children's behavior. There are also a number of self-report inventories, most of which fall within the category of "personality inventories" and, as such, unlike most of the parent scales already discussed, are not necessarily developed on or intended for abnormal populations. Examples are the California Personality Inventories, the MMPI, the Junior Eysenck Personality Inventory (Eysenck & Rachman, 1965), and the Cattell 16 PF tests. None of these seems to have achieved much lasting popularity in children's clinics, possibly because most of the children seen there are too young, too disturbed, or otherwise unable to read and/or verbalize well. Another difficulty lies in the failure of most clinicians to produce results that fit within diagnostic, psychodynamic, behavioral, or other conceptual modes prevalent clinically. It is of interest to note, however, that two that have been factor analyzed, the Junior Eysenck (Eysenck & Rachman, 1965) and the Bugenthal, Whalen, and Henker (1977) scale, yield single factors relating to anxiety, similar to the parent factors mentioned previously.

Because of their apparent failure to make much impact on the clinical field, such self-report inventories are difficult to evaluate, particularly since studies suggest that correlations with adult-completed scales are rather low, and this area seems to need more research (Herjanic, Herjanic, Brown, & Wheatt, 1975; O'Leary & Johnson, 1979; Rutter, 1976). Peer ratings similarly seem to have attracted little attention, despite evidence that they may be powerful detectors of disorder (see O'Leary & Johnson, 1979; Pekarik, Prinz, Liebert, Weintraub, & Neale, 1976).

Anxiety Scales

In contrast to general scales, most anxiety scales are self-report types, and although in theory they could be answered by a parent, data to date suggest that parent–child correlations are low (Barrios, Hartmann, & Shigetomi, 1981; Johnson & Melamed, 1979). The most-used and best-studied scales are discussed in the following paragraphs.

The *Children's Manifest Anxiety Scale* (CMAS) (Castenada, McCandless, & Palermo, 1956) is the child equivalent of the adult one. This is a 53-item scale of which 42 items relate to anxiety and 11 to a lie scale. The properties of this scale have been reviewed in detail by Johnson and Melamed (1979) and Werry (1978). It has good test–retest reliability and correlates modestly with other similar scales and poorly with adult estimates; it discriminates between normal and various clinical populations (although, as all too common in such studies, diagnostic eponyms are vague or simply defined as attending a clinic), but is insensitive to stress. Norms exist, but these seem to vary by locality. Factor analysis has revealed two or three similar factors, depending on the study, as follows: one reflecting overanxiousness; one reflecting physiologic anxiety; and one, sometimes combined with the latter, reflecting cognitive anxiety (e.g., inattentiveness, preoccupation, etc.).

The *State–Trait Anxiety Scale* (Spielberger, 1973) has also been well reviewed by Johnson and Melamed (1979). As the name suggests, this scale was designed to differentiate situational from trait anxiety and thus to deal with the failure of the CMAS to respond to acute stress. Unfortunately, the data validating the difference between the two scales is at best mixed and at worst contradictory. For example state anxiety had a higher test–retest reliability at 3 months than trait anxiety, and responses to acute stress have been less than unambiguous. Norms have not been checked for their generality across regions.

A number of *situation-specific scales* are available, covering a variety of specific situations (see Barrios *et al.,* 1981). One of the best known is the Test Anxiety Scale for Children (Sarason, Davidson, Lighthall, Waite, & Ruebush, 1960). This was designed to assess the effect of anxiety on test scores, primarily those of achievement and intelligence. It has been discussed in detail by Johnson and Malemed (1979). It is reasonably reliable and of modest validity. Most of the use of this scale, however, has been in educational rather than clinical settings. Others described by Barrios *et al.* (1981) include some for assessing anxiety associated with peer interactions, medical procedures, and hospitalization.

Two *fear survey schedules* (FSS) for itemizing fears in children exist—the 80-item FSS for Children (Scherer & Nakamura, 1968) based on a similar one for adults and the 81-item Louisville FSS (Miller *et al.,* 1971, 1972). Both have been reviewed in more detail by Barrios *et al.* (1981) and Johnson and Melamed (1979). Both scales group fears into certain *a priori* categories (school, home, social, etc.) and both have been factor analyzed and yield three classes of fears—physical injury and personal disaster, natural and supernatural dangers, and social fears. Reliability and validity data on both are very limited, although both offer some interesting data on the distribution of fears in normal children that attest to the validity of the now-classic study by Jersild and Holmes (1935) both as to type and wide occurrence. In passing, it may be noted that, while anxiety disorders are more common in boys, fears are more common in girls, suggesting considerable caution about equating fear and anxiety disorders.

PSYCHOLOGICAL TESTS

A psychological test is defined here as requiring the child to perform within some unusual structured situation, the nature of which is dictated by, and the results interpreted within, some theory of human behavior in its broadest sense. A test assumes that the behavior it evokes is typical of the individual or reflects some currently or permanently stable characteristics. The difference between this and a behavioral assessment is discussed in this chapter in the section entitled "Behavioral Methods." The distinction from self-report symptom inventories or checklists discussed previously is rather nice, but symptom measures are excluded here, as are tests of other than psychological function such as motor or physiological responses.

There are two main categories of psychological tests, projective and intellectual–cognitive. The first group includes such tests as the Rorschach, Children's Thematic Apperception Test, and so on, which are characterized by their reliance upon a matrix or set of instructions on to which the person can "project" his or her fantasies or thoughts. The second group includes the standard intelligence, achievement, and cognitive tests such as the WISC, Bender–Gestalt, and perceptuomotor tests. One or two tests seem to straddle both (e.g., the Goodenough Draw-a-Person Test).

An adequate review of the role of these tests in the assessment of anxiety in children is quite beyond this review and this reviewer. Fortunately, the role of projective tests and some cognitive tests in diagnosis has been reviewed cogently in detail by Gittelman (1980) and somewhat more broadly by O'Leary and Johnson (1979).

Gittelman (1980) raises the following criticisms. Most of the work with projective tests has been poorly controlled, particularly for IQ. Diagnosis, especially reliably made and meaningfully categorized, has seldom appeared as a validating criterion. While the tests do discriminate children seen in psychiatric clinics from those not, there is a large overlap, so that "clinical significance of the findings is nil" (p. 432). Their prognostic ability is, as far as it has been studied, poor. Despite the clear indication that many childhood disorders (especially anxiety disorders) are quite distinct from those of adults, extrapolation from work with adults to children is common. The relationship of the underlying concepts and assumptions to psychiatric symptoms, disorders, or personality is often obscure. Rather similar conclusions were reached by O'Leary and Johnson (1979), who because their brief was rather larger, also indicated the failure of such tests to indicate how treatment should proceed.

Gittelman's comments about the WISC deserve direct quotation: ". . . it is clear that anyone who claims that the WISC subtest scatter is relevant to personality diagnosis or psychopathology has to catch up on some reading" (1980, p. 433).

On the light of these criticisms, there does not seem to be much role at present for the use of psychological tests in the diagnosis and assessment of anxiety symptoms, traits, disorders, or states in children. Possible exceptions to this summary statement, in keeping with

Gittelman's (1980) caveat, are the tests not discussed by her. In particular, this would include the various laboratory tests of cognitive function that have figured in the study of hyperactivity and of its pharmacotherapy such as the Continuous Performance Test, the Porteus Mazes, and Paired Associate Learning (see Aman, 1978; Douglas & Peters, 1979). To date, their role in the diagnosis and assessment of anxiety in children has not been adequately explored.

BEHAVIORAL METHODS

Behavioral methods of assessment differ from rating scales in their emphasis on recording behavior as actually observed, rather than as retrospective, preaveraged estimates; they differ from psychological tests in their empirical and naturalistic nature and, usually, from both by attempting also to define immediately antecedent (eliciting and discriminative stimuli) and consequent (punishing and reinforcing contingencies) environmental events. There is also another difference from both, which is neither necessary nor absolute: Most behavioral methods are idiographic rather than nomothetic, both in design and in application.

Whatever the particular behavioral method, the process is usually much the same. First, target behaviors are defined, next their eliciting stimuli and contingencies, then who is to do the observing and recording (self, significant other, or neutral observer), where (home, school, playground, clinic, etc.), and for how long. Target behaviors are then counted as they occur.

Behavioral assessment has shown spectacular growth in the last decade, as reflected in monographs (Ciminero, Calhoun, & Adams, 1977; Cone & Hawkins, 1977; Mash & Terdal, 1981b) and even in a journal (*Behavioral Assessment*) devoted specifically to this topic. It is also the assessment method that has been most conscientiously checked for reliability and utility. Because of its emphasis on the empirical and molecular aspects of behavior, however, it has contributed less to theory in childhood psychopathology than rating scales. In addition, the emphasis on overt behavior has left certain areas such as anxiety relatively untouched. Detailed reviews of behavioral assessment in children can be found in Mash and Terdal (1981a), O'Leary and Johnson (1979), Wells (1981), and Werry (1978).

The Behavioral Interview

Reviews of the behavioral interview can be found in Mash and Terdal (1981a) and Wells (1981). After vilifying the interview at first, behaviorists have been forced to admit that it is an integral part of their own assessment procedures and thus a subject worthy of study (Wells, 1981). The way behaviorists structure such an interview, however, is exactly as one would predict; emphasis is on the here and now rather than past history, on molecular, observable behaviors rather than internal and more global constructs, and with close attention to antecedent and consequent environmental responses. A new and interesting development pioneered by Wahler (Wahler, 1980; Wahler, House, & Stambaugh, 1976) is the idea of "setting events" (such as maternal mood), which expands the behavioral interview to include an assessment of the social ecology—family and community. Such developments close the gap between the traditional clinical and the behavioral interview somewhat, although the more structured style and goals still differentiate the two. The goals (problem behavior, stimulus, and contingency definition vs. diagnosis) also differentiate it from the structured interviews described previously.

General Purpose Codes

Because of the ideology of the behavioral approach, general purpose instruments are infrequent, and perhaps because of the emphasis on the observable, most items in such codes are of a conduct and/or hyperactive type that is ill-suited to the assessment of anxiety. Some scales are beginning to include a new approach, avoidant, and interactional items that may be more suitable. Examples of such instruments are the Ecobehavioral assessment of Wahler *et al.* (1976) and the Family Interaction Coding System (Patterson, Reid, & Maerov, 1978). Others are described by Wells (1981).

Anxiety Codes

The fear survey schedules discussed previously are not true behavioral assessments, although they are often called so. In actuality they are self-ratings, not here-and-now observations. Neither do they define eliciting stimuli and/or contingencies with any precision. The behavioral methods most germane here are described in the following paragraphs.

Behavioral avoidance tests have been listed and described in detail by Barrios *et al.* (1981). Most are centered on one specific phobic situation or object (such as animals, medical procedures, darkness, water, or separation), to which the child is then exposed, and the degree of anxiety is assessed by the closeness to the phobic stimulus that the child reaches before stopping, by the latencies of responding, and so on. These techniques have been criticized by Barrios *et al.* (1981) for lack of systemization in such matters as the number of steps and instructions to the child, the lack of research about procedural and other variables, and for a general failure to present reliability and validity data. It is clear too, that their use with anxiety in children would be most useful in, but restricted to, simple phobias.

An example from an *observational code* is the Timed Behavior Checklist for adults, which was originally developed for anxiety about public speaking (see Barrios *et al.*, 1981) and has been adapted to children. It provides the prototype for other observational codes for separation anxiety, surgery, and dental procedures (see Barrios *et al.*, 1981; Johnson & Melamed, 1979). Here, a list of objective signs of anxiety is compiled, the child is put in the situation, and the items are checked off as occurring or not at specified intervals over a time period. Again, this technique is most suited to specific phobic situations.

Because of their preoccupation with disturbing behaviors, it is only lately that behaviorists have begun to evince much interest in assessment of social interaction (Wells, 1981). In addition to application of standard methods used with other behaviors, some more novel techniques such as role play have been used in *social interaction codes*. Characteristically, anxiety in children results in escape or avoidant behavior (social isolation or withdrawal). Unlike anxiety, this is susceptible to observation and thus is more suitable for behavioral assessment. All of the techniques of behavioral assessment of social interaction have been described in works by Wells (1981) and Johnson and Melamed (1979), to which readers are referred.

Summary of Behavioral Measures

There can be little doubt that behavioral measures offer a major advance in the assessment of anxiety in children, and these measures have only recently begun to be exploited. Their great advantages center on high reliability, relevance to treatment, and potential as research measures. They also have a number of problems, however, which have been outlined by Barrios *et al.,* (1981), Wells (1981), and Werry (1978). They are inclined to be cumbersome, time-consuming, and as a result, expensive and generate consumer resistance. They are often intrusive (in the classroom or home) and thus may create reactivity or distortion of the naturalness of the behavior. Although initially reliable, they tend to show a "drift" with time unless unannounced spot checks are made. They do not add as many data as might be expected when compared with simpler ratings. There is the problem of adequate sampling over time and over situations, which is necessary to minimize variance. They also are not free of the problem, seen in other measures, of discrepancies between different observers and between observers and self-ratings. Last, they are most suited to individual children and/or situations and thus pose some difficulties in adaptation for research purposes.

PHYSIOLOGICAL MEASURES

As is well known, anxiety is accompanied by certain physiological changes affecting a wide variety of systems and levels of function. Studies of these effects are of two types. In the first the acute effects of stress are studied in nonclinical populations such as paratroopers undergoing their first jump or normal volunteers being subjected to unpleasant stimuli like shock or plunging the hand into ice-cold water. This type of study has established the normal psychophysiology of anxiety. In the second these measures have been used to see what differences there are between patients with anxiety symptoms or disorders and those without, including both normal controls and patients. The thesis is, of course, that those who exhibit anxiety as adjudged by other methods will have higher psychophysiological scores, similar to those seen in normal volunteers under conditions of acute stress.

The types of physiological changes and the studies testing the validity of this hypothesis have been reviewed by Lader (1980), whose conclusions can be summarized as follows:

1. *Cardiovascular*: increased pulse rate, vasoconstriction in the fingers, raised blood pressure

2. *Pupilary*: longer dilatation duration under stress

3. *Respiratory*: increased respiratory rate, less efficient utilization of inspired oxygen

4. *Musculoskeletal*: increased amplitude of finger tremor, raised muscle tension

5. *Electroencephalogram* (EEG): decreased amounts of alpha and increased beta rhythms, diminished Contingent Negative Variation (CNV)

6. *Endocrine*: elevated blood cortisol, urinary 17-hydroxy corticosteroids and aldosterone, blood and urinary catecholamines

7. *Palmar sweat glands*: increased conductance, increased spontaneous fluctions in conductance, slower habituation to novel stimuli

Not only are the absolute levels of many of these responses higher in anxious patients, but return to basal levels after acute stress is slower. In general, the changes are more sustained in patients with chronic free-floating anxiety than in those with phobias or other situation-specific anxiety, who tend to exhibit them only in the feared situation or contemplation thereof.

In summarizing these findings, Lader (1980) concluded that almost all studies had shown that anxious patients exhibit "overalertness, overarousal and overpreparedness" (p. 238) in all physiological modalities described in the preceding list. Lader also concluded that the more clinically anxious the patient, the higher the levels. Finally, clinical improvement is accompanied by reduction in levels. While these results were held to be consistent with the popular neuropsychological concept of a nonspecific arousal continuum energizing emotion, he stressed that each measure is subject to a number of constraints that give it a limited range of usefulness within the overall arousal range. He also pointed out that while each stimulus contributes nonspecifically to arousal level, each is invested with a specific affective state, which in turn feeds back to increase or decrease the arousal level.

Critics of the arousal concept are numerous (see Barrios *et al.,* 1981) and draw attention to problems of response specificity, unreliability of measures across individuals (as opposed to group trends summarized above) and across situations, and the methodological and technical problems presented by artifacts, initial values, adaptation, the orienting response, and the obtrusion of overriding physiological demands such as temperature regulation with palmar sweating and digestion for heart rate. They caution that this area is for experts only and refer the reader to weighty technical tomes.

Perhaps for these reasons reviews of physiological assessment of anxiety in children (Barrios *et al.*, 1981; Johnson & Melamed, 1979; Taylor, 1980; Wells, 1981) find few such studies, although more have been done in children with other kinds of disorders such as attention deficit. Nevertheless, these reviews find that the few studies of anxious children suggest that the same pattern occurs as in adults, but no firm generalizations appear in order until more study has been undertaken. These reviewers point out that certain simplified reports of physiological variables may obviate the need for complicated apparatus. This seems somewhat at variance with the caveat about multiple measures and the general complexity of the area.

SUMMARY OF ASSESSMENT

The assessment of anxiety in children is intimately tied to the theoretical frame of reference and the purposes of the assessor. A variety of measures exist, although some are better developed and more useful in specific situations than others.

The unstructured interview is still the most widely used tool and has the advantage of flexibility, naturalness, and comprehensiveness, but suffers from variability of information gained and from differing response sets, even among interviewers of ostensibly similar theoretical orientation, all of which impair reliability and validity and make it unsuitable as a research instrument. Structuring the interview can overcome some of these problems, but the price is rigidity and artificiality. Reasonably suitable structured interviews exist for diagnosis, whether of the simple Isle of Wight type or of the complex DSM-III-oriented type. Behaviorists have been slower to develop the structured interview, but there are signs that their interest is quickening. While the interview is used widely to assess change in anxiety, no structured interview specifically for this purpose seems to exist. If clinicians are to be persuaded to adopt the structured diagnostic interview as a routine procedure, it will first be necessary to demonstrate that considerable benefits will accrue. Nowhere is this more evident than in the area of DSM-III diagnosis, where the clear gains in reliability that would result remain to be matched by demonstration of the clinical value of such diagnoses (Werry, 1985).

For enumeration of children's fears, differential diagnosis of anxiety disorder, and the normative assessment of children's fears, trait, state, and situation-specific anxiety, rating scales are relatively numerous when compared with other assessment measures. Most rating scales are for parents, teachers, or other adult raters. However, in those scales aimed at anxiety alone rather than all types of symptoms, self-reports are more common. Nearly all the well-known rating scales have been subject to empirical–statistical analysis and to varying degrees of psychometric evaluation. Of all the measures suited to anxiety, they are the most practical, economic and best studied, but they are bedevilled by, at least, only relatively modest agreement among raters. Some—especially those by Conners, which were developed for psychopharmacologic studies (see Goyette et al., 1978)—are among the best for assessing changes in anxiety, especially of the trait type. Their greatest usefulness, however, is at the normative-diagnostic level for trait anxiety.

The utility of psychological tests in the assessment of anxiety is unimpressive, although some of the better laboratory tests of cognitive functions that have figured so prominently in the study of hyperactivity and its pharmacotherapy have not been applied to anxiety. Because of the subjectively reported effects of anxiety on cognitive functions such as attention and memory, they deserve investigation, particularly in attempts to validate the distinctiveness of the anxiety disorders and in assessing the effects of treatment.

Behavioral assessment methods are the most reliable (at least initially) and the most clearly relevant to treatment. However, the admirable emphasis on the externally observable and the direct counting of behaviors by neutral observers constrains the acceptability, cost-effectiveness, and comprehensiveness of these methods. Self and parent recordings and the extension of observed domains to the social ecology and internal behaviors offer the prospect of improvement. Reliability drift with repeated measures is a problem that detracts from their value as change measures, and their advantages over other measures such as ratings, is not as impressive as once thought. These methods are most suitable for individualized assessment and treatment but can also be used for nomothetic studies.

Physiological measures are ideologically attractive but complex to implement and difficult to interpret. No single measure appears robust enough to serve, on its own, as a measure of anxiety. Such methods have not figured largely to date in the diagnosis or assessment of anxiety in children but, as technological devices become smaller and less expensive and able to reduce and interpret data, their role may grow. They are among the most objective of measures of anxiety and, unlike behavioral measures, are closely tied to the anxiety affective system.

Certain general problems in the area of assessment remain. The most difficult is the low reliability among different measures and measurers. While multivariate statistical techniques can assist in the resolution of some of these problems, especially at the research level, they cannot easily determine the validating criterion in the clinical situation. For example if observations by parents, teachers, doctors, and child disagree, then which is to serve as the validating criterion? To some extent, this problem is inevitable, since all observers and measures are to a significant degree situation-specific; so unless the behavior completely transcends environments, some disagreement is inevitable and not necessarily attributable to the measure or rater. The essence of clinical judgment is to weigh all these factors appropriately and combine them into a diagnostic or treatment decision.

The second problem is the lack of knowledge about anxiety in children, which has received much less systematic study than some other problems such as hyperactivity, autism, and latterly, depression. The systematic study of these disorders has been responsible for much of the advance in theory, therapy, and measurement of childhood psychopathology. It is now time to apply this technology to the study of anxiety.

ACKNOWLEDGMENTS

The preparation of this chapter was assisted by NICHD Grant HD-10570, "The Neuropharmacology of Developmental of Disorders," George Breese and C. T. Gualtieri, Principal Investigators; USPHS Grant No. HD-03110 to the Biological Sciences Research Center; and MCH Project 916 to the Division of Disorders of Development and Learning, University of North Carolina, Chapel Hill, North Carolina.

REFERENCES

Achenbach, T. M. The Child Behavior Profile. I. Boys aged 3–11. *Journal of Consulting and Clinical Psychology*, 1978, *46*, 478–488.
Achenbach, T. M. DSM-III in light of empirical research on classification of child psychopathology. *Journal of the American Academy of Child Psychiatry*, 1980, *19*, 395–412.

Aman, M. G. Drugs, learning and the psychotherapies. In J. S. Werry (Ed.), *Pediatric psychopharmacology: The use of behavior modifying drugs in children.* New York: Brunner/Mazel, 1978.

American Psychiatric Association. *Diagnostic and statistical manual of mental disorders* (3rd ed.). Washington, D.C.: Author, 1980.

Barrios, B. A., Hartmann, D. P. & Shigetomi, C. Fears and anxieties in children. In E. J. Mash & L. G. Terdal (Eds.), *Behavioral assessment of childhood disorders.* New York: Guilford, 1981.

Borkovec, T. D., Weerts, T. C., & Berstein, D. A. Assessment of anxiety. In A. R. Ciminero, K. R. Calhoun, & H. E. Adams (Eds.), *Handbook of behavioral assessment.* New York: Wiley, 1977.

Bugenthal, D. B., Whalen, C. K., & Henker, B. Causal attributions of hyperactive children and motivational assumptions of two behavior-change approaches: Evidence for an interactionist position. *Child Development,* 1977, *48,* 874–884.

Castenada, A., McCandless, B., & Palermo, D. The children's form of the Manifest Anxiety Scale. *Child Development,* 1956, *27,* 317–326.

Ciminero, A. R., Calhoun, K. S., & Adams, H. E. (Eds.). *Handbook of behavioral assessment.* New York: Wiley, 1977.

Cone, J. D., & Hawkins, R. P. (Eds.). *Behavioral assessment: New directions in clinical psychology.* New York: Brunner/Mazel, 1977.

Conners, C. K., & Werry, J. S. Pharmacotherapy. In H. C. Quay & J. S. Werry (Eds.), *Psychopathological disorders of childhood* (2nd ed.). New York: Wiley, 1979.

Douglas, V. I., & Peters, K. G. Toward a clearer definition of the attentional deficit of hyperactive children. In G. A. Hale & M. Lewis (Eds.), *Attention and the development of cognitive skills.* New York: Plenum Press, 1979.

Eysenck, H. J., & Rachman, S. *The causes and cures of neurosis.* London: Routledge & Kegan Paul, 1965.

Gittelman, R. The role of psychological tests for differential diagnosis in child psychiatry. *Journal of the American Academy of Child Psychiatry,* 1980, *19,* 413–438.

Gittelman-Klein, R., Spitzer, R. L., & Cantwell, D. P. Diagnostic classifications and psychopharmacological indications. In J. S. Werry (Ed.), *Pediatric psychopharmacology: The use of behavior modifying drugs in children.* New York: Brunner/Mazel, 1978.

Goyette, C. H., Conners, C. K., & Ulrich, R. F. Normative data on the revised Conners parent and teacher rating scales. *Journal of Abnormal Child Psychology,* 1978, *6,* 221–236.

Graham, P., & Rutter, M. The reliability and validity of the psychiatric assessment of the child. II. Interview with the parents. *British Journal of Psychiatry,* 1968, *114,* 581–592.

Herjanic, B., & Campbell, W. Differentiating psychiatrically disturbed children on the basis of a structured interview. *Journal of Abnormal Child Psychology,* 1977, *5,* 127–134.

Herjanic, B., Herjanic, M., Brown, F., & Wheatt, T. Are children reliable reporters? *Journal of Abnormal Child Psychology,* 1975, *3,* 41–48.

Herjanic, B., & Reich, W. Development of a structured psychiatric interview for children: Agreement between child and parent on individual symptoms. *Journal of Abnormal Child Psychology,* 1982, *10,* 307–324.

Humphries, L. E., & Ciminero, A. R. Parent report measures of child behavior: A review. *Journal of Clinical Child Psychology,* 1979, *7*, 56–63.

Jersild, A. T., & Holmes, F. B. Children's fears. *Child Development Monographs,* No. 20, 1935.

Johnson, S. B., & Melamed, B. G. The assessment and treatment of children's fears. In B. B. Lahey & A. E. Kazdin, (Eds.), *Advances in clinical psychology* (Vol. 2). New York: Plenum Press, 1979.

Klein, D. F. Anxiety reconceptualized. In D. F. Klein & J. Rabkin (Eds.), *Anxiety: New research and changing concepts.* New York: Raven Press, 1981.

Kolvin, I., & Nicol, A. R. Child psychiatry. In K. Granville-Grossman (Ed.), *Recent advances in clinical psychiatry* (Vol. 3). Edinburgh: Churchill-Livingstone, 1979.

Lader, M. H. The psychophysiology of anxiety. In H. M. Van Praag, M. H. Lader, O. J. Rafaelsen, & E. J. Sachar (Eds.), *Handbook of biological psychiatry.* Part II: *Brain mechanisms and abnormal behavior—psychophysiology.* New York: Marcel Dekker, 1980.

Mash, E. J., & Terdal, L. G. Behavioral assessment of childhood disturbance. In E. J. Mash & L. G. Terdal (Eds.), *Behavioral assessment of childhood disorders.* New York: Guilford, 1981. (a)

Mash, E. J., & Terdal, L. G. (Eds.). *Behavioral assessment of childhood disorders.* New York: Guilford, 1981. (b)

Miller, L. C., Barrett C. L., Hampe, E., & Noble, H. Revised anxiety scales for the Louisville Behavior Checklist. *Psychological Reports,* 1971, *29*, 503–511.

Miller, L. C., Barrett, C. L., Hampe, E., & Noble, H. Factor structure of childhood fears. *Journal of Consulting and Clinical Psychology,* 1972, *39*, 264–268.

O'Leary, K. D., & Johnson, S. B. Psychological assessment. In H. C. Quay & J. S. Werry (Eds.), *Psychopathological disorders of childhood* (2nd ed.). New York: Wiley, 1979.

Patterson, G. R., Reid, J. B., & Maerov, S. L. Development of the family interaction coding system (FICS). In J. B. Reid (Ed.), *A social learning approach to family intervention* (Vol. 2: *Observations in home settings*). Eugene, Ore.: Castalia Press, 1978.

Pekarik, E., Prinz, R., Liebert, D., Weintraub, S., & Neale, J. The Pupil Evaluation Inventory: A sociometric technique for assessing children's behavior. *Journal of Abnormal Child Psychology,* 1976, *4*, 83–97.

Quay, H. C. Classification. In H. C. Quay & J. S. Werry (Eds.), *Psychopathological disorders of childhood* (3rd ed.). New York: Wiley, in press. (a)

Quay, H. C. A critical analysis of DSM-III as a taxonomy of psychopathology in childhood and adolescence. In T. Millon & G. Klerman (Eds.), *Contemporary issues in psychopathology.* New York: Guilford, in press. (b)

Reich, W., Herjanic, B., Welner, Z., & Gandhy, P. R. Development of a structured psychiatric interview for children: Agreement on diagnosis comparing child and parent interviews. *Journal of Abnormal Child Psychology,* 1982, *10*, 325–336.

Rutter, M. Research report: Institute of Psychiatry Department of Child and Adolescent Psychiatry. *Psychological Medicine,* 1976, *6*, 505–516.

Rutter, M., & Graham, P. The reliability and validity of the psychiatric assessment of the child. I. Interview with the child. *British Journal of Psychiatry,* 1968, *114*, 563–579.

Rutter, M., & Shaffer, D. DSM-III: A step forward or back in terms of classification of child psychiatric disorders? *Journal of the American Academy of Child Psychiatry*, 1980, *19*, 371–394.

Rutter, M., Tizard, J., Yule, W., Graham, P., & Whitmore, K. Research report: The Isle of Wight studies, 1964–1974. *Psychological Medicine*, 1976, *6*, 313–332.

Sarason, S. B., Davidson, K. S., Lighthall, F. F., Waite, R. R., & Ruebush, B. K. *Anxiety in elementary school children*. New York: Wiley, 1960.

Scherer, M. W., & Nakamura, C. Y. A fear survey schedule for children (FSS-FC): A factor analytic comparison with manifest anxiety (CMAS). *Behaviour Research and Therapy*, 1968, *6*, 173–182.

Shaffer, D. The association between enuresis and emotional disorder. In I. Kolvin, R. McKeith, & S. Meadow (Eds.), *Bladder control and enuresis*. London: William Heinemann, 1973.

Spielberger, C. D. *Manual for the state-trait anxiety inventory for children*. Palo Alto, Calif.: Consulting Psychologists Press, 1973.

Strober, M., Green, J., & Carlson, G. The reliability of psychiatric diagnosis in hospitalized adolescents: Inter-rater agreement using the DSM-III. *Archives of General Psychiatry*, 1981, *38*, 141–145.

Taylor, E. Childhood disorders. In H. M. Van Praag, M. H. Lader, O. J. Rafaelsen, & E. J. Sachar (Eds.), *Handbook of biological psychiatry* (Part II: *Brain mechanisms and abnormal behavior—psychophysiology*). New York: Marcel Dekker, 1980.

Wahler, R. G. The insular mother: Her problems in parent–child treatment. *Journal of Applied Behaviorl Analysis*, 1980, *13*, 207–220.

Wahler, R. G., House, A. E., & Stambaugh, E. E. *Ecological assessment of child problem behavior*. New York: Pergamon Press, 1976.

Wells, K. C. Assessment of children in outpatient settings. In M. Hersen & A. S. Bellak (Eds.), *Behavioral assessment: A practical handbook* (2nd ed.). New York: Pergamon Press, 1981.

Werry, J. S. Measures in pediatric psychopharmacology. In J. S. Werry (Ed.), *Pediatric psychopharmacology: The use of behavior modifying drugs in children*. New York: Brunner/Mazel, 1978.

Werry, J. S. Psychosomatic disorders, psychogenic symptoms and hospitalization. In H. C. Quay & J. S. Werry (Eds.), *Psychopathological disorders of childhood* (3rd ed.). New York: Wiley, in press.

Werry, J. S. ICD 9 or DSM-III: Classification for the clinician. *Journal of Child Psychology*, 1985, *26*.

Werry, J. S., & Aman, M. G. Anxiety in children. In G. D. Burrows & B. Davies (Eds.), *Handbook of studies on anxiety*. Amsterdam: Elsevier/North Holland, 1980.

Werry, J. S., Methven, R. J., Fitzpatrick, J., & Dixon, H. The interrater reliability of the DSM-III in children. *Journal of Abnormal Child Psychology*, 1983, *11*, 341–354.

World Health Organization. *The international classification of diseases* (9th revision). Geneva: Author, 1980.

‡ 5 ‡

CHILDHOOD ANXIETY DISORDERS: CORRELATES AND OUTCOME

RACHEL GITTELMAN

INTRODUCTION

A single chapter on both the factors that have been studied in association with childhood anxiety disorders and the disorders' outcome is dictated by the paucity of information regarding any one of the topics reviewed. It is hoped that this situation is temporary, and we look forward to discrete chapters on the genetics, outcome, and pertinent social factors of childhood anxiety disorders when more empirical information is obtained. Until then it seems unjustified to provide distinct reviews of each issue. The amalgam of the diverse topics included in this chapter therefore represents a historical necessity.

One of the problems in attempting to provide a systematic summary of what is known about childhood anxiety disorders stems from the lack of synchrony in the vocabularies and concepts of diverse approaches in the study of anxiety. The psychological phenomenon of anxiety has been critical to most theories of psychopathology. In spite of its long history in psychology, anxiety remains a vague, poorly specified, construct (Klein, 1981). The most recent diagnostic schema as reflected in DSM-III (American Psychiatric Association, 1980) represents the first formal refinement of the broad concept of anxiety.

Rachel Gittelman. New York State Psychiatric Institute, and College of Physicians and Surgeons, Columbia University, New York, New York.

It stipulates a number of anxiety diagnoses, but the research antecedes this classification. Were it possible to establish retrospectively DSM-III diagnoses that correspond to clinical conditions reported, it would be possible to present the literature pertaining to each diagnosis. Since this approach is on the whole not feasible, it is not attempted for the purposes of this review. Issues are discussed for children with anxiety disorders in general. Whenever possible the type of disorder studied is indicated.

Further clouding the precise reporting of the state of knowledge regarding childhood anxiety disorders is the use of the even vaguer concept of "emotional disorder" used in the British literature. This class of psychiatric diagnoses seems best defined by exclusion; it consists of a variety of poorly defined symptoms that cannot be categorized as reflecting a psychotic disorder or a conduct disorder, the latter of which includes truancy, aggression, oppositional behavior, stealing, and so on. The use of the nonspecific emotional disorders category is deliberate on the part of British child psychiatrists. They have held, for the most part, that although much evidence exists that corroborates the merits of distinguishing between the conduct and emotional disorders of childhood, none exists that justifies the further refinement of these two classes of disorder (Rutter & Shaffer, 1980). It is evident from clinical reports that anxiety disorders account for the great majority of emotional disorders. Their classification is a current controversy deserving of attention, albeit brief, in this chapter, the main interests of which lie elsewhere.

CLASSIFICATION OF CHILDHOOD ANXIETY DISORDERS

In general, very little work has been done to formulate, and much less to validate, various classificatory schemes in child psychopathology. A striking exception is the delineation of infantile autism as separate from the overall group of childhood psychoses and childhood schizophrenia. This practice followed investigation of the cognitive deficits, natural history, family history, treatment response, as well as other aspects of infantile autism. (Nevertheless, this distinction is still deplored by some.) No similar effort has been conducted to refine the overall group of emotional disorders that, as noted above, consists mainly of children with anxiety symptoms. It may be argued, therefore, that DSM-III is providing clinical distinctions where none, or perhaps others, are warranted.

In the absence of scientific data, one may wonder what was the basis for the DSM-III classification of children's anxiety disorders. Because the DSM-III provides definitions of the anxiety disorders and their major symptoms, this information is not repeated here. It should be noted, however, that in DSM-III the obsessive–compulsive disorders are included with the anxiety disorders. This practice complicates an overall discussion of anxiety disorders, since there is no clinical basis at this time to consider the obsessive–compulsive disorders as types of anxiety disorders. It is true that individuals with obsessions and compulsions are often highly anxious, but that is the case for patients with many other mental disorders as well. Putting obsessive–compulsive disorders under the rubic of anxiety disorders was an arbitrary step, but perhaps a necessary one in that obsessive–compulsive disorders fit best in the anxiety group, though still not well. In this discussion obsessive–compulsive disorders are not included as part and parcel of anxiety disorders.

The isolation of separation anxiety from other forms of anxiety disorders in children stems from its developmental significance when it occurs in nonpathological form at appropriate ages. It is widely recognized that separation anxiety has relevance to the development of social bonding and attachment in young children. It seems to have different psychological meaning from other forms of anxiety such as specific fears (simple phobias) or social anxiety (avoidant disorder). It is not unreasonable, therefore, to expect the pathological variant also to have specific features.

The other anxiety diagnoses applicable to children—avoidant, overanxious, simple phobic, and obsessive–compulsive disorders— have distinguishable clinical features. Their phenomenology often overlaps, however, and it is not clear to what extent they exist in pure form.

The potential value of the classification is that it will provide the impetus to examine the merits of the clinical distinctions on grounds other than the fact that they are recognizably different. The apparent face validity of the classification is certainly necessary, but clearly not sufficient to justify its existence. As long as the nomenclature of childhood anxiety disorders is viewed as a working model (and one that may not work), it is believed to be an advance in the classification of childhood psychopathology.

CORRELATES OF CHILDHOOD ANXIETY DISORDERS

Information regarding the factors associated with childhood anxiety disorders is, for the most part, derived from treated cases. This situation has clear disadvantages, since biases may have been introduced by restricting the investigation to individuals who have sought professional help. Those with similar afflictions who have not come for treatment may be quite dissimilar. Therefore, treated children may be unlike untreated ones, and conclusions may be accepted erroneously as factual. These issues are presented more fully in Chapter 3. Potential differences between clinical and nonclinical groups seem all the more relevant to the anxiety disorders, since the latter do not regularly require special therapeutic, educational, or legal interventions, as is mostly the case for psychotic or severe conduct disorders. Nevertheless, the study of treated cases is useful in that it allows for the formulation of hypotheses regarding various aspects of the anxiety disorders. These notions may, in time, be put to the test in other clinical samples and in epidemiologic surveys. For a proper perspective, however, it is important not to confuse the sources of data.

DEMOGRAPHIC CHARACTERISTICS

The concept of demographics is used loosely for the purposes of this discussion. It refers to the usual factors of social class, gender, and age; IQ is also included here, for convenience.

Social Class

Several clinical investigators have reported that referred cases of anxious children come from more socially advantaged groups than general clinic populations (Gittelman-Klein & Klein, 1973; Miller, Barrett, Hampe, & Noble, 1972). More white children and children from higher socioeconomic classes have been found represented in children with anxiety disorders treated in clinics. In other cases anxious children in clinics were no different from the general population (Berney et al., 1981). However, since the lower social classes tend to be more common among clinic attendees, the anxious group would still seem to be relatively more middle class.

Population surveys have not reported a higher rate of anxiety symptoms in children from the higher classes (Richman, Stevenson, & Graham, 1982: Rutter, Tizard, & Whitmore, 1981; Ziv & Luz, 1973). In a large sample surveyed from the general population, however, the types of fears among children from upper compared with lower classes differed (Angelino, Dollins, & Mech, 1956).

Gender

Clinical samples of anxious children do not present a consistent pattern of sex distribution. In some cases, boys are more numerous (Baker & Wills, 1978; Miller *et al.*, 1972; Hersov, 1960); in others, the reverse is the case (Berney *et al.*, 1981; Coolidge, Brodie, & Feeney, 1964); and in still others there is no difference (Berg, 1970; Berg, Butler, Fairbairn, & McGuire, 1981; Gittelman-Klein & Klein, 1980; Roberts, 1975; Smith, 1970; Warren, 1965a). It appears that both sexes are about equally vulnerable to anxiety disorders in childhood. This pattern of sex distribution is clearly atypical of overall child clinic populations, where referred boys greatly and regularly outnumber girls before adolescence. Anxiety ratings in unselected groups, however, frequently report that girls are somewhat more frequently affected by anxiety (Abe & Masui, 1981; Bledsoe, 1973; Douglas & Rice, 1979; Olah, Stettin, & Magnusson, 1978; Ziv & Luz, 1973), or neurotic disorders (Rutter *et al.*, 1981). Though this sex difference is not consistently found (Miller, Barrett, Hampe, & Noble, 1971), an excess of reported anxiety in girls in the general population seems to be a stable phenomenon, since it has been observed in several European countries, as well as in the United States and Japan. It is not clear whether this is due to the fact that girls express fears more readily than boys, or whether they are truly more anxious. Furthermore, girls might experience more anxiety and fears than boys, but might not as a result become functionally impaired more frequently than boys. If so, anxious girls would not become patients more often than boys.

In summary, referral patterns may affect the observed distributions of socioeconomic status and gender. However, the effect is slight, leading to somewhat higher social status and perhaps more boys being treated.

Birth Order

One epidemiologic study has reported a higher frequency of anxiety disorders in firstborns (Rutter *et al.*, 1981). This finding has not been well-documented in clinical studies, which have reported no consistent pattern of anxiety regarding birth order (Berg, Butler, & McGuire, 1972; Hersov, 1960; Smith, 1970).

Age

Children may become fearful at any age, but different types of fears and anxiety tend to emerge at different developmental stages. The same is most likely true of the anxiety disorders. No data have been obtained to document this possible phenomenon in studies of affected children. From retrospective reports of adults suffering from anxiety disorders, simple phobic disorders appear early in childhood, and social phobias appear in adolescence (Marks & Gelder, 1966). Separation anxiety disorder varies in age of onset. Several clinical reports have indicated that its severe form, school phobia, peaks around age 11 (Berg, 1970; Gittelman-Klein & Klein, 1973; Tyrer & Tyrer, 1974). An increase in a variety of fears at age 11 has also been reported in population surveys (Angelino et al., 1956; MacFarlane, Allen, & Honzik, 1954). In most Western countries this age coincides with a transfer from primary to secondary school. It is possible that this event may be a stress precipitant in vulnerable children.

Age of onset has been considered an important factor in school phobia. It has been argued that a later age of onset indicates a much more pernicious pathological process and that it affects prognosis adversely (Eisenberg, 1958b). The early and late onsets are also believed to have different familial correlates, with family deviance being more marked in groups with later onset (Coolidge et al., 1964; Eisenberg, 1958b; Prince, 1968). (The issue of family characteristics is reviewed in this chapter in a following section.)

Another demographic feature, family size, has not been found to be specifically related to anxiety disorder in children (Berg et al., 1972; Hersov, 1960).

IQ

There is no compelling a priori reason to believe that the cognitive development of children who develop anxiety disorders is compromised. However, the possibility remains. It is not inconceivable that impairment in central nervous system function could lead to anxiety via a number of pathways. Brain damage or dysfunction could have a direct influence on the physiological propensity for anxiety. Alternately, brain dysfunction could lead to some nonspecific limitations that, in turn, would make it likely for children thus affected to become anxious, either as a result of their difficulties, or of the differential social treatment they might be subjected to in contrast to children without any brain damage. There is evidence that children with frank brain damage are at greater risk for a variety of psychiatric disorders than are normal children (for a summary, see Rutter, 1981). Since IQ may be used as an estimate of the intactness of the central nervous system in groups of children, an examination of IQ in children with anxiety disorders might be suggestive. (Alternately, should relatively low IQ be a characteristic of anxiety disorders, it might be secondary to interference in test performance due to the emotional turmoil experienced by anxious children during testing.)

In a British sample of 11-year-olds, IQ was lower in "neurotic" children than controls, especially so in girls (Rutter *et al.,* 1981).

Contrary findings were reported in another population survey of British children. Richman *et al.* (1982) reported that "neurotic" girls had higher performance IQs than well-matched controls. This finding was not observed in the boys.

Controlled investigations of IQ in clinical samples of children with anxiety disorders have been few. Berg and co-workers compared the IQs of 100 consecutive school phobic children to those of other hospitalized children (Berg, Collins, McGuire, & O'Melia, 1975). The school phobic children who were above average in IQ (mean full IQ, 106) had significantly higher IQs. The use of other psychiatric groups for comparative purposes is not ideal, since ill children are likely to be subject to a number of influences that may lower IQ scores. Contrasting 50 school phobic children and normals, Hersov found no IQ differences (Hersov, 1960).

In summary the two population surveys report conflicting results; one found lower IQs in "neurotic" girls, the other the opposite. Clinical studies do not report lower IQs in either gender. It seems reasonable to assume that impaired intellectual development is not a correlate of childhood anxiety disorders.

Traumatic Experiences

A few investigators have sought a relationship between traumatic events and anxiety symptoms in children (Gordon, 1977; Martinez-Monfort & Dreger, 1972; Ziv & Israeli, 1973). The three studies identified have yielded negative results. Following a cyclone in Australia, children's fears were infrequent, and negatively correlated with age (Gordon, 1977). Black high school students transferred to white schools following desegregation orders in the South of the United States were not found to have an exceptional level of anxiety symptoms (Martinez-Monfort & Dreger, 1972). In the third study children living in Israel in an area under frequent shelling were reported to be no different in levels of self-rated anxiety from children who lived in peaceful areas (Ziv & Israeli, 1973). A consistent methodological limitation of these investigations is the exclusive reliance on self-ratings to assess anxious symptomatology. In the absence of adequate validation of these measures, it is difficult to interpret results they generate. We are not sure that children reveal their affective states adequately on paper-and-pencil checklists.

From the above studies it would appear that children and adolescents are quite invulnerable to catastrophic or traumatic events that are shared by their social group. Even if these findings were based on sound methodology, it would be erroneous to assume that all forms of trauma bear similarly benign consequences. The studies of the social stresses might dispel the notion that such events regularly have a catastrophic impact on young people's emotional stability. However, it is possible that other stresses, such as parents' divorce or death of a close relative, are associated with the development of anxiety symptoms and disorders in children.

In a study by Gittelman-Klein and Klein (1980), severe separation anxiety had occurred following the illness or death of a loved one, a move of the child's home, or a change of school in 80% of the children and adolescents. A major disruption of the children's pattern of attachment had occurred in most cases. The undefined notion of stress therefore may not contribute to an understanding of the psychological factors that may lead to the development of anxiety disorders in children. Cyclones and desegregation may not be important factors, but in children who are already vulnerable, other seemingly more innocuous events that are perceived as threatening to the integrity of the family may contribute to the development of an anxiety disorder.

PERSONALITY CORRELATES

The study of personality in anxiety disorders has potential theoretical importance. For instance if it were found that personality organizations differed for various types of anxiety disorders, it would argue for the merits of distinguishing among the disorders. Therefore, the study of personality could be a validating tool in the classification of anxiety disorders. A report of anxiety in normal 3-year-olds exemplifies this approach (Doris, McIntyre, Kelsey, & Lehman, 1971). Parents rated their children prior to the children's entry in nursery school, on a scale whose content tapped separation anxiety and other anxieties, such as fear of animals, falling, and the like. Nursery school teachers rated the children's level of separation anxiety throughout the school year. The children's level of separation anxiety, prior to the start of school, was predictive of separation anxiety in nursery school throughout the year. In contrast, other anxieties did not predict separation anxiety in school. As a result, the authors propose that separation anxiety and general proneness to anxiety have different psychological significance and merit separate study. Unfortunately, the above findings have not been replicated, nor have they been extended to the study of anxiety disorders. However, they point to the possibility that there may be some specificity to the longitudinal aspects of anxiety in normal children.

One of the obvious difficulties in interpreting associations between personality characteristics and psychiatric diagnoses is the lack of temporal independence between the two in the studies conducted so far. Unless children's personalities are investigated *before* they develop anxiety disorders, it is impossible to extricate one from the other, in order to determine which is cause and which is effect.

To test the theory advanced by Leventhal and Sills (1964) that school phobic children have grandiose self-images, leading them to avoid school where this view of themselves is challenged, Nichols and Berg (1970) compared self-esteem ratings of children with school phobia and fear of leaving home to children with other disorders. They found a significant difference between the two types of disturbance in the number of children with good versus poor ratings of self, but in the direction opposite from that expected. The notion of an unrealistic overvaluing in children with school phobia is ruled out by this study. Apart from this conclusion, however, very little else is to be learned. It cannot be assumed that poor self-image is a factor that predisposes children to school phobia or to fear of leaving home.

In reports of school phobic youngsters who were inpatients, Berg and coauthors reported that school phobic children were immature and overly dependent on their mothers (Berg & McGuire, 1971) but not unduly willful or obstinate (Berg & Collins, 1974). Similarly, Hersov (1960) reported that school phobic children were more passive, dependent, and inhibited as compared with normal controls.

Berg, Nichols, and Pritchard (1969) contrasted personality correlates of small groups of acute and chronic school phobic adolescents who were also inpatients. The chronic cases were rated as more dependent and had higher neuroticism scores than the cases with recent onset.

Besides the limitations of the above studies due to the very small sample sizes, the clinical cases included are atypical of school phobic children, since they focused on inpatients and school phobics are very rarely hospitalized. Moreover, the personality ratings were all done at the time of inpatient admission. Ratings therefore were most likely conducted at a point of crisis when the disorder was very handicapping and disruptive of the usual functioning of the child and his or her family. The degree to which the findings are true of children with school phobia is unknown. It is also unclear whether these personality characteristics—dependency, immaturity, and neuroticism—have any relevance to the development of anxiety related to school attendance in children.

In searching for personality characteristics that predispose to anxiety disorders in children, it seems reasonable to assume that if a personality trait is not found during the active phase of a disorder, it is most unlikely to be a causal or influencing agent. The interpretation of positive studies is more complicated. If certain personality characteristics, such as excessive dependency, are found when the child is brought for treatment, it is not possible to assert that they contribute to the evolution of the disorder. Such positive results are only heuristic, permitting the hypothesis or conjecture that a causal relationship may exist between the trait and the disorder. As a result, we are in the unusual situation where only negative studies provide definite information. The cliché that correlation in no way implies causation seems to be forgotten frequently for the convenient formulation of psychological theories. Prospective studies of children before they have developed anxiety disorders would be informative in providing information as to the psychological precursors of anxiety disorders. Such studies are uneconomical and present formidable practical as well as conceptual challenges. The practical difficulties are related to the costs of studying very large samples over time. Even more problematic are the conceptual issues that include the selection of appropriate groups at risk for anxiety disorders, children of proper ages so that they are most likely not to have the disorder yet but are not too far from it, and relevant personality characteristics. The absence of prospective studies is hardly surprising. What is more regrettable is the lack of study of clinical cases after they have remitted. If personality deviance were ameliorated during remission of the disorder, it would be difficult to argue for an etiologic role of the personality trait. If it persisted, a question would still remain regarding the sequence of events, since the personality difficulties arising during the clinical phase could devlop functional autonomy. In such cases, there would be justification for examining the possibility that the personality characteristics pre-dispose to the disorder.

FAMILY CHARACTERISTICS

An animal experiment suggests that maternal behavior may influence the infant's vulnerability to separation. Smotherman, Hunt, McGinnis, and Levine (1979) report that infant rhesus macaques of highly dominant mothers had the greatest adrenocorticol response to separation from their mothers. Yet, the studies of nonpatients that have attempted to relate parental discipline and anxiety level to children's anxiety have not revealed a significant association between the parent and child characteristics (Byrne, 1964; Perry & Millimet, 1975).

It is often stated as a given that families of children with anxiety disorders are psychologically deviant and that their psychopathology plays an etiologic role in the child's symptoms (e.g., Prince, 1968). Mothers of children with separation anxiety have been described as being highly anxious of letting go of the child and of transmitting separation anxiety to the child to maintain proximity with the child (Eisenberg, 1958a). In this model the pathology resides primarily in the parent. Understandably, appropriate treatment for the child is to force separation from the anxiogenic mother.

Many other characteristics have been attributed to the immediate families of youngsters with separation anxious disorders. Mothers have been described, in turn, as overdependent on their own mothers, immature, ambivalent toward their child, overprotective, perfec-tionistic, depressed, overindulgent, dissatisfied with their marital relationship and therefore using the child as a lover-substitute, and socially isolated (Davidson, 1961; Eisenberg, 1958a, 1958b, 1959; Johnson, Falstein, Stanislaus, & Svendsen, 1941; Talbot, 1957). Fathers have not been reported to have as much psychopathology as mothers.

The views that mothers' difficulties have a causal influence in the development of their children's anxiety disorders are important, since they have carried specific therapeutic messages (Davidson, 1961; Eisenberg, 1959; Sperling, 1967).

Berg *et al.* (1969) used the Eysenck Personality Inventory to evaluate parents of hospitalized school phobic youngsters. They report that mothers, but not fathers, had elevated neuroticism scores compared to population norms. Unfortunately, population norms are unsatisfactory as standards of comparison when assessing an experimental group. Controls matched on relevant characteristics such as social status, age, number of children of similar ages, and other important measures are required for proper evaluation.

Hersov (1960) reported that mothers of school phobic children were rated as significantly more overprotective than normal controls and also had a greater prevalence of neurotic illness.

Berg *et al.* (1981) interviewed the parents of a small group of hospitalized school phobic children, parents of children with other nonpsychotic disorders, and parents of normals to investigate the family function in school phobic children. Contrary to expectation, the families did not have different patterns of social behavior or of decision making about child rearing. It is possible that the number of cases in each group was not large enough to detect group differences in familial patterns.

It has been suggested by Bowlby (1961) that separating from the mother early in life makes children vulnerable to later anxiety states. Support for the notion that separation from parents is associated with maladjustment in children is provided by results from Shepherd, Oppenheim, and Mitchell (1971). These authors found that the rate of deviance among children who have been separated for at least 1 month was about twice what it was in other youngsters. Whether anxiety itself was more salient than other symptoms in the separated children is not specified.

Although it is tempting to conjecture that separation causes deviance, the relationship between these two phenomena is not simple. Many children were separated because they had to be hospitalized. The illness therefore may have been responsible for both the separation and the subsquently identified behavioral problems. That early separation is an important phenomenon in the development of anxiety disorders in children has not been observed by clinicians working with children with separation anxiety disorders. Quite the contrary, clinicians have reported consistently that, at least in the disorder of separation anxiety, families seem especially close-knit and seem to have a lesser history of separation. In the single study that examined this issue systematically, children with school phobia had experienced significantly less separation than controls (Hersov, 1960).

MEDICAL FACTORS

A relationship between medical illness and the development of anxiety disorders has been suggested. Lansky, Lowman, Voto, and Gyulay (1975) reported that about 10% of children treated for malignant neoplasms developed severe separation anxiety. This anxiety was most frequent in children over the age of 10. It is possible that an appreciation of the concept of death is not developed in younger children and that they may be protected thereby from some of the psychological consequences of a lethal disease.

Sermet (1974) found that children with severe fear of dental care had many other forms of anxiety as well and that they had experienced significantly more hospital admissions than had controls. In this particular instance it is not known whether the medical conditions had anteceded the onset of the anxiety symptoms; therefore, the contributing role of children's medical illness in anxiety is unclear.

Shaffer *et al.* (1985) investigated the relationship between behavioral and neurologic findings at age 7 and psychiatric status at age 17 in an unselected group of black children who were originally studied as part of a large prospective study of prenatal care in a large urban medical center. Anxiety disorders at the age of 17 were significantly associated with the presence of soft neurologic signs at age 7. The greatest risk for anxiety at age 17, however, was among those who at age 7 had had both neurologic signs and deviant behavioral ratings during psychometric testing. Overanxious disorders were the most frequently diagnosed. This study suggests that neurodevelopment plays a role in the evolution of anxiety disorders. Shaffer *et al.* note that the origins of soft signs are unknown but may well be genetic.

GENETIC FACTORS

There is considerable evidence that anxious behavior can be bred selectively in animals. In human adults and children, the tendency to experience anxiety has also been reported to be, at least in part, under genetic control (Goldsmith & Gottesman, 1981; Torgersen, 1979; for reviews, see Carey & Gottesman, 1981; Marks 1973). In addition, the adult anxiety disorder, panic anxiety, has been reported to be influenced by genetic factors (Crowe, Pauls, Slyman, & Noyes, 1980; Torgersen, 1983). In contrast, no evidence of genetic transmission for generalized anxiety, another adult anxiety disorder, has been observed (Torgersen, 1983). The positive genetic findings for one anxiety disorder and the negative findings for another, support the merits of distinguishing various types of anxiety states. These results also emphasize the need for delineating the characteristics of the "anxious," "neurotic," or "emotional" disorders studied.

Two strategies have been used to investigate familial concordance for anxiety in children. One has consisted of studying the parents of anxious children; the other has evaluated the offsprings of adults with anxiety disorders.

Berg (1976) reported on the status of the children of a very large group of agoraphobic women. He found a prevalence of 14% for school phobia in the 11- to 15-year-old children, a rate much higher than that expected in the general population.

In a similar but small study of agoraphobic women, the rate of psychiatric disorder in the children and in children of controls did not differ (Buglass, Clarke, Henderson, Kreitman, & Presley, 1977). No case of school phobia occurred in either group. As noted, Berg (1976) found a 14% rate of school phobia in adolescent offspring of agoraphobics. (Buglass et al. do not report the number of children between 11 and 15 years of age in their total sample of 27 cases. It is possible for no case of school phobia to occur in a very small sample if the expected rate is 10%-15%).

Weissman, Leckman, Merikangas, Gammon, and Prusoff (1984) studied the psychiatric status of children of normal and depressed women. The depressed patients were dichotomized into those with a history of anxiety disorders (i.e., generalized anxiety, phobic and panic disorders) and those without anxiety disorders (i.e., with pure depression). The rate of anxiety symptoms was much higher among the children of the depressed/anxious individuals than among the children of the pure depressives and the children of normal controls. This study suggests that anxiety symptoms are more likely to occur in children whose parents have an anxiety disorder and that parental depression alone is not associated with anxiety disorders in the offspring. The most prevalent form of anxiety in the children was separation anxiety. Furthermore, not all forms of anxiety in the parents had the same association with anxiety in the offspring. Panic disorder, compared with generalized anxiety, bore a significantly greater risk for separation anxiety in the children.

Only two studies have reported on parents of children with anxiety disorders. Both cases reported on parents of children with school phobias, therefore mostly children with separation anxiety were studied (Berg, Butler, & Pritchard, 1974; Gittelman-Klein, 1975).

Berg and associates (Berg, Butler, & Pritchard, 1974) obtained information from parents of hospitalized adolescents consisting of school-phobic and other types of patients. If a history of psychiatric problems was elicited from the mother, her physician was contacted for details. Half the mothers in both groups were considered psychiatrically ill, the most common condition being affective disorders whose clinical content included phobic symptoms. These results do not indicate an increase in anxiety disorders in parents of children with school phobia. Unfortunately, the presence of anxiety symptoms was not ruled out in the controls, and the procedures for diagnosing the parents are not given.

The second study (Gittelman-Klein, 1975) compared the psychiatric status of parents and siblings of school phobic and hyperactive children. The parents were interviewed about themselves and their other children. The rate of depression did not differ between the parents of the anxious and hyperactive children. Parents' anxiety symptoms were divided between simple phobias and separation anxiety. Parents of the school phobic and hyperactive children did not differ significantly with regard to prevalence or type of simple phobias. In contrast, separation anxiety was much more frequent in the parents of school phobic children than in the parents of hyperactive youngsters (19% vs. 2%, respectively). The siblings of the patients also differed significantly. The brothers and sisters of the school-phobic children, compared with those of the hyperactive, children, had had much more school phobia (16% vs. 0%, respectively). These results also point to the desirability of distinguishing among various forms of anxiety symptoms.

The family data on childhood anxiety states is ambiguous. There are some positive as well as negative findings. However, there are enough positive results from preliminary studies to warrant systematic inquiry regarding familial concordance of various childhood anxiety disorders.

OUTCOME

If the common childhood fears are evanescent phenomena associated with various developmental phases, they are unlikely to be of clinical importance. However, it would be important to know if they represent early signs of long-lasting anxiety symptoms. (This issue is also discussed in Chapter 3 of this volume.)

Several investigations have noted that fears and shyness, a form of early social anxiety, are relatively stable phenomena in children (Eme & Schmidt, 1978; MacFarlane *et al.*, 1954). In a general population study, Richman *et al.* (1982) found that fears at age 3 were associated with the development of "neurotic" disorders 5 years later. Thus, it appears that fears and anxieties in early childhood are not regularly innocuous events. It is striking that fears and anxieties seem to predict similar clinical symptoms. The fearful, anxious 3-year-olds studied by Richman and associates were not at greater risk than the other children for all types of psychiatric disorder at the age of 8; they were only more likely to have "neurotic" disorders at age 8.

In the classic epidemiologic study of the Isle of Wight (Rutter *et al.*, 1981), children with "emotional" disorder at age 11 were twice as likely to have psychiatric problems in adolescence than other youngsters. In this instance, as well, the outcome was not random; children with emotional disorders retained the same type of disturbance (Rutter, 1980). In fact, none of the 11-year-olds with an emotional disorder had developed a conduct disorder at the age of 15.

The above studies have reported on the long-term correlates of nonclinical anxiety states. An early clinical report of the adult outcome of 34 children treated for shy, withdrawn behavior reported that most were functioning well (Morris, Soroker, & Burruss, 1954). This early report generated considerable optimism concerning the long-term significance of anxious childhood disorders.

Little other inquiry of the long-term outcome of childhood anxiety disorders has been undertaken. An early study of 41 school phobic children relied on telephone and mail responses from the family and school, conducted from 1 to 7 years following outpatient treatment (Rodriguez, Rodriguez, & Eisenberg, 1959). Regular school attendance had resumed in 70% of the group. The children below the age of 11 had a better outcome than those aged 11 and older. It seems that moderate to severe maladjustment was present in 30% of the children, three cases being considered schizophrenic. The nature of the psychiatric features at follow-up is ambiguous, because of the lack of clinical evaluations and diagnostic standards.

Coolidge *et al.* (1964) interviewed the mothers and most of 49 children, 9 years after the children had been treated for school phobia. Sixty percent were judged to have some problems in adjustment, 20% with serious difficulty ranging from character disorder to psychosis, in spite of renewed school attendance. In this study only a minority were felt to have no particular limitation at follow-up.

An early study of the status of 67 "neurotic" youngsters 6 years after admission to an inpatient unit reports that, of the 16 cases admitted with school phobia, 9 (56%) were well at follow-up; therefore, a relatively large proportion continued to be in difficulty due to phobic symptoms (whose nature is not specified) (Warren, 1965b). No other information is provided for this patient subgroup. Of the whole "neurotic" group, a sizeable proportion (32%) had further serious psychiatric illness. Half had required further treatment. Of those who had been ill during the follow-up interval, 58% had developed other conditions. In this respect the neurotic children showed a more variable outcome than those with conduct disorders, who always retained the same symptoms if they failed to recover. As has been found in studies of fears in nonpatient groups, the outcome of the "neurotic" youngsters suggests that patterns of early and late psychopathology are relatively consistent. Unfortunately, this study suffers from marked diversity in clinical composition. The young patients had a broad mixture of "neurotic" psychopathology, such as obsessive–compulsive, anorectic, and phobic symptoms. Since these conditions are likely to have contrasting clinical courses, results of the combined patients provides little useful information.

A prospective study by Waldron (1976) compared 24 children who had had a school phobia with 18 other neurotic children and with a small group of carefully selected normal controls. At follow-up, no difference was found between the school phobic and neurotic children. Both patient groups had more frequent diagnoses of neurosis and personality disorders than controls. Also, they were felt to have worse occupational and interpersonal adjustments. Curiously, none of the controls received a psychiatric diagnosis. This finding points to the necessity of using relatively large control groups so that the expected population rate of psychiatric disorder is detected. Studies using small groups of normals may under- or overestimate the prevalence of emotional disorders. Also problematic is the lack of diagnostic refinement in the patient groups. It is possible that both the school phobic and neurotic children suffered from similar anxiety disorders, since school refusal was the only distinguishing feature between them.

An extended follow-up by Herman, Stickler, and Lucas (1982) of children with a hyperventilation syndrome, which is believed to be a form of anxiety neurosis, suggests that these children continue to have anxiety symptoms well into adulthood. The results of this uncontrolled report should stimulate further systematic research in the role of anxiety in a syndrome often treated by medical specialists.

Several uncontrolled studies of the outcome of previously hospitalized school phobic children have been reported. In a large series of carefully evaluated 100 youngsters, Berg, Butler, and Hall (1976) found that many were experiencing clinically significant difficulty 3 years after discharge. Half had difficulties in school attendance, and depending on the degree of functional incapacitation applied, between 50% and 70% were experiencing other symptomatology. Five (5%) had developed agoraphobia. IQ was significantly associated with quality of adjustment, with brighter youngsters having worse outcomes. A subgroup of the sample had been examined 1 year after discharge (Berg, 1970); their condition was worse after 3 years (Berg et al., 1976). It remains to be elucidated whether the post-treatment outcome of school phobic children may deteriorate over time.

In a report of the posthospital adjustment of 14 school phobic children, Weiss and Burke (1970) indicate that only one could be considered free of serious neurotic or personality problems. Yet, the group's overall functioning was satisfactory.

Roberts (1975) obtained follow-up information on less than half of 131 younsters hospitalized for school phobia, 5–18 years after discharge. All were judged to suffer from anxiety, but only 25% from separation anxiety. In this incomplete sample, over half the patients continued to have impaired school attendance, and half rated themselves as having poor adjustment. Age of onset was not predictive of eventual outcome.

Another questionnaire study of 54 hospitalized school phobic children (80% of the original group), followed up at least 2 years after discharge, found that 22% reported having difficulty going out alone; in 6% it was severe. Other outcome measures, including those pertaining to mood, friendship patterns, and school or work attendance, yielded low rates of disturbance (Boreham, 1983).

Baker and Wills (1979) examined the occupational status of 67 school phobic children who were past 16 years of age, the school-leaving age in Britain. An average of 6 years had elapsed since their discharge from an outpatient psychiatric clinic. A sizeable proportion (almost 20%) had never resumed school. However, 85% were working or attending school full-time. The work and educational status of the group was only slightly worse than that of the general population of similar sex and age. Return to school during treatment was not associated with a more favorable work outcome.

Most of the outcome studies have focused on hospitalized cases, yet it is unusual for the clinical management of school phobic children to include inpatient care. Therefore, little is known of the outcome of the more typical clinical cases of school phobia.

The follow-up studies presented have all consisted of clinical cases. Since these are likely to represent relatively severe or chronic cases, they do not provide information about the outcome of school phobic children in the general population. Only one investigation was found dealing with the outcome of school phobic children in a total school population (Ono, 1972). In this Japanese group, 1 year after the identification of 95 school phobic children, half were frequently absent from school. The short-term follow-up of this study limits its usefulness in predicting outcome; nevertheless, it suggests that continued difficulties in school attendance are not exceptional, at least in the short run, as has been found in studies of referred children.

The overview of the outcome studies does not provide a clear picture of the psychiatrict sequelae of childhood and adolescent anxiety disorders. Several investigators report a high rate of "neurotic" disturbance in the subsequent adjustment of school phobic children. However, the nature of the emotional impairment is unclear. The single study of the later work history of school phobic children does not indicate the likelihood of occupational handicaps in most cases (Baker

& Wills, 1979). No predictors of outcome have been identified. Early age of onset has not been found consistently to portend a more favorable outlook than later onset. Successful short-term clinical management has also failed to predispose to a better long-term outcome.

FOLLOW-BACK STUDIES

If the presence of an anxiety disorder puts children at risk for similar conditions in adulthood, it would follow that the childhood histories of adult patients with anxiety disorders should have a disproportionate prevalence of anxiety disorders.

In a survey of mothers who brought their 3-year-olds to a public health clinic, Abe (1972) reports that the presence of anxiety symptoms in adulthood was strongly associated with anxiety in childhood. Anxiety symptoms did not appear to start *de novo* in adulthood. (Chapter 3 of this volume discusses these data more fully.)

Klein (1964) noted a high prevalence of separation anxiety disorders in the childhoods of inpatient agoraphobics compared with other patients. Berg, Marks, McGuire, and Lipsedge (1974) examined the frequency of reported previous school phobia among the English nationwide sample of nearly 800 agoraphobic women compared with a group of 57 neurotic outpatients. Both groups reported a very high frequency of school phobia in childhood (22%). The authors conclude that childhood school phobia is a precursor of later neurotic illness but not specifically of agoraphobia. This report would have benefited from a more detailed description of the neurotic group. It is not impossible that the agoraphobes and neurotics shared similar anxiety disorders. If so, it would blur differences between them.

In a large study of adult neurotics, Tyrer and Tyrer (1974) found that adults with anxiety and those with depressive disorders reported having had more school avoidance in childhood than controls (9% vs. 2%, respectively. The anxious and depressive "neurotics," however, did not differ from each other in rate of childhood school avoidance.

In a recent study (Gittelman & Klein, 1985) women with panic disorders and agoraphobia were found to have a significantly greater rate of early separation anxiety than women with simple phobic disorders. This relationship was not observed among male patients.

The retrospective, follow-back studies of adult patients with anxiety disorders are inconsistent in suggesting a specific association between adult panic or agoraphobic disorders and childhood separation anxiety. It is unknown whether other forms of childhood anxiety are also associated with these adult conditions.

The results support the likelihood of a relationship between childhood and later anxiety disorders. This association does not follow for an estimate of the magnitude of the risk for a later disorder for children affected with anxiety disorders. What it does contribute is some confidence in the notion that early and late anxiety conditions are not independent clinical phenomena. The degree to which they are associated remains to be elucidated.

REFERENCES

Abe, K. Phobias and nervous symptoms in childhood and maturity: Resistance and associations. *British Journal of Psychiatry*, 1972, *120*, 275–283.

Abe, K., & Masui, T. Age–sex trends of phobic and anxiety symptoms in adolescents. *British Journal of Psychiatry*, 1981, *138*, 297–302.

American Psychiatric Association. *Diagnostic and statistical manual of mental disorders* (3rd ed.). Washington, D.C.: Author, 1980.

Angelino, H., Dollins, J., & Mech, E. Trends in the fears and worries of school children as related to socio-economic status and age. *Journal of Genetic Psychology*, 1956, *89*, 263–276.

Baker, H., & Wills, U. School phobia: Classification and treatment. *British Journal of Psychiatry*, 1978, *132*, 492–499.

Baker, H., & Wills, U. School phobic children at work. *British Journal of Psychiatry*, 1979, *135*, 561–564.

Berg, I. A follow-up study of school phobic adolescents admitted to an in-patient unit. *Journal of Child Psychology and Psychiatry*, 1970, *11*, 37–47.

Berg, I. School phobia in the children of agoraphobic women. *British Journal of Psychiatry*, 1976, *128*, 86–89.

Berg, I., Butler, A., Fairbairn, I., & McGuire, R. The parents of school phobic adolescents—A preliminary investigation of family life variables. *Psychological Medicine*, 1981, *11*, 79–83.

Berg, I., Butler, A., & Hall, G. The outcome of adolescent school phobia. *British Journal of Psychiatry*, 1976, *128*, 80–85.

Berg, I., Butler, A., & McGuire, R. Birth order and family size of school phobic adolescents. *British Journal of Psychiatry*, 1972, *121*, 509–514.

Berg, I., Butler, A., & Pritchard, J. Psychiatric illness in the mothers of school phobic adolescents. *British Journal of Psychiatry*, 1974, *125*, 466–467.

Berg, I., & Collins, T. Wilfulness in school phobic adolescents. *British Journal of Psychiatry*, 1974, *125*, 468–469.

Berg, I., Collins, T., McGuire, R., & O'Melia, J. Educational attainment in adolescent school phobia. *British Journal of Psychiatry*, 1975, *126*, 435–438.

Berg, I., Marks, I., McGuire, R., & Lipsedge, M. School phobia and agoraphobia. *Psychological Medicine*, 1974, *4*, 428–434.

Berg, I., & McGuire, R. Are school phobic adolescents overdependent? *British Journal of Psychiatry*, 1971, *119*, 167–168.

Berg, I., Nichols, K., & Pritchard, C. School phobia—Its classification and relationship to dependency. *Journal of Child Psychology and Psychiatry*, 1969, *10*, 123–141.

Berney, T., Kolvin, L., Bhate, S., Garside, R., Jeans, J., Kay, B., & Scarth, L. School phobia: A therapeutic trial with clomipramine and short-term outcome. *British Journal of Psychiatry*, 1981, *138*, 110–118.

Bledsoe, J. Sex and grade difference in children's manifest anxiety. *Psychological Reports*, 1973, *32*, 285–286.

Boreham, J. A follow-up study of 54 persistent school refusers. *Association for Child Psychology and Psychiatry News*, 1983, *15*, 8–14.

Bowlby, J. Childhood mourning and its implications for psychiatry. *American Journal of Psychiatry*, 1961, *118*, 481–498.

Buglass, D., Clarke, J., Henderson, A. S., Kreitman, N., & Presley, A. S. A study of agoraphobic housewives. *Psychological Medicine*, 1977, *7*, 73–86.

Byrne, D. Repression-sensitization as a dimension of personality. In B. A. Maher (Ed.), *Progress in experimental personality research* (Vol. 7). New York: Academic Press, 1964, pp. 170–220.

Carey, G., & Gottesman, I. I. Twin and family studies of anxiety, phobic, and obsessive disorders. In D. F. Klein & J. G. Rabkin (Eds.), *Anxiety: New research and changing concepts*. New York: Raven Press, 1982, pp. 117–136.

Coolidge, J. C., Brodie, R. D., & Feeney, B. A ten-year follow-up study of sixty-six school-phobic children. *American Journal of Orthopsychiatry*, 1964, *34*, 675–684.

Crowe, R. R., Pauls, D. L., Slymen, D. J., & Noyes, R. A family study of anxiety neurosis. *Archives of General Psychiatry*, 1980, *37*, 77–79.

Davidson, S. School phobia as a manifestation of family disturbance: Its structure and treatment. *Journal of Child Psychology and Psychiatry*, 1961, *1*, 270–287.

Doris, J., McIntyre, A., Kelsey, C., & Lehman, E. Separation anxiety in nursery school children. *Proceedings of the Annual Meeting of the American Psychological Association*, 1971, pp. 145–146.

Douglas, J. D., & Rice, K. M. Sex differences in children's anxiety and defensiveness measures. *Developmental Psychology*, 1979, *15*, 223–224.

Eisenberg, L. School phobia: Diagnosis, genesis and clinical management. *Pediatric Clinics of North America*, 1958, *4*, 645–666. (a)

Eisenberg, L. School phobia: A study in the communication of anxiety. *American Journal of Psychiatry*, 1958, *114*, 712–718.

Eisenberg, L. The pediatric management of school phobia. *Journal of Pediatrics*, 1959, *55*, 758–766.

Eme, R. F., & Schmidt, D. The stability of children's fears. *Child Development*, 1978, *49*, 1277–1279.

Gittelman, R., & Klein, D. F. Childhood separation anxiety and adult agoraphobia. In A. Y. Tuma & J. D. Maser (Eds.), *Anxiety and the anxiety disorders*. Hillsdale, N.J.: Erlbaum, 1985, pp. 389–402.

Gittelman-Klein, R. Psychiatric characteristics of the relatives of school phobic children. In D. V. S. Sankar (Ed.), *Mental health in children* (Vol. 1). Westbury, N.Y.: PJD Publications, 1975, pp. 325–334.

Gittelman-Klein, R., & Klein, D. F. School phobia: Diagnostic considerations in the light of imipramine effects. *Journal of Nervous and Mental Disease*, 1973, *156*, 199–215.

Gittelman-Klein, R., & Klein, D. F. Separation anxiety in school refusal and its treatment with drugs. In L. Hersov & I. Berg (Eds.), *Out of school*. London: Wiley, 1980, pp. 321–341.

Goldsmith, H. H., & Gottesman, I. I. Origins of variation in behavioral style: A longitudinal study of temperament in young twins. *Child Development*, 1981, *52*, 91–103.

Gordon, M. Cyclone Tracey. II. The effects on Darwin. *Australian Psychologist*, 1977, *12*, 55–82.

Herman, S. P., Stickler, G. B., & Lucas, A. R. Hyperventilation syndrome in children and adolescents: Long-term follow-up. *Pediatrics*, 1982, *67*, 183–187.

Hersov, L. A. Persistent non-attendance at school. *Child Psychology and Psychiatry*, 1960, *1*, 130–136.

Johnson, A. M., Falstein, E., I., Stanislaus, A. S., & Svendsen, M. School phobia. *American Journal of Orthopsychiatry*, 1941, *11*, 702–708.

Klein, D. F. Delineation of two drug-responsive anxiety syndromes. *Psychopharmacologia*, 1964, *3*, 397–408.

Klein, D. F. Anxiety reconceptualized. In D. F. Klein & J. G. Rabkin (Eds.), *Anxiety: New research and changing concepts*. New York: Raven Press, 1981, pp. 235–263.

Lansky, S. B., Lowman, J. T., Voto, T. & Gyulay, J. School phobia in children with malignant neoplasms. *American Journal of the Disabled Child*, 1975, *129*, 42–46.

Leventhal, T., & Sills, M. Self-image in school phobia. *American Journal of Orthopsychiatry*, 1964, *34*, 685–695.

MacFarlane, J. W., Allen, L., & Honzik, M. *A Developmental study of the behavior problems of normal children*. Berkeley, Calif.: University of California Press, 1954.

Marks, I. M. Research in neurosis: A selective review. 1. Causes and courses. *Psychological Medicine*, 1973, *3*, 436–454.

Marks, I. M., & Gelder, M. G. Different ages of onset in varieties of phobia. *American Journal of Psychiatry*, 1966, *123*, 218–221.

Martinez-Monfort, A., & Dreger, R. M. Reactions of high school students in school desegregation in a Southern metropolitan area. *Psychological Reports*, 1972, *30*, 543–565.

Miller, L. C., Barrett, C. L., Hampe, E., & Noble, H. Revised anxiety scales in the Louisville Behavior Checklist. *Psychological Reports*, 1971, *29*, 503–511.

Miller, L. C., Barrett, C. L., Hampe, E., & Noble, H. Comparison of reciprocal inhibition, psychotherapy and waiting list control for phobic children. *Journal of Abnormal Psychology*, 1972, *79*, 269–279.

Morris, D. P., Soroker, E., & Burruss, G. Follow-up studies of shy, withdrawn children. I. Evaluation of later adjustment. *American Journal of Orthopsychiatry*, 1954, *24*, 743–754.

Nichols, K. A., & Berg, I. School phobia and self-examination. *Journal of Child Psychology and Psychiatry*, 1970, *11*, 133–141.

Olah, A., Stettin, H., & Magnusson, D. *Comparison of anxiety patterns of Swedish and Hungarian youngsters.* Report No. 523 for the Department of Psychology, University of Stockholm, Stockholm, Sweden, 1978.

Ono, O. Basic studies in school phobia: An investigation in a local area (Kagawa Prefecture). *Japanese Journal of Child Psychiatry*, 1972, *13*, 249–260. (Abstract)

Perry, N. W., & Millimet, C. R. Child rearing antecedents and high anxiety eighth grade children. In C. Spielberger & I. Sarason (Eds.), *Stress and anxiety* (Vol. 4). Washington, D.C.: Halstead, 1975, pp. 189–204.

Prince, G. S. School phobia. In E. Miller (Ed.), *Foundations of child psychiatry.* London: Pergamon Press, 1968, pp. 413–434.

Richman, N., Stevenson, J., & Graham, P. J. *Preschool to school: A behavioral study.* London: Academic Press, 1982.

Roberts, M. Persistent school refusal among children and adolescents. In D. R. Wirt, G. Winokur, & M. Roff (Eds.), *Life history research in psychopathology* (Vol. 4). Minneapolis, Minn.: University of Minnesota Press, 1975, pp. 79–108.

Rodriguez, A., Rodriguez, M., & Eisenberg, L. The outcome of school phobia: A follow-up study based on 41 cases. *American Journal of Psychiatry*, 1959, *116*, 540–544.

Rutter, M. *Changing youth in a changing society.* Cambridge, Mass.: Harvard University Press, 1980.

Rutter, M. Psychological sequelae of brain damage in children. *American Journal of Psychiatry*, 1981, *138*, 1533–1544.

Rutter, M., & Shaffer, D. DSM III: A step forward or back in terms of the classification of child psychiatric disorders? *Journal of the American Academy of Child Psychiatry*, 1980, *19*, 371–394.

Rutter, M., Tizard, J., & Whitmore, K. *Education, health and behaviour.* New York: Krieger, 1981.

Sermet, O. Emotional and medical factors in child dental anxiety. *Journal of Child Psychology and Psychiatry*, 1974, *15*, 313–321.

Shaffer, D., Schonfeld, I., O'Connor, P. A., Stokman, C., Trautman, P., Shafer, S., & Ng, S. Neurological soft signs: Their relationship to psychiatric disorder and intelligence in childhood and adolescence. *Archives of General Psychiatry*, 1985, *42*, 342–351.

Shepherd, M., Oppenheim, B., & Mitchell, S. (Eds.). *Childhood behavior and mental health.* London: University of London Press 1971.

Smith, S. L. School refusal with anxiety: A review of sixty-three cases. *Canadian Psychiatric Association Journal*, 1970, *15*, 257–264.

Smotherman, W. P., Hunt, L., McGinnis, L. M., & Levine, S. Mother-infant separation in group living rhesus macaques: A hormonal analysis. *Developmental Psychobiology*, 1979, *12*, 211–217.

Sperling, M. School phobias: Classification, dynamics, and treatment. *Psychoanalytic Study of the Child*, 1967, *22*, 375–401.

Talbot, M. Panic in school phobia. *American Journal of Orthopsychiatry*, 1957, *27*, 286–295.

Torgersen, S. The nature and origin of common phobic fears. *British Journal of Psychiatry*, 1979, *134*, 343–351.

Torgersen, S. Genetic factors in anxiety disorders. *Archives of General Psychiatry*, 1983, *40*, 1085–1089.

Tyrer, P., & Tyrer, S. School refusal, truancy, and adult neurotic illness. *Psychological Medicine*, 1974, *4*, 416–421.

Waldron, S. The significance of childhood neurosis for adult mental health: A follow-up study. *American Journal of Psychiatry*, 1976, *133*, 532–538.

Warren, W. A study of adolescent psychiatric in-patients and the outcome six or more years later. I. Clinical histories and hospital findings. *Journal of Child Psychology and Psychiatry*, 1965, *6*, 1–17. (a)

Warren, W. A study of adolescent psychiatric in-patients and the outcome six or more years later. II. The follow-up study. *Journal of Child Psychology and Psychiatry*, 1965, *6*, 141–160. (b)

Weiss, M., & Burke, A. A 5- to 10-year follow-up of hospitalized school phobic children and adolescents. *American Journal of Orthopsychiatry*, 1970, *40*, 672–676.

Weissman, M. M., Leckman, J. F., Merikangas, K. R., Gammon, G. B., & Prusoff, B. A. Depression and anxiety disorders in parents and children. *Archives of General Psychiatry*, 1984, *41*, 845–852.

Ziv, A., & Israeli, R. Effects of bombardment on the manifest anxiety level of children living in kibbutzim. *Journal of Consulting and Clinical Psychology*, 1973, *40*, 287–291.

Ziv, A., & Luz, M. Manifest anxiety in children of different socioeconomic levels. *Human Development*, 1973, *16*, 224–232.

✝6✝

CHILDHOOD OBSESSIVE–COMPULSIVE DISORDER: AN ANXIETY DISORDER?

CAROL J. BERG
THEODORE P. ZAHN
DAVID BEHAR
JUDITH L. RAPOPORT

INTRODUCTION

Historically, the symptomatology of obsessive–compulsive disorder (OCD) and anxiety have been linked. Jastrowitz (1878) stated that compulsions were dependent on anxiety. Freud (1924) conceptualized compulsive symptoms as being, at least partially, in response to anxiety, while others felt the occurrence of anxiety was secondary. Learning theorists (Dollard & Miller, 1950) regarded compulsive symptoms as conditioned responses to anxiety-provoking events with reinforcement by anxiety reduction. In examining physiological responses, Carr (1974) concluded that compulsive behaviors take place at high levels of anxiety and serve to reduce these levels to those characteristic of the individual in a resting state. Beech (1974) postulated that obsessives have a predisposition to states of pathological arousal and some mechanism by which such states lead to

Carol J. Berg and Judith L. Rapoport. Child Psychiatry Branch, National Institute of Mental Health, Bethesda, Maryland.

Theodore P. Zahn. Laboratory of Psychology and Psychopathology, National Institute of Mental Health, Bethesda, Maryland.

David Behar. Department of Psychiatry, Medical College of Pennsylvania, Philadelphia, Pennsylvania.

morbid thoughts and aberrant behavior. A certain confusion continues to exist in lumping together obsessive–compulsive–ruminative states with anxiety states despite our nosology being reasonably accurate from a descriptive point of view (Margetts, 1977). More recent speculation about biological aspects of OCD suggest independence from anxiety disorders (Behar et al., 1984; Rapoport et al., 1981).

Anxiety disorders of childhood, considered common, are classified as separation, avoidant, and overanxious disorders with phobic and panic disorder diagnosed using adult criteria (DSM-III; American Psychiatric Association, 1980). In contrast, childhood OCD has been considered a relatively rare childhood psychiatric disorder although it is increasingly being recognized and studied (Behar et al., 1984; Rapoport et al., 1981). Judd (1965), in his description of five cases of childhood OCD (found among 405 children seen at the University of California at Los Angeles patient services) did not stress anxiety as prominent. Prevalent family characteristics of obsessive patients have included significant pathology (Hollingsworth, Tanquay, Grossman, & Pabst, 1980; Judd, 1965; Lewis, 1936; Lo, 1967), but have not included diagnosed cases of anxiety disorder. Kringlen (1965), in a long-term follow-up of adults with OCD, determined 25% had anxiety and obsessive symptoms at the onset of their illness but none developed an anxiety disorder several years later.

As part of an ongoing study of childhood OCD, an unusually large sample of children and adolescents with pure OCD has been evaluated. This report addresses the relationship between obsessive–compulsive symptoms and signs of anxiety collected for this group.

METHODS

SUBJECTS

Thirty adolescent patients (aged 8–18, M 14 $\pm$ 2.46 years; 21 boys, 9 girls) were provisionally diagnosed as having severe primary OCD by two child psychiatrists during a screening interview at the Clinical Center of the National Institutes of Health. Inclusion criteria were rituals and/or repetitive thoughts considered unreasonable by the patient, experienced as distressful and causing significant interference in home, school, or interpersonal functioning with symptoms present for 1 year. Individuals were excluded if they had a Wechsler Full Scale IQ less than 85, would not cooperate with the testing program, had psychotic symptoms, primary depressive illness, definite neurological disease, or symptoms too mild to interfere significantly with academic or personal functioning. The 30 adolescent patients participated in a 5-day assessment phase that included a structured clinical interview for children (Herjanic, Herjanic, Brown, & Wheatt, 1975; Herjanic & Campbell, 1977), direct observations by ward and other clinical personnel, the Child Behavioral Checklist (Achenbach, 1979) for parents, and physiological measures.

Twenty-three adolescent controls (aged 10–17, M 14 ± 2.2 years; 14 boys, 9 girls), of comparable age and matched as nearly as possible for IQ, participated in the physiological measures. None of the children or their families had histories of psychiatric problems or had developmental problems. All controls spent approximately 5 days as inpatients on the same ward during evaluation.

All living parents (one parent was dead) and 61 siblings were evaluated in nonblind personal interviews with several siblings being interviewed by telephone. The majority of siblings under 18 years of age were interviewed with the same clinical interview as the patients while the siblings over 18 years of age and the parents were interviewed with the Schedule for Affective Disorders and Schizophrenia (Spitzer & Endicott, 1978).

ASSESSMENT

Ward and staff interviewing physician ratings included:

  • *Leyton Obsessional Inventory—Child Version* (Berg, Rapoport, & Flament, in press). This inventory gave yes–no answers to 44 obsessional symptoms as well as resistance and interference scores with respect to symptoms present.

  • *Obsessive–Compulsive Rating Scale* (Rapoport, Elkins, & Mikkelson, 1980). This four-item scale, scored 1 to 5, rated preoccupation, number, interference, and time spent resisting compulsive rituals.

  • *Comprehensive Psychopathological Rating Scale—* Obsessive–Compulsive Disorder subscale (Thoren, Asberg, Cronholm, Jornestedt, & Traskman, 1980). This eight-item scale, scored 0 to 3, rated severity of obsessive–compulsive symptoms.

• *NIMH Global Scales* (Murphy, Pickar, & Alterman, 1982). These scales, scored 1 to 15, rated severity of anxiety and obsessive–compulsive symptoms (Rapoport & Elkins, unpublished).

• *Brief Psychiatric Rating Scale* (Overall & Gorham, 1962). Item 2, anxiety, was selected and rated based on the patient's verbal report and rated 1 to 7.

• *NIMH Self-Rating Scale* (Kotin, Post, & Goodwin, 1973). Item 4, "feel anxious," was selected and rated on a scale of 0 to 6.

• *Child Behavior Checklist* (Achenbach, 1979). The checklist contained seven areas of social competencies and 113 items of behavioral problems, scored 0 to 2, which were rated by parents.

• *Physiological Measures* (Zahn, Rapoport, & Thompson, 1980). Skin conductance (SC) and heart rate were recorded during a 3-minute rest period and a series of 75-dB, 500-Hz nonsignal tones were presented at 20- to 30-second intervals. The indices of autonomic arousal examined were frequency of spontaneous SC responses (SCRs) per minute, SC level, number of SCRs elicited by the tones, and the mean heart rate.

STATISTICS

Two-way analyses of variance were computed to compare the means of group and sex on each of the four autonomic measures. Interactions were analyzed using tests for simple effects (Winer, 1971). Pearson product–moment correlations were performed for obsessive and anxiety scores.

RESULTS

CLINICAL INTERVIEW (PATIENTS)

All 30 children were diagnosed as having primary childhood OCD. In addition, four patients met DSM-III criteria for overanxious disorder; five patients had at least four positive symptoms that did not meet duration criteria (6 months). One patient met criteria for separation anxiety. Phobias were considered but not diagnosed since no cases were seen in which the phobic thought was independent of the obsessional disorder.

CHILD BEHAVIOR CHECKLIST

Twenty-four parents completed the checklist. Internalizing scores (> 70) were clearly more prominent for four out of five girls and eight of 19 boys. Four of these patients (one girl, three boys) were also higher (> 70) on the Externalizing band.

WARD RATINGS

Obsessional ratings (Obsessive–Compulsive Rating Scale, Comprehensive Psychopathological Rating Scale—Obsessive–Compulsive Disorder subscale, NIMH Global obsessive–compulsive item) correlated significantly with the ratings of anxiety (Brief Psychiatric Rating Scale anxiety item, NIMH Self-Rating Scale anxiety item, and NIMH Global anxiety item), r = .48–.74 (p < .04–.0001). However, the Leyton obsessional measures did not correlate with the anxiety measures.

PHYSIOLOGICAL MEASURES

Obsessive patients and normal controls were compared for four conventional indices of autonomic arousal averaged for the rest and tone periods (Table 6.1). None of the differences between the groups as a whole were significant, but there was a trend (p < .1) for controls to give more SC orienting responses. However, there were statistically significant differences on three variables. The obsessive–compulsive boys were higher than control boys on all four variables whereas the converse was true for the girls. That is, boys showed an autonomic profile resembling anxiety disorder, whereas girls did not. The autonomic measures, reanalyzed removing two boys with secondary anxiety, remained unchanged. Correlations between the physiological and anxiety measures as a group and by sex were not significant.

CLINICAL INTERVIEW (FAMILY)

Diagnosis of 60 parents did not indicate familial loading for anxiety disorders. Diagnosis included only three parents with anxiety

TABLE 6.1. Means and Significance Tests of Baseline Autonomic Variables for Obsessive Adolescents and Controls

Variable	Obsessives (M ± SD)	Controls (M ± SD)	Group × sex		
			F	df	p
SCRs/minute					
Boys	4.64 ± 4.13	2.17 ± 1.38[a]			
Girls	.88 ± 1.02	1.38 ± 2.23[b]	8.26	1,43	.01
Total	2.76 ± 2.57	2.62 ± 1.80			
SC level (μmho)					
Boys	9.44 ± 6.48	7.33 ± 3.94			
Girls	3.62 ± 2.39	7.12 ± 4.39[b]	3.78	1,43	.10
Total	6.53 ± 4.44	7.22 ± 4.17			
Heart rate (beats/minute)					
Boys	77.70 ± 10.20	67.80 ± 7.80[a]			
Girls	75.00 ± 7.10	78.80 ± 15.70	4.80	1,43	.05
Total	73.30 ± 8.70	73.30 ± 11.70			
Number of orienting SCRs					
Boys	5.10 ± 2.20	4.40 ± 2.60			
Girls	1.70 ± 1.30	5.10 ± 2.90[a]	8.84	1,43	.005
Total	3.40 ± 1.80	4.70 ± 2.70[b]			

[a] $p < .05$.
[b] $p < .10$.

disorders (and only two with major affective disorder). Similarly, of 61 siblings interviewed, only three received diagnosis of anxiety disorder as one of their diagnoses.

DISCUSSION

Diagnostically, only five of 30 adolescent obsessive patients qualified for an additional DSM-III diagnosis of anxiety disorder. Moreover, family loading for anxiety disorder was not high, particularly in view of the increasing recognition of the frequency of these disorders in the general population (Robins et al., 1984).

The autonomic data are more complex. Although overall results of the psychophysiological tests are consistent with the hypothesis that obsessive–compulsive and control children do not differ in autonomic arousal, they are complicated by marked sex differences. The obsessive–compulsive boys were consistently higher on the arousal indices than control boys, while their female counterparts were low in arousal compared to controls. These effects are shown by both

SC and heart rate measures apparently ruling out peripheral mechanisms as a factor.

The results for the boys are consistent with the hypothesis that OCD is an anxiety disorder since similar elevations in these same indices of arousal are common findings in anxiety disorders (Lader, 1975; Zahn, in press). In addition, they are consistent with the results of a similar study on adult obsessive–compulsive patients in which the patients had significantly higher SCR frequency, SC and heart rate rest than controls (Insel, Zahn, & Murphy, 1984). This was shown by both men and women, with the women generally showing a stronger effect of diagnosis than the men.

In contrast, the results for the obsessive–compulsive girls are consistent with neither the anxiety disorder hypothesis nor the data from the adult study. Low arousal indices have been observed in a subgroup of patients with endogenous depression (Lader, 1975; Zahn, in press), consistent with the hypothesis that OCD may be part of an affective disorder spectrum. However, this does not address the apparent inconsistency with the data from adult women and the developmental implications of that finding.

Despite all the questions they raise, the present data do suggest the high autonomic activity is not a primary etiologic factor in OCD as suggested by Beech and Perigault (Beech, 1974). If this were true, both boys and girls would be expected to manifest high arousal. If it is assumed that obsessive–compulsive symptoms develop to alleviate feelings of discomfort, then our data suggest that those feelings are more likely to be fear and anxiety in boys and perhaps, shame and guilt in girls. Alternatively, it might be hypothesized that at an early stage of the disorder, both boys and girls are hyperaroused, but the symptoms of the girls are more successful (or overly successful) in lowering arousal. The close relationship between the anxiety and obsessive measures during the assessment phase only indicated that a subjective state of worry or apprehension was present concurrent with the obsessive symptoms as judged by both the patient and clinician. However, since the anxiety ratings did not correlate with the physiological measures, the "state" of anxiety may be qualitatively different.

Other approaches will be needed to settle the question of whether childhood OCD is anxiety disorder. To date, pharmacologic success with antianxiety agents has not been striking. Clomipramine, on the other hand, appears to have specific benefit for childhood OCD (Flament *et al.,* in press) but has not been evaluated for anxiety disorders. Thus, pharmacologic distinction has only partially been demonstrated.

Long-term follow-up studies have not reported an excess of anxiety disorders (Kringlen, 1965). Our preliminary follow-up data with this sample suggest that, over time, anxiety may play a more prominent role in the symptom picture. Whether this represents continuity with anxiety disorders is unclear as secondary anxiety may develop in response to continuing disability from the obsessions.

Finally, as with other disorders, OCD may be heterogeneous. Our data for children indicate that at least these subjects' disorder may be more independent from anxiety or depressive disorders than is their adult counterpart.

REFERENCES

Achenbach, T. The Child Behavior Profile: An empirically based system for assessing children's behavioral problems and competencies. *International Journal of Mental Health,* 1979, *7,* 24–42.

American Psychiatric Association. *Diagnostic and statistical manual of mental disorders* (3rd ed.). Washington, D.C.: Author, 1980.

Beech, H. R. (Ed.). *Obsessional states.* London: Methuen, 1974.

Behar, D., Rapoport, J. L., Berg, C. J., Denckla, M. B., Mann, L., Cox, C., Fedrico, P., Zahn, T., & Wolfman, M. G. Computerized tomography and neuropsychological test measures in adolescents with obsessive–compulsive disorder. *American Journal of Psychiatry,* 1984, *141*(3), 363–369.

Berg, C. J., Rapoport, J. L., & Flament, M. F. The Leyton Obsessional Inventory— Child version. *Journal of the American Academy of Child Psychiatry,* in press.

Carr, A. T. Compulsive neurosis: A review of the literature. *Psychological Bulletin,* 1974, *81,*(5), 311–318.

Dollard, J., & Miller, N. E. *Personality and psychotherapy: An analysis in terms of learning, thinking and culture.* New York: McGraw-Hill, 1950.

Flament, M. F., Rapoport, J. L., Berg, C. J., Sceery, W., Kilts, C., Mellstrom, B., & Linnoila, M. Clomipramine treatment of childhood obsessive compulsive disorder: A double-blind controlled study. *Archives of General Psychiatry,* in press.

Freud, S. *Standard edition* (Vol. 1). London: Hogarth Press, 1924.

Herjanic, B., & Campbell, W. Differentiating psychiatrically disturbed children on the basis of a structured psychiatric interview. *Journal of Abnormal Child Psychology,* 1977, *5,* 127–135.

Herjanic, B., Herjanic, M., Brown, F., & Wheatt, T. Are children realiable reporters? *Journal of Abnormal Child Psychology,* 1975, *3,* 41–49.

Hollingsworth, C. E., Tanquay, P. E., Grossman, L., & Pabst, P. Longterm outcome of obsessive–compulsive disorder in childhood. *Journal of the American Academy of Child Psychiatry,* 1980, *19,* 127–135.

Insel, T. P., Zahn, T. P., & Murphy, D. L. Obsessive–compulsive disorder: An anxiety disorder? In A. H. Tuma & J. D. Maser (Eds.), *Anxiety and anxiety disorders.* Hillsdale, N.J.: Erlbaum, 1984, pp. 577–589.

Jastrowitz, H. Discussions with Westphal. *Archiv für Psychiatrie und Nervenkrankheiten,* 1878, *8,* 750–755.

Judd, L. Obsessive compulsive neurosis in children. *Archives of General Psychiatry,* 1965, *12,* 136–143.

Kotin, J., Post, R. M., & Goodwin, F. K. Tetrahydrocannabinol in depressed patients. *Archives of General Psychiatry,* 1973, *28,* 345–352.

Kringlen, E. Obsessional neurotics: A long-term follow-up. *British Journal of Psychiatry,* 1965, *111,* 709–722.

Lader, M. H. *The psychophysiology of mental illness.* London: Routledge & Kegan Paul, 1975.

Lewis, A. Problems of obsessional illness. *Proceedings of the Royal Society of Medicine,* 1936, *29,* 325–366.

Lo, W. H. A follow-up study of obsessional neurotics in Hong Kong Chinese. *British Journal of Psychiatry,* 1967, *113,* 823–832.

Margetts, E. L. Closing remarks. *Journal of International Medical Research,* 1977, *5*(5), 126–128.

Murphy, D. L., Pickar, D., & Alterman, I. S. Methods for the quantitative assessment of depressive and manic behavior. In E. L. Burdock, A. Sudilousky, & S. Gershon (Eds.), *The behavior of psychiatric patients.* New York: Marcel Dekker, 1982, pp. 355–392.

Overall, J. E., & Gorham, D. R. The Brief Psychiatric Rating Scale. *Psychological Reports,* 1962, *10,* 799–812.

Rapoport, J. L., & Elkins, R. *NIMH obsessive–compulsive subscale.* Unpublished.

Rapoport, J. L., Elkins, R., & Mikkelson, E. Clinical controlled trial of chlorimipramine in adolescents with obsessive–compulsive disorder. *Psychopharmacology Bulletin,* 1980, *16,* 61–63.

Rapoport, J. L., Elkins, R., Langer, D. H., Sceery, W., Buchsbaum, M. S., Gillin, J. C., Murphy, D. L., Zahn, T. P., Lake, R., Ludlow, C., & Mendelson, W. Childhood obsessive–compulsive disorder. *American Journal of Psychiatry,* 1981, *138*(12), 1545–1554.

Robins, L. N., Helzer, J. E., Weissman, M. M., Orvaschel, H., Gruenberg, E., Burke, J. D., & Regier, D. A. Lifetime prevalence of specific pschiatric disorders in three sites. *Archives of General Psychiatry,* 1984, *41*(10), 949–958.

Spitzer, R. L., & Endicott, J. *Schedule for Affective Disorders and Schizophrenia.* New York: New York State Psychiatric Institute, 1978.

Thoren, P., Asberg, M., Cronholm, B., Jornestedt, L., & Traskman, L. Clomipramine treatment of obsessive–compulsive disorder. *Archives of General Psychiatry,* 1980, *37,* 1281–1285.

Winer, B. J. *Statistical principles in experimental design.* New York: McGraw-Hill, 1971.

Zahn, T. P., Rapoport, J. L., & Thompson, C. L. Autonomic and behavioral effects of dextroamphetamine and placebo in normal and hyperactive prepubertal boys. *Journal of Abnormal Child Psychology,* 1980, *8,* 145–160.

Zahn, T. P. Psychophysiological approaches to psychopathology. In M. G. H. Coles, E. Donchin, & S. W. Porges (Eds.), *Psychophysiology: Systems, processes, and application.* New York: Guilford, in press.

‡ 7 ‡

RELATIONSHIP BETWEEN AFFECTIVE AND ANXIETY DISORDERS IN CHILDHOOD

JOAQUIM PUIG-ANTICH
HARRIS RABINOVICH

In this chapter we explore the relationship between anxiety and depressive disorders in childhood. We review first what is known about the differences between depressed and nondepressed emotional disorders and then examine the overlap between these two types of symptoms and diagnoses. To this purpose we use our data from a study of prepubertal major depression. Since the data were not collected for the analyses we report, these must be considered post hoc and exploratory.

DISSECTING THE EMOTIONAL DISORDERS

The classic child psychiatric nosology that separated emotional disorders from conduct disorders has been validated by a variety of demographic and follow-up data (Rutter, 1979). The overall category of childhood emotional disorders, however, is clearly not a homogeneous entity (Puig-Antich & Gittelman-Klein, 1982). We have argued that emotional disorders should be separated into depressive and nondepressive types (Puig-Antich, 1982). The validity of such distinction is receiving increasing support from a variety of studies, summarized here briefly.

Joaquim Puig-Antich. Department of Psychiatry, University of Pittsburgh School of Medicine, Western Psychiatric Institute and Clinic, Pittsburgh, Pennsylvania.
Harris Rabinovich. New York State Psychiatric Institute, and College of Physicians and Surgeons, Columbia University, New York, New York.

FAMILIAL AGGREGATION STUDIES

In a controlled family history study of prepubertal major depression (Puig-Antich, Tabrizi, *et al.,* unpublished), we found significant familial aggregation of major depression in the relatives of prepubertal children with major depressive disorders when compared with the families of normal controls. Familial morbidity risks for alcoholism were also significantly higher in the families of the children with major depression than in the families of normal controls.

Families of children with nondepressed emotional disorder occupied an intermediate position regarding prevalence of lifetime major depression in the adult relatives. These families did not differ significantly from those of either children with major depression or normal children. On the other hand the families of children with nondepressed disorders have a significantly lower morbidity risk for alcoholism than families of children with major depression and are indistinguishable from families of normal children on this measure.

"Other psychiatric disorder," a catch-all Family History–Research Diagnostic Criteria diagnostic category that, in this study, comprised mostly anxiety disorders, was found to be equally as prevalent among the adult relatives of both depressive and nondepressive psychiatric children (Andreasen, Endicott, Spitzer, & Winokur, 1977). In all psychiatric groups, mobidity risks for "other" diagnosis were significantly higher than in the families of normal controls. No significant evidence of familial aggregation was found for mania, antisocial personality, substance use disorders, or schizophrenia.

Similar findings were obtained among second-degree relatives. This depth of familiar disorder indicates the extent of pedigree loading among children with major depressive disorder. It also suggests that high density of the pedigree for affective disorder and alcoholism may be a characteristic of early age of onset of depression. Thus, there were only minor differences among the three psychiatric groups in the proportion of relatives with any psychiatric disorder. However, first- and second-degree relatives of depressed children had significantly higher morbidity risks for the diagnoses subsumed under the "depressive spectrum disease" (Winokur, 1972) than the relatives in either of the control groups. Depressive spectrum disease includes any subject with at least one of the following lifetime diagnoses: major depression, alcoholism, or antisocial personality disorder. Familial aggregation of alcoholism in first- and second-degree relatives clearly differentiates prepubertal major depression from nondepressed emotional disorders. However, no conclusions can be reached at present regarding familial aggregation of major depression between these two diagnostic groups. The use of the more sensitive family study method (Andreasen *et al.*, 1977) in larger groups will be necessary to determine if there are in fact significant differences between them.

FOLLOW-UP STUDIES

Follow-up into adolescence of the heterogeneous group of emotional disorders identified at midchildhood has given a picture of substantial variability of clinical outcome. Thus, Rutter (1979) found that only about half (54%) of these children were free of psychiatric problems in adolescence. Thirty-one percent showed persistent emotional disorder, and 10% presented mixed disorder (emotional *and* conduct symptomatology).

There are no follow-up studies of strictly nondepressed emotional disorders in the literature. Although follow-up studies have been reported of children with emotional disorders, such as obsessional disorder (Adams, 1973), no distinction was made between those with and without depression.

The persistence of major depression and dysthymic disorders in nonpharmacologically treated children has been found to be remarkable. The DSM-III diagnostic criteria for dysthymia in children are identical to those for adults, the validity of which is strongly supported by the work of Akiskal *et al.* (1979) and Keller, Shapiro, Lavori, and Wolfe (1982a, 1982b). Kovacs, Feinberg, Crouse-Novak, Paulauskas, and Finkelstein (1984), in a 5-year follow-up of such children, have found that the mean duration of an episode of prepubertal dysthymia is 3 years, while that of prepubertal depression is 1½ years. In addition, those authors found that approximately one half of major depressive episodes occur in children who already have dysthymic disorder. Once recovery from the initial major depressive and/or dysthymic episode sets in, these patients return to dysthymia and have a 70% probability of developing a second dysthymic and/or major depressive episode in the next few years (Kovacs, Feinberg, Crouse-Novak, Paulauskas, Pollock, & Finkelstein, 1984). Furthermore, among nondepressed children with other psychiatric disorders, matched for age and sex, none developed an affective episode over the same period of time. Children with an initial diagnosis of adjustment disorder with depressive features did not go on to develop psychiatric syndromes.

Thus, it appears that childhood affective disorders present with a remarkable long-term stability that may be lacking in the emotional disorders without affective illness.

NEUROENDOCRINE STUDIES

Abnormalities of growth hormone secretion have been found in prepubertal children with major depressive disorder in two different experimental designs. Like their adult counterparts (Gregoire, Branman, DeBuck, & Corvillain, 1977; Gruen, Sachar, Altman, & Sassin, 1975), prepubertal children with endogenous depression hyposecrete growth hormone in response to insulin-induced hypoglycemia (Puig-Antich et al., 1981; Puig-Antich, Novacenko, et al., 1984). Growth hormone hyposecretion in response to insulin tolerance tests (ITT) occurs not only in the endogenous group but also in one third of children with nonendogenous depression in the same age group. This marker is, therefore, more frequent than in adult depressives, a fact that may reflect both the severity of the illness when its onset is so early in life and the virtual lack of circulating estrogens before puberty (Frantz & Rabkin, 1965; Merimee & Feinberg, 1971).

In addition, we have found that prepubertal children with major depression, both endogenous and nonendogenous, secrete significantly more growth hormone during sleep than normal and psychiatric, nondepressed, controls (Puig-Antich, Goetz, Davies, Novacenko, et al., 1984). Interestingly, there is little overlap between these two phenomena. Approximately 85% of our sample of prepubertal major depression can be identified by having at least one of these two growth hormone secretion abnormalities. It is of great significance that both growth hormone abnormalities persist in the recovered drug-free state (Puig-Antich, Goetz, Davies, Novacenko, et al., 1984; Puig-Antich, Goetz, Davies, Tabrizi, et al., 1984). These findings suggest that true trait markers of the disorder may be identifiable.

SLEEP STUDIES

We have reported that fully recovered drug-free prepubertal patients with major depression show significantly shortened latency from sleep onset to the first rapid eye movement period (REMP) than patients with nondepressed emotional disorders and normals, and than themselves during the depressive episode (Puig-Antich, Goetz, *et al.,* 1983). Therefore, first REMP latency may also be a marker of trait for major depressive disorder in prepuberty.

The lack of polysomnographic differences at pretreatment (Puig-Antich *et al.,* 1982) and the lack of sleep studies in fully recovered, drug-free children with nondepressed emotional disorders, preclude any conclusions regarding the differentiation of affective and nonaffective emotional disorders based on current knowledge of sleep function in these childhood conditions.

It is concluded, therefore, that there is sufficient evidence to support the validity of separating the emotional disorders of childhood into the categories of depressed and nondepressed.

BRIEF DESCRIPTION OF CLINICAL ASSESSMENT AND DIAGNOSTIC ISSUES AND METHODS

The two main diagnostic classes addressed in this chapter, anxiety disorders and depressive disorders of childhood, have been defined in DSM-III (American Psychiatric Association, 1980).

The diagnosis of major depression in children and adolescents is made using the same unmodified diagnostic criteria for major depression used in older age groups (Puig-Antich, Blau, Marx, Greenhill, & Chambers, 1978). The presence of depressive mood and/or pervasive anhedonia or lack of interest is necessary but not sufficient to make the diagnosis of major depressive disorder. Also required are the presence of at least four out of the eight associated symptoms that are diagnostic of the depressive syndrome. The symptoms include an appetite disturbance; sleep disturbance; loss of energy, fatigability, or tiredness; psychomotor agitation or retardation; feelings of excessive or inappropriate guilt; difficulty concentrating or slowed down thinking; and thoughts of death or suicide or any suicidal behavior. Features commonly associated with depressive disorders but not included in the diagnostic criteria include depressed appearance, low self-esteem, tearfulness, somatic complaints (aches and pains), anger/irritability, and brooding. The disorder should have been present for at least 2 weeks and accompanied by functional impairment at home, at school and/or with peers.

A full description of the method of our assessment of depressive sympatomatology in children has been published elsewhere (Puig-Antich, Chambers, & Tabrizi, 1983). Children were assessed using the Schedule for Affective Disorders and Schizophrenia for School-Aged Children—Present Episode (Kiddie SADS-P, K-SADS-P) by means of parent and child symptom-oriented interviews. The reliability of which is described elsewhere (Chambers *et al.,* in press). The diagnoses of major depression were made by Research Diagnostic Criteria (RDC), and those of nondepressed emotional disorders were made by DSM-III. It is helpful to describe the decision rules we used for diagnosis. The minimum severity of depressive mood is a report of three periods of continuous depressive mood per week, each period lasting for at least 3 consecutive hours. Some children report frequent, short periods of sadness, but on further questioning their "mood baseline" is constantly low, always considerably lower than their peers, upon which negative mood spikes are superimposed. Once this pattern is clarified, these children should be counted positive for depressed mood.

Depressive mood that was totally and completely relieved by the presence of the main attachment figure(s) was not considered a symptom of depression. These children rarely experienced depressive mood in the presence of the parent and without an impending separation. Such children always presented pathological separation anxiety and were accepted in the nondepressed emotional disorder group. On the other hand children who presented anxiety symptoms or one of the anxiety disorders plus dysphoric mood in the presence of the parent were excluded from the study if they did not fit criteria for major depressive disorder. If they did fit such criteria, they were accepted as major depressives. Children with dysthymia without major depression and children with adjustment disorder with depressive mood were excluded. In this study, therefore, nondepressed emotional disorders were free of depressive mood. Depressed emotional disorders were all major depression.

THE OVERLAP BETWEEN ANXIETY AND DEPRESSIVE PICTURES

In Kovacs's follow-up study of children with major depression and/or dysthymic disorder, practically all children presented with accompanying anxiety *symptoms* (Kovacs, personal communication, 1983). Hershberg, Carlson, Cantwell, and Strober (1982) have reported similar findings. They compared children and adolescents who had anxiety disorders with depressed youngsters in the same age range. The depressive group presented high symptomatic levels of generalized anxiety, somatic complaints, and obsessive–compulsive phenomena. They showed lower but still elevated prevalences of phobic and observed anxiety.

In our studies of children with major depression, we found very similar patterns. Most depressive children present with anxiety symptoms. Table 7.1 shows the rates for each anxiety symptom found in our sample of 80 children with major depressive disorder and 43 nondepressed prepubertal children with emotional disorders. No differences were found in the rate of each anxiety symptom between the two samples.

When one considers anxiety disorder *diagnoses,* the rates are lower but still quite high. Thus, in Kovacs's sample of 54 children with dysthymic disorder and/or major depressive disorder, 35% presented a concomitant anxiety disorder diagnosis. This overlap is almost complete in the case of obsessive–compulsive disorder in youngsters. Rapoport *et al.* (1981) have found that most youngsters with obsessive–compulsive disorder also have a past or current diagnosis of major depression.

TABLE 7.1. Presence of K-SADS-P Neurotic Symptoms in Nondepressed, Neurotic, and Major Depressive Prepubertal Children

	Major depressive disorder ($n = 80$)			Nondepressed emotional disorder ($n = 43$)		
	Not present	Mild	Moderate/ severe	Not present	Mild	Moderate/ severe
Phobia	27%	25%	48%	23%	19%	58%
Separation anxiety	23%	18%	59%	20%	19%	61%
Obsessive–compulsive	73%	16%	11%	79%	14.0%	7%
Depersonal	91%	5%	4%	95%	4.7%	0%
Worrying	11%	19%	70%	23%	19%	58%

It is concluded that the main clinical difference between children with anxiety disorders and children with depressive disorders is the presence of depressive symptoms, not the anxiety manifestations, since the latter are quite often present in affectively disordered children. It is as if, in most cases, the affective picture is superimposed on a background of anxiety symptoms/disorder. Hershberg et al. (1982) suggest that the level of anxiety complaints in depressive children is not generally recognized because the depressive symptomatology is more circumscribed and easy to assess. Although children with "pure" major depression without anxiety symptoms exist, most investigators agree that they are a minority. Adult depressives frequently present both anxiety symptoms and disorders (Akiskal et al., 1979; Weissman, Leckman, Merikangas, Gammon, & Prusoff, 1984).

The question of overlap is most complex in the case of separation anxiety disorder and major depression. It is clear today that there are patients with clear-cut major depression without separation anxiety and patients with separation anxiety disorder without either major depressive disorder or dysthymic disorder. A substantial proportion of children, however, present both types of symptoms, either concomitantly or at different times in the course of childhood and/or adolescence. In light of this, and also in view of the effectiveness of imipramine (Gittelman-Klein & Klein, 1973) and also other antidepressants in reducing pathological separation anxiety, the argument has been raised repeatedly that separation anxiety disorder may be a form of depression in childhood (Hersov, 1977) beginning with the old notion that school phobia may have "masked" depression and, therefore, may be a "depressive equivalent." These arguments have withstood neither the test of time nor the new evidence produced by improved assessment techniques for affective symptoms in children (Carlson & Cantwell, 1980; Puig-Antich, 1982). As a result, the concept of masked depression has been retracted (Cytryn, McKnew, & Bunney, 1980), as with proper use of semistructured phenomenological symptom-oriented interviews, the presence of depressive mood or disorder can be demonstrated.

Nevertheless, the question of the relationship between these two disorders remains. Puig-Antich and Gittelman-Klein (1982) have discussed the following three different possible strategies to differentiate clinically one syndrome from the other and to elicit the relationship between the two disorders when they coexist: (1) to make a primary–secondary distinction based on differential chronological onset of each syndrome; (2) to use intensity of each syndrome as a guideline; thus a child with major endogenous depression and mild separation anxiety would be considered primarily depressed; (3) to limit the diagnosis of separation anxiety disorder to children whose symptomatology remits when separation is neither current nor in the offing.

Although these guidelines are logical and can be helpful, a substantial gray area remains regarding the specific limits of each disorder when they coexist. In addition, none of these guidelines offers any light regarding the relationship between the two disorders, although by defining precisely how experimental groups are constructed and improving assessment and diagnostic procedures, they may aid in gathering new information about this association.

It was concluded (Puig-Antich & Gittelman-Klein, 1982) that when a child fits criteria for both disorders simultaneously both diagnoses should be made. It was also noted that psychobiological correlates may be helpful in eliciting which diagnosis should be primary. A design was proposed comparing children who have major depression and moderate to severe separation anxiety disorder with children who have major depression without separation anxiety ("pure" major depression) and to nondepressed children with separation anxiety ("pure" separation anxiety).

PSYCHOBIOLOGICAL OVERLAP

Our prepubertal depression psychobiological study, although not designed to answer these questions, offers an opportunity to conduct exploratory analyses that can serve as preliminary hypotheses-generating evidence. We present the results of these analyses and also review other investigators' data that bear on these questions. Of all anxiety manifestations, separation anxiety was chosen as the key clinical symptom because of its empirically and theoretically likely association with affective disorders, because it was by far the most reliable anxiety symptom measured by the K-SADS-P (Chambers et al., in press), and also because of its very high prevalence among the nondepressed emotional disorder group.

FAMILIAL AGGREGATION

An exploratory analysis of the relevant data from a family history study
of prepubertal major depressive disorder (Puig-Antich, Tabrizi, *et al.,*
unpublished) is presented in Table 7.2. The groups did not differ
significantly for age, sex, or socioeconomic status. The main findings
are as follows: (1) Nondepressed children with separation anxiety

TABLE 7.2. Age-Corrected Estimates of Morbidity Risk: Both Sexes Combined

	MDD with separation anxiety (n = 28)	MDD without separation anxiety (n = 19)	Separation anxiety without MDD (n = 12)	p^b	Paired contrasts
Major depressive disorder					
First-degree relatives	.43	.55	.39	NS	
Second-degree relatives	.09	.10	.11	NS	
Mania					
First-degree relatives	.07	.04	.05	NS	
Second-degree relatives	.02	.01	.03	NS	
Alcoholism					
First-degree relatives	.34	.18	.09	< .05	1 versus 3 (.05)
Second-degree relatives	.17	.15	.07	< .06	1 versus 3 (.05)
Antisocial personality[a]					
First-degree relatives	.07	.08	.13	NS	
Second-degree relatives	.05	.04	.02	NS	
Substance abuse					
First-degree relatives	.06	.03	.07	NS	
Second-degree relatives	.03	.04	.02	NS	
Other[a]					
First-degree relatives	.29	.28	.27	NS	
Second-degree relatives	.09	.18	.12	< .05	1 versus 2 (.03)
Schizophrenia					
First-degree relatives	.00	.00	.00	NS	
Second-degree relatives	.03	.00	.03	NS	
Affective spectrum[a]					
First-degree relatives	.49	.50	.37	NS	
Second-degree relatives	.24	.20	.15	NS	
Any psychiatric diagnosis[a]					
First-degree relatives	.65	.67	.53	NS	
Second-degree relatives	.31	.35	.29	NS	

Note. MDD, major depressive disorder; NS, not significant.

[a] Not age corrected.

[b] Chi-square.

symptoms have age-corrected morbidity risks for major depression in first- and second-degree relatives indistinguishable from major depressive children. (2) The presence of separation anxiety in a depressive child has no significant effect regarding aggregation of major depression in first- and second-degree relatives. (3) The age-corrected prevalence of alcoholism in first- and second-degree relatives of children with major depression is significantly higher in major depressive children with separation anxiety than in nondepressed separation anxiety children. Pure major depressive children fall in between and do not differ significantly from the pure separation anxiety group. (4) There are no differences in prevalence of "other" (mostly anxiety) diagnoses among first-degree relatives of the three groups. (5) Children with pure major depression have significantly more "other" diagnoses in their second-degree relatives than children with major depression and separation anxiety. (6) There are no differences in morbidity risks among the three groups for any of the other psychiatric diagnoses surveyed.

Overall these data suggest that contrary to a prior report (Gittelman-Klein, 1975), affective disorder among parents may predispose the children to separation anxiety disorder. It also suggests that separation anxiety in some cases may be a precursor to depressive illness. Furthermore, the higher prevalence of alcoholism in affectively loaded families, the higher the chances that the children will be affected with separation anxiety before puberty. In a similar vein, the more alcoholism in the family, the higher the chances that separation anxious offspring will develop a concomitant major depression. As is the case of the children, anxiety symptoms were equally prevalent in the family members of all psychiatric groups, including depressive and nondepressive.

POLYSOMNOGRAPHY

Children with major depression and separation anxiety showed no differences from children with pure separation anxiety or children with pure major depression in any of the polysomnographic variables when the mean of three consecutive nights was considered. Number of awakenings during the second half of the night were higher (nonsignificant trend) in children with major depression and separation anxiety than in the other two groups (Table 7.3).

TABLE 7.3. Sleep Function during Depressive Episode: Three-Night Means

	MDD with separation anxiety ($n = 32$)	MDD without separation anxiety ($n = 21$)	Separation anxiety without MDD ($n = 17$)	p
Total sleep time (min)	494.30 ± 36.10	486.20 ± 56.10	472.20 ± 51.80	< .290
Sleep period time (min)	533.30 ± 43.10	513.90 ± 58.00	502.70 ± 41.50	< .090
Total rest period (min)	561.60 ± 42.70	549.20 ± 44.90	532.70 ± 37.20	< .080
Sleep latency (min)	28.30 ± 14.80	35.40 ± 25.70	30.00 ± 26.80	< .510
Number of first half awakenings	1.00 ± 1.20	0.48 ± 0.98	0.88 ± 0.93	< .210
Number of second half awakenings	2.90 ± 2.20	1.76 ± 1.09	1.88 ± 1.65	< .055
Stage 1 (min)	33.50 ± 15.10	39.50 ± 19.30	32.20 ± 14.30	< .300
Stage 2 (min)	251.90 ± 32.80	240.90 ± 39.40	227.90 ± 46.30	< .120
Stage 3 (min)	40.30 ± 12.10	35.70 ± 13.60	38.70 ± 12.70	< .440
Stage 4 (min)	90.10 ± 20.80	87.30 ± 26.00	98.10 ± 13.40	< .270
Delta (min)	130.40 ± 26.20	122.90 ± 34.20	136.80 ± 20.80	< .310
REM (min)	78.60 ± 16.90	82.80 ± 18.10	75.30 ± 20.50	< .440
Sleep efficiency (min)	92.70 ± 3.80	94.60 ± 3.34	93.70 ± 4.19	< .210
Number of REMPs	4.25 ± 0.92	4.52 ± 0.75	4.35 ± 0.93	< .540
REMP latency (min)	161.80 ± 58.30	142.00 ± 45.80	147.00 ± 38.50	< .340
REM efficiency (min)	84.40 ± 7.65	82.60 ± 5.81	80.50 ± 7.74	< .190
REM density (min)	3.05 ± 1.09	3.24 ± 1.17	3.22 ± 1.06	< .800

Note. MDD, major depressive disorder; REMP, rapid eye movement period.

147

The same pattern was found when the first night alone was considered (Table 7.4). Children with pure major depression presented significantly higher total sleep time, sleep period time, and total rest period than nondepressed children with separation anxiety. Nevertheless, the presence of separation anxiety in children with major depression made no difference regarding sleep variables. Children with major depression, as reported before, presented no adaptation effects. Even when separation anxiety was present, children with major depression showed no adaptation effects (Table 7.4).

We did not find any differences either in REMP latencies or in any other sleep variable between fully recovered, drug-free, major depressive children who had significant separation anxiety during the episode, and children recovered from "pure" major depressive episode. The only exception is that the number of awakenings in the first half of the night was significantly higher in the mixed depression and separation anxiety group (Table 7.5).

In summary, the presence of associated separation anxiety does not appear to modify in any major way the sleep function of children with major depression, neither during illness nor during a recovered state.

GROWTH HORMONE SECRETION

The introduction of separation anxiety as a variable to subdivide children with major depression into two groups was not followed by significant differences in either growth hormone response to ITT or in the secretion of this hormone during the sleep period (Table 7.6). There is, however, the possibility of a type II error in this comparison. Analyses during recovery were not conducted because of high test–retest correlation shown by these variables from the depressed to the nondepressed state (Puig-Antich, Davies, et al., 1984; Puig-Antich, Goetz, Davies, Tabrizi, et al., 1984), combined with the lower sample size of children fully recovered from a major depressive episode.

PSYCHOPHARMACOLOGY

We have reported before that the symptom of separation anxiety associated with major depression in children does not predict

TABLE 7.4. Sleep Function during Depressive Episode: Night 1 Sleep

	MDD with separation anxiety (n = 31)	MDD without separation anxiety (n = 20)	Separation anxiety without MDD (n = 17)	T
Total sleep time (min)	472.90 ± 54.90	471.30 ± 88.50	436.10 ± 67.20	0.018
Sleep period time (min)	517.10 ± 52.40	503.90 ± 84.00	468.60 ± 49.40	0.043
Total rest period (min)	550.50 ± 57.50	547.10 ± 65.00	499.70 ± 53.30	0.014
Sleep latency (min)	33.50 ± 24.50	43.20 ± 39.20	31.10 ± 42.10	0.497
Number of first half awakenings	2.26 ± 1.69	0.50 ± 1.19	0.77 ± 1.35	0.190
Number of second half awakenings	2.27 ± 2.39	1.55 ± 1.23	1.76 ± 2.02	0.070
Stage 1 (min)	30.80 ± 17.30	41.70 ± 26.00	28.10 ± 19.00	0.100
Stage 2 (min)	240.60 ± 42.00	231.30 ± 62.90	202.90 ± 67.90	0.090
Stage 3 (min)	38.30 ± 17.20	32.70 ± 13.60	39.00 ± 19.60	0.440
Stage 4 (min)	88.50 ± 24.20	89.20 ± 28.20	103.10 ± 17.20	0.110
Delta (min)	126.80 ± 31.10	121.90 ± 37.90	142.10 ± 28.60	0.160
REM (min)	74.80 ± 23.00	76.40 ± 27.30	63.20 ± 25.20	0.210
Sleep efficiency (min)	91.50 ± 5.84	93.30 ± 5.69	92.80 ± 7.55	0.570
Number of REMPs	3.97 ± 1.05	3.85 ± 1.36	3.76 ± 1.20	0.840
REMP latency (min)	170.10 ± 60.30	160.80 ± 50.80	141.90 ± 60.00	0.270
REM efficiency (min)	83.60 ± 9.92	89.30 ± 6.40	78.80 ± 14.09	0.150
REM density (min)	3.97 ± 1.16	3.72 ± 0.96	3.75 ± 1.36	0.830

Note. MDD, major depressive disorder; REMP, rapid eye movement period.

TABLE 7.5. Sleep Function in Recovered Children

	MDD with separation anxiety ($n = 20$)	MDD without separation anxiety ($n = 8$)	T	p
Total sleep time (min)	500.20 ± 47.80	480.80 ± 35.80	1.04	NS
Sleep period time (min)	526.70 ± 48.00	503.20 ± 38.90	1.23	NS
Total rest period (min)	550.10 ± 44.30	527.10 ± 39.70	1.27	NS
Sleep latency (min)	23.40 ± 11.60	23.90 ± 19.70	0.09	NS
Number of first half awakenings	0.95 ± 1.05	0.00 ± 0.00	2.53	<.001
Number of second half awakenings	2.00 ± 1.21	1.62 ± 0.92	0.79	NS
Stage 1 (min)	35.20 ± 11.50	34.60 ± 14.60	0.12	NS
Stage 2 (min)	252.10 ± 34.80	229.70 ± 29.00	1.60	NS
Stage 3 (min)	41.70 ± 16.90	39.90 ± 11.70	0.27	NS
Stage 4 (min)	85.30 ± 17.60	92.70 ± 24.80	0.90	NS
Delta (min)	127.00 ± 29.30	132.60 ± 23.50	0.48	NS
REM (min)	86.00 ± 18.40	83.80 ± 18.50	0.28	NS
Sleep efficiency (min)	94.70 ± 2.30	95.70 ± 2.10	1.13	NS
Number of REMPs	4.90 ± 0.79	4.75 ± 0.71	0.47	NS
REMP latency (min)	116.50 ± 40.10	126.90 ± 32.80	0.65	NS
REM efficiency (min)	83.70 ± 6.15	84.30 ± 6.10	0.21	NS
REM density (min)	3.16 ± 1.37	3.16 ± 1.43	0.00	NS

Note. MDD, major depressive disorder; REMP, rapid eye movement period.

TABLE 7.6. Diagnosis of Major Depression and/or Separation Anxiety for Growth Hormone Variables

	MDD with separation anxiety	MDD without separation anxiety	Neurotics with separation anxiety	Statistics (KW)	p
Illness ITT AUC	203.8 ± 192.7	155.2 ± 155.2	306.7 ± 236.6	$\chi^2 = 4.75$	< .09
$n =$	16	14	12		
Illness sleep AUC	2146 ± 1212	2042 ± 1292	1528 ± 914	$\chi^2 = 2.19$	NS
$n =$	21	18	13		
Illness peak	15.4 ± 8.87	14.72 ± 7.59	11.67 ± 5.29	$\chi^2 = 1.31$	NS
$n =$	23	19	15		

Note. MDD, major depressive disorder; KW, Kruskal–Wallis; ITT, insulin tolerance test; AUC. area under the curve; NS, not significant.

antidepressant response to imipramine (Puig-Antich, Perel, *et al.,* in press). Out of 30 prepubertal children with major depressive disorder in a plasma level/clinical response study, 11 were found not separation anxious, of whom 8 (73%) responded to imipramine. The other 19 children were found to present associated separation anxiety, of whom 12 (63%) responded to imipramine. Similarly, separation anxiety did not predict placebo response at 5 weeks in 22 children with major depression who were randomly assigned to placebo. Of those without separation anxiety 75% (6 of 8) responded. Of those with associated separation anxiety 64% (9 of 14) responded.

DISCUSSION

The analyses presented in this chapter suggest that separation anxiety associated with prepubertal major depression has no detectable influence on the psychobiologic correlates of affective illness in children. This could easily lead to a premature conclusion that depression should be the primary diagnosis when these two syndromes are associated, but this conclusion would probably not be correct. First of all, there are as yet no established specific correlates of separation anxiety disorder in children. Therefore, the reverse test—to study separation anxious children with and without depression to see whether affective illness can influence the psychobiologic correlates of separation anxiety—cannot be performed. In the absence of this, issues of diagnostic primacy cannot be solved. In fact, diagnostic "primacy" is probably not a real issue. The key is to find the mechanisms underlying the associations reported. What can be said, though, is that so far there is no substantial evidence indicating that the nature of depressive illness in children is affected by the presence of associated separation anxiety.

Weissman *et al.* (1984) have reported that among the offspring of major depressive parents, children who develop separation anxiety (whether or not associated with major depression) come from parents who, besides major depression, also had a history of agoraphobia or panic attacks. Furthermore, these authors found that, similar to the adults (Leckman, Merikangas, Pauls, Prusoff, & Weissman, 1983; Leckman, Weissman, Merikangas, Pauls, & Prusoff, 1983) offspring of parents with major depression plus agoraphobia or plus panic attacks were also more likely to present the syndrome of major depression than children from depressive parents without anxiety diagnoses. These findings were independent of which disorder was chronologically primary or secondary in the offspring. The findings in children did not have any relationship to differential onset of these psychiatric diagnoses when they coexisted in the same parent whether they occurred simultaneously or independently.

The design of study, however, did not include a group of parents with anxiety diagnoses and without affective disorders. The possibility of a parallel "synergistic" effect of parental affective disorder in the transmission of anxiety disorders to children therefore could not be explored.

The preliminary evidence from the studies reviewed in this chapter suggest that anxiety and depressive symptomatology show a high degree of association in families and also in individuals. This association is at present better delineated in samples selected for affective disorder than in patients selected for anxiety disorders. To understand the mechanisms underlying this association, studies should be carried out both at the individual and family level, with both children and adults, in which pure forms of either disorder are separated out from those where both diagnostic classes overlap.

In our family history study we found that the age-corrected prevalence of depression but not alcoholism tended to be higher in families of children with nondepressed emotional disorders than in the sample of normal controls (Puig-Antich, Tabrizi, *et al.,* unpublished). If confirmed in our ongoing family study, using a larger sample size, this would suggest that one of the factors predisposing to separation anxiety disorder is a moderate increase in familial aggregation of affective illness. Nevertheless, this interpretation may be too circumscribed. The moderate increase found might reflect the families of those children who at present report separation anxiety disorder and who will develop dysthymia and/or major depression in the course of their lives. Thus, such moderate pedigree loading may only predispose to separation anxiety disorder in cases where the latter will ultimately be shown to have a forerunner of full-fledged affective illness. In order to answer this and other questions, it would be helpful to have follow-up data, using modern assessment methods, on nondepressed children who have emotional disorders, but such data are not available at present.

Overall, the exploratory analyses presented in this chapter and data from relevant studies suggest the following preliminary conclusions: (1) Among major depressive and/or dysthymic children, the overlap of depressive and anxiety symptoms is very high. Only a small minority show no anxiety symptoms, and about one third of prepubertal major depressive children have a coexisting diagnosis of an anxiety disorder, frequently separation anxiety. (2) We are still unable to explain the nature of the association between depressive and anxiety disorders, which is likely to be much more frequent than can be explained by chance alone. (3) Children with emotional disorders (depressed and nondepressed) come from families with high morbidity risks for anxiety disorders among their adult members. (4) Children with affective (depressed) emotional disorders come from families whose members are likely to suffer from, in addition to anxiety disorders, major depression and/or alcoholism. (5) Children with nondepressed emotional disorders also show a lesser, moderate increase of affective disorder, but not alcoholism among their relatives. (6) The presence or absence of separation anxiety does not have any detectable influence on the psychobiological correlates of prepubertal depressive illness we studied. (7) In our view a strategy combining family studies and follow-up of children and adolescents with "pure" major depressive disorders, "pure" anxiety disorders, and with both conditions holds the best promise to elucidate the mechanisms of the association. In fact a major problem in the analyses referred to here as well as those from Weissman *et al.* (1982), is that they were designed with other purposes in mind; namely, to study affective disorder not anxiety disorder. Studies focusing on anxiety disorders with and without depression and also depression with and without anxiety, and designed with this purpose, are likely to be more productive.

ACKNOWLEDGMENTS

The writing of this chapter was partially supported by National Institute of Mental Health Grant Nos. MH-30838 and MH-30839, and by Mental Health Clinical Research Center Grant No. MH-30906 to the New York State Psychiatric Institute. We thank Deborah Goetz, Raymond Goetz, and Mark Davies for technical and statistical assistance.

REFERENCES

Adams, P. L. *Obsessive children: A sociopsychiatric study.* New York: Brunner/Mazel, 1973.

Akiskal, H. S., Rosenthal, R. H., Rosenthal, T. L., Kashgarian, M., Khani, M. K., & Puzantian, V. R. Differentiation of primary affective illness from situational, symptomatic, and secondary depressions. *Archives of General Psychiatry,* 1979, *36,* 635–643.

American Psychiatric Association. *Diagnostic and statistical manual of mental disorders* (3rd ed.). Washington, D.C.: Author, 1980.

Andreasen, N. C., Endicott, J., Spitzer, R. L., & Winokur, G. Family history method using research diagnostic criteria. *Archives of General Psychiatry,* 1977, *34,* 1229–1223.

Carlson, G. A., & Cantwell, D. P. Unmasking masked depression in children and adults. *American Journal of Psychiatry,* 1980, *137,* 445–449.

Chambers, W. J., Puig-Antich, J., Hirsch, M., Paez, P., Ambrosini, P. J., Tabrizi, M. A., & Davies, M. The assessment of affective disorders in children and adolescents by semistructured interview: Test–retest reliability of the K-SADS-P. *Archives of General Psychiatry,* in press.

Cytryn, L., McKnew, D., & Bunney, W. Diagnosis of depression in children: Reassessment. *American Journal of Psychiatry,* 1980, *137,* 22–25.

Frantz, A. G., & Rabkin, M. T. Effects of estrogen and sex difference on secretion of human growth hormone. *Journal of Clinical Endocrinology and Metabolism,* 1965, *25,* 1470–1480.

Gittelman-Klein, R. Psychiatric characteristics of the relatives of school phobic children. In D. V. Sankar (Ed.), *Mental health in children.* Westbury, N.Y.: PJD Publisher, 1975, pp. 325–334.

Gittelman-Klein, R. Psychiatric characteristics of the relatives of school phobic children. In D. V. Sankar (Ed.), *Mental health in children.* Westbury, N.Y.: PJD Publisher, 1975.

Gregoire, F., Branman, G., DeBuck, R., & Corvillain, J. Hormone release in depressed patients before and after recovery. *Psychoneuroendocrinology,* 1977, *2,* 303–312.

Gruen, P. H., Sachar, E. J., Altman, N., & Sassin, J. Growth hormone responses to hypoglycemia in postmenopausal depressed women. *Archives of General Psychiatry,* 1975, *32,* 31–33.

Hershberg, S., Carlson, G. A., Cantwell, D., & Strober, M. Anxiety and depressive disorders in psychiatrically disturbed children. *Journal of Clinical Psychiatry,* 1982, *43,* 358–361.

Hersov, L. Depression and school refusal. In M. Rutter & L. Hersov (Eds.), *Child psychiatry: Modern approaches.* Oxford: Blackwell, 1977.

Keller, M. B., Shapiro, R. W., Lavori, P. W., & Wolfe, N. Recovery in major depressive disorder. *Archives of General Psychiatry,* 1982, *39,* 8, 905–910. (a)

Keller, M. B., Shapiro, R. W., Lavori, P. W., & Wolfe, N. Relapse in major depressive disorder. *Archives of General Psychiatry,* 1982, *39,* (8), 911–920. (b)

Kovacs, M., Feinberg, T. L., Crouse-Novak, M. A., Paulauskas, S., & Finkelstein, R. Depressive disorders in childhood. I. A longitudinal prospective study of characteristics and recovery. *Archives of General Psychiatry*, 1974, *41*, 229–237.

Kovacs, M., Feinberg, T. L., Crouse-Novak, M. A., Paulauskas, S., Pollock, M., & Finkelstein, R. Depressive disorders in childhood. II. A logitudinal study of the risk for a subsequent major depression. *Archives of General Psychiatry*, 1984, *41*, 643–649.

Leckman, J. F., Merikangas, K. R., Pauls, D. L., Prusoff, B. A., & Weissman, M. N. Anxiety disorders and depression: Contradictions between family study data and DSM-III conventions. *American Journal of Psychiatry*, 1983, *140*, 880–882.

Leckman, J. F., Weissman, M. M., Merikangas, K. R., Pauls, D. L., & Prusoff, B. A. Panic disorder and major depression: Increased risk of depression, alcoholism, panic, and phobic disorders in families of depressed probands with panic disorder. *Archives of General Psychiatry*, 1983, *40*, 1055–1060.

Merimee, T. J., & Feinberg, S. E. Studies of the sex based variation of human growth hormone secretion. *Journal of Clinical Endocrinology and Metablism*, 1971, *33*, 896–902.

Puig-Antich, J. Major depression and conduct disorder in prepuberty. *Journal of the American Academy of Child Psychiatry*, 1982, *21*, 118–128.

Puig-Antich, J., Blau, S., Marx, N., Greenhill, L., & Chambers, W. Prepubertal major depressive disorder: A pilot study. *Journal of the American Academy of Child Psychiatry*, 1978, *17*, 695–707.

Puig-Antich, J., Chambers, W., & Tabrizi, M. A. The clinical assessment of current depressive episodes in children and adolescents: Interviews with parents and children. In D. Cantwell & G. Carlson (Eds.), *Childhood Depression*. New York: Spectrum, 1983, pp. 157–179.

Puig-Antich, J., Davies, M., Novacenko, H., Tabrizi, M. A., Ambrosini, P., Goetz, R., Bianaca, J., Goetz, D., & Sachar, E. J. Growth hormone secretion in prepubertal children with a major depression. III. Response to insulin induced hypoglycemia after recovery from a depressive episode. *Archives of General Psychiatry*, 1984, *41*, 471–475.

Puig-Antich, J., & Gittelman-Klein, R. Depression in children and adolescents. In E. S. Paykel (Ed.), *Handbook of affective disorders*, New York, Churchill Livingstone, 1982.

Puig-Antich, J., Goetz, R., Davies, M., Novacenko, H., Chambers, W. J., Tabrizi, M. A., Krawiec, V., Ambrosini, P. J., & Sachar, E. J. Growth hormone secretion in prepubertal children with major depression. II. Sleep related plasma concentrations during a depressive episode. *Archives of General Psychiatry*, 1984, *41*, 463–466.

Puig-Antich, J., Goetz, R., Davies, M., Tabrizi, M. A., Novacenko, H., Hanlon, C., Sachar, E. J., & Weitzman, E. D. Growth hormone secretion in prepubertal children with major depression. IV. Sleep related plasma concentrations in a drug-free, fully recovered, clinical state. *Archives of General Psychiatry*, 1984, *41*, 479–483.

Puig-Antich, J., Goetz, R., Hanlon, C., Davies, M., Thompson, J., Chambers, W. J., Tabrizi, M. A., & Weitzman, E. D. Sleep architecture and REM sleep measures in prepubertal major depressives during an episode. *Archives of General Psychiatry*, 1982, *39*, 932–939.

Puig-Antich, J., Goetz, R., Hanlon, C., Tabrizi, M. A., Davies, M., & Weitzman, E. D. Sleep architecture and REM sleep measures in prepubertal major depressives: Studies during recovery from a major depressive episode in a drug free state. *Archives of General Psychiatry*, 1983, *40*, 187–192.

Puig-Antich, J., Novacenko, H., Davies, M., Chambers, W. J., Tabrizi, M. A., Krawiec, V., Ambrosini, P. J., & Sachar, E. J. Growth hormone secretion in prepubertal children with major depression I. Final report on response to insulin-induced hypoglycemia during a depressive episode. *Archives of General Psychiatry*, 1984, *41*, 455–460.

Puig-Antich, J., Perel, J., Lupatkin, W., Chambers, W. J., Tabrizi, M. A., Davies, M., King, J., Johnson, R., & Stiller, R. Imipramine in prepubertal major depression. *Archives of General Psychiatry*, in press.

Puig-Antich, J., Tabrizi, M. A., Davies, M., Goetz, R., Chambers, W., Halpern, F., & Sachar, E. J. Prepubertal endogenous major depressives hyposecrete growth hormone in response to insulin induced hypoglycemia. *Biological Psychiatry*, 1981, *16*, 801–818.

Rapoport, J., Elkins, R., Langer, D. H. Sceery, W., Bushsbaum, M. W., Gillin, J. C., Murphy, D. L., Zahn, T. P., Lake, R., Ludlow, C., & Mendelson, W. Childhood obsessive-compulsive disorder. *American Journal of Psychiatry*, 1981, *138*, 1545–1554.

Rutter, M. *Changing youth in a changing society*. London: Nuffield Provincial Hospitals Trust, 1979.

Weissman, M. M., Leckman, J. F., Merikangas, K. R., Gammon, G. D., & Prusoff, B. A. Depression and anxiety disorders in parents and children. *Archives of General Psychiatry*, 1984, *41*, 845–852.

Winokur, G. Depressive spectrum disease: Description and family study. *Comprehensive Psychiatry*, 1972, *13*, 3–8.

‡ 8 ‡

LEARNING THEORIES OF ANXIETY

DAVID SHAFFER

INTRODUCTION

There are two major psychological theories of anxiety. The psychoanalytic theories are described in Chapter 9 of this volume. The present chapter deals with the theories that have been derived from Pavlov's (1927) original conditioning model. Although the two theoretical systems have many differences, they also bear some striking similarities. Both assign primary importance to the role of early traumatic experience, both invoke a mechanism whereby one specific fear becomes the source of another (through displacement in the analytic and through stimulus generalization in learning theory), and although both models clearly recognize that there is "normal" and "abnormal" anxiety, neither can account for the difference in a way that is likely to satisfy a contemporary clinician. However, the contemporary clinician *will* probably choose between very different treatments, each of which have been developed from one of these theoretical models.

This chapter does not further contrast psychoanalytical and learning theories. It describes the experiments that led to the initial formulation of the learning theory of anxiety, how the theory was challenged, and the adaptations that it has undergone in response to these challenges, and discusses the value of the theories for the clinician.

David Shaffer. Division of Child Psychiatry, New York State Psychiatric Institute, and Departments of Clinical Psychiatry and Pediatrics, College of Physicians and Surgeons, Columbia University, New York, New York.

THE CLASSICAL CONDITIONING MODEL

In 1920 John B. Watson and Rosalie Rayner published an account in the *Journal of Experimental Psychology* of an experiment that they had conducted at the Johns Hopkins Hospital on a "healthy and unemotional" infant boy, Albert B. The article was entitled "Conditioned Emotional Reactions," and it forms the basis for the earliest explanation of anxiety based on learning theory.

At the age of 9 months, Albert was "pretested" to establish whether he showed anxiety when confronted with various stimuli including a live white rat and a rabbit and other furry and nonfurry inanimate objects. He did not. However, he was distressed by the noise of a hammer striking a piece of metal behind his back. Two months later, Albert, now aged 11 months, was again exposed to these stimuli, and on an unspecified number of times, exposure to the white rat was *coupled* with the loud noise behind his back. After several trials, Albert B. showed a distress response when faced with the white rat *without* the accompanying noise. This response persisted when he was tested several weeks later and was also evident when he was shown other furry objects and animals. At this point, Albert B.'s mother withdrew him from the hospital and the experiment came to an end, prematurely from the experimenters' point of view, because they were now unable to study the extinction characteristics of Albert's acquired fear(s) (Harris, 1979).

After this experiment, Watson and Rayner applied a Pavlovian paradigm to Albert's acquisition of anxiety. The loud noise was the unconditioned stimulus (UCS), which produced the unconditioned response (UCR), fear. The paired exposure of the white rat and the loud noise had given the rat the property of a conditioned stimulus (CS) and subsequent exposure to the CS alone elicited fear as a conditioned response (CR).

In later writings (see Cornwell & Hobbs, 1976; Harris, 1979; Prytula, Oster, & Davis, 1977, for more complete and critical accounts) Watson and Rayner (1920) proposed that neurotic anxiety arises from experiences in which a neutral stimulus has been paired, serendipitously, with an anxiety-provoking stimulus (UCS). Wolpe and Rachman (1960) applied this model to Freud's case of "Little Hans" (1909/1950). Wolpe recalls that Hans, "a nervous boy, never unmoved if someone wept in his presence, who had earlier been upset at seeing a horse in the merry-go-round being beaten," developed his fear of horses after experiencing distress when the horse drawing a bus that he was in fell down. Freud's explanation of Hans's symptom was that Hans had displaced his (oedipal) fear of his father onto the horse. Wolpe and Rachman explained Hans's fear as being due to the pairing of an anxiety-provoking experience with the sight of the falling horse. A psycho-biologist might have made more of Hans's predisposition to anxiety.

OBJECTIONS TO THE CLASSICAL CONDITIONING MODEL

There are a number of objections to the classical conditioning model (see Eysenck, 1980, for a review).

1. Watson and Rayner's experiment (1920) itself can be criticized (see Harris, 1979). It was carried out before modern techniques were available to measure the physiological concomitants of anxiety. Albert's infant distress may or may not have been the equivalent of anxiety. Only one of the objects to which Albert was successfully exposed was *not* a furry object; Watson's suggestion that Albert's fears had generalized only to furry objects, therefore, could not have been satisfactorily demonstrated, as Albert's fears may have generalized to all stimuli presented at the examination. Because the experiment ended prematurely, persistence of the fears was not demonstrated; and there is no evidence that Albert went on to develop a clinically recognizable anxiety disorder.

Attempts to replicate Watson's and Rayner's experiment (Bregman, 1934; English, 1929; Valentine, 1930) met with mixed success and have been criticized for both their methods and interpretation (Delprato, 1980).

2. Marks (1969) has commented on how most phobias arise from a relatively narrow range of stimuli, for example, snakes, spiders, heights, closed spaces, and so on. This is *not* what one would expect if abnormal fears arise from the serendipitous pairing of fear or anxious affect with other experiences. Similarly, there are many objects or situations that are clearly anxiety provoking but do not form the basis of commonly encountered clinical syndromes, for example, fear of automobiles or gas burners. Just as there appears to be some variation in individual susceptibility to fears, so it would seem that not all objects are equipotent in their fear-eliciting capabilities.

3. According to classical conditioning theory, an unreinforced conditioned response should extinguish rapidly if the conditioned

stimulus is not followed by the unconditioned stimulus. This should be the case with most fears in clinical patients, which are rarely, if ever, followed by the disastrous consequences that the patient fears. Yet, it is a common clinical experience that the fears of anxious patients, if anything, increase rather then decrease with time.

4. Classical conditioning theory posits that exposure to a single traumatic experience, that is, single-trial learning, is the most common source of most neurotic fears. However, clinical and laboratory experience indicates that single-trial learning of anxiety responses is uncommon except as a consequence of a potentially catastrophic event, for example, fear of flying after surviving an airplane accident.

5. In classical conditioning, the acquisition of a conditioned response requires that the CS and the UCS be paired within a very narrow space of time. In real life, this must be unusual.

These objections have led to various modifications of classical conditioning theory.

THE ADAPTIVE EVOLUTIONARY–PREPAREDNESS THEORY

An adaptive evolutionary theory was proposed by Garcia and Koelling (1966) and elaborated by Seligman (1970, 1971) to explain why relatively few stimuli give rise to phobic anxiety.

Garcia undertook experiments on taste aversion in animals. In the paradigmatic experiment, Garcia and Koelling (1966) taught rats to take flavored water from a laboratory apparatus. The availability of the flavored water was paired with a stimulus in the form of a click and flashing light. Once trained, the rats either (1) drank flavored water to which had been added a toxic dose of lithium carbonate, (2) were irradiated while drinking (these two conditions would be expected to lead to internal—interoceptive—malaise or nausea), or (3) received a foot shock (exteroceptive trauma). It was found that the rats who experienced the interoceptive consequences developed a conditioned aversive response to the flavored water but not to the audiovisual warning, whereas those who had been subject to the electric shock did the reverse. Garcia concluded that experiencing internal malaise had taught the rats to avoid the food even though the noxious effect (UCS) was widely separated in time (in conditioning terms) from drinking the flavored water (CS). He suggested that these different responses to unpleasant experiences were biologically determined and served the process of natural selection.

Seligman (1970, 1971) extended this idea, suggesting that fears were inherited much as any other instinctual behavior and that the objects of fear could be ranged on a continuum of "preparedness" that was related to their biological value for early man. Preparedness is defined operationally so that a more prepared fear is one that is acquired more rapidly, slower to extinguish, and more resistant to cognitive explanation (e.g., reassuring the subject in an experiment that the UCS will *not* follow the CS).

Experiments have been carried out to test the preparedness theory. If a small but aversive electric shock is linked to a picture of a spider or a snake (hypothesized as being highly prepared) or flowers or geometrical designs (hypothesized as unprepared), conditioned responses to the prepared stimuli occur despite rational explanation and reassurance and extinguish more slowly than responses to unprepared stimuli (Hugdahl, Fredrickson, & Ohman, 1977; McNally & Reiss, 1982; Ohman, Fredrickson, Hugdahl, & Rimmo, 1976). However, there is no consistent evidence that "prepared stimuli" are learned more rapidly. Furthermore, slowness to extinguish could be due to associative learning that had taken place outside of the experiment, that is, that a fear of spiders had been learned independently, before the experiment. In some cases there was evidence for this, with higher baseline readings for electrodermal activity when the subjects were exposed to the hypothetically "prepared" stimuli before the conditioning experiment.

Although all of the research has shown that "unprepared" stimuli extinguish more rapidly than prepared stimuli, it is precisely in the area of extinction that *clinical* observations are in conflict with the preparedness hypothesis. Thus, Rachman and Seligman (1976) reported on two patients with prototypically unprepared phobias— one with a fear of chocolate, the other with a fear of vegetable and plant leaves—both of which should have extinguished rapidly (as indicated by the time taken to respond to desensitization therapy). However, both were extremely *resistant* to desensitization treatment. Extending this finding, deSilva, Rachman, and Seligman (1977) reviewed phobic cases treated with behavior therapy at the Maudsley Hospital and found no relationship between their hypothetical evolutionary utility (their preparedness) and the rapidity with which they responded to treatment.

WHY DON'T "NEUROTIC" FEARS EXTINGUISH?

It is difficult to reconcile with learning theory the observation that the fears of neurotically anxious individuals often increase over time, because learning theory would predict that when pairing of the CS and US occur rarely, if at all, fears should diminish or extinguish.

Seligman (1971) has pointed out that this might take place in some instances because the individual is consistently "successful" in avoidance behavior. For example, if a child with school phobia remains *away* from school, the child will not be *able* to learn that his or her presence at school (CS) does not lead to the feared consequence, whether it be humiliation at school, harm befalling the parent while the child is away from home, or whatever other anxiety staying at home and not going to school may be imagined to prevent. If the individual never learns that being in school does not result in the feared consequence (UCS), extinction cannot be expected to follow. When this situation is elicited in the laboratory, a "response prevention" strategy coupled with the unlinking of the CS and UCS will usually lead to rapid extinction. An analogy in clinical practice could be the use of implosion or flooding therapy for phobic anxiety.

However, in clinical anxiety states and phobias, avoidance behavior is not invariably present, and even if it is, it is not usually complete. For example, a child with snake phobia, even if he or she manages to avoid zoos and terrain where snakes might be found, is still likely to be exposed to images of snakes or to snakes in imagination without experiencing any adverse consequences. Yet without treatment, fear of snakes will not diminish.

Eysenck (1976, 1980) has attempted to explain this phenomenon. He draws attention to two variations, A and B, of the Pavlovian Conditioning Model (Grant, 1964). In Pavlovian A conditioning, the subject displays motivated behavior as part of the conditioned response. For example, in the classical Pavlovian experiment (a dog is presented with food [UCS], preceded by the sound of a bell [CS] and then learns to salivate [CR] in response to the bell alone), the CR does not occur if the animal is satiated, and if it does occur the induced salivation will normally be followed by the dog going on to search for food and then to eat it.

In Pavlovian B conditioning, the appearance of the CR does not require motivation or any willful act by the animal. An example provided by Eysenck (1980) is the development of salivation, nausea, and vomiting as a UCR to the stimulus of an injection of morphine. The animal is powerless to prevent those effects. When conditioned, the animal will show these responses at the sight of the needle without any willful intervention of its own.

It is Eysenck's proposition that anxiety is the result of Pavlovian B conditioning. Not only is the UCS (the experience of anxiety) independent of the person's motivation (which is another feature of type B conditioning), but there is a good deal of overlap between the CR and the UCR. This, he suggests, is why it is possible for anxiety to increase even in the absence of a coupling of CS and UCS. Because the CR is the same as the UCR, it acts to reinforce the CS even in the absence of the UCS–UCR system. To give a concrete example, a child sees a dog (CS) that snarls or otherwise menaces him (UCS), this in turn produces fear (UCR). When the child next sees a dog (CS), a precisely *similar* feeling of anxiety (CR) is experienced. If the sight or thought of a dog produces fear that is similar to the UCR, then every exposure to a dog, whether in reality or in imagination, will serve to *reinforce* the response and fear should increase. Eysenck provides examples from the experimental literature to support the phenomenon along with evidence that this process is most likely to occur after single trial learning of *mild* intensity. This formulation conveniently addresses another objection to classical learning theories, that is, that relatively few phobias can be attributed to a single identifiable traumatic incident.

SUMMARY AND CONCLUSIONS

Several features strike the clinician reviewing the literature on the psychological theories of anxiety. First, there is a good deal of confusion about what type of disorder the theories are trying to explain. Most usually, there is a comment to the effect that fears and phobias and neurotic anxiety will be regarded as a single entity. This poses a real problem for the child psychiatrist because of the high proportion of normal children and adolescents who show a number of fears but who have little other evidence of maladjustment or psychiatric disturbance. For example, Lapouse and Monk (1959) found that 40% of 7- to 12-year-olds in a general community sample had more than seven fears. Rutter, Tizard, and Whitmore (1970) found that "fearfulness" was almost as common in psychiatrically disturbed boys aged 10–11 as in the general population (although the differences among girls were significant). Costello, Edelbrock, and Costello (1984) using the Diagnostic Interview Schedule for Children (DISC) found that phobic symptoms were actually more prevalent in a small nondisturbed pediatric population of 7- to 11-year-olds than in a group of age-matched psychiatric patients.

Avoidance behavior, perhaps as much as subjective distress, seems to determine whether or not a particular child will present as a patient, and there is no satisfactory explanation about what differentiates the child who does and does not show this behavior. Is avoidance behavior an epiphenomenon of a normal psychological event (anxiety)? Does it only occur when reinforced socially? Or is it a more fundamental index of severity, signifying perhaps that the anxious–avoidant individual has experienced a more severe or more unpleasant psychophysiological response that has led to the avoidance, whereas the anxious nonavoidant individual has had a less distressing experience? A satisfactory theory would address this question and might even predict the distinguishing features of "normal" and abnormal anxiety. However, the theories do not do this.

Second, for those interested in the origins of psychopathology, the psychological theories, whether psychoanalytic or learning, stretch credibility by attempting to explain relatively rare outcomes by the experience of everyday events. The oedipal "family romance" is held to be universal, and the serendipitous pairing of emotion and a given object or situation must be as well. Clearly, neither are enough to explain why only a few individuals will develop handicapping anxiety symptoms. Some other modifying factor, an "individual difference," must play a role.

The purely psychological theories offer little to explain these individual differences. Why is a fear accepted as unpleasant but tolerable by some children, whereas in others it will lead to a distortion of social behavior? The individual difference could lie in the child's experience, for example, the quality (secure or insecure) of an early attachment. Equally plausibly, it could lie in some constitutional difference such as having a low threshold for the psychophysiological expression of anxiety.

A biological modifier seems more plausible. Epidemiological studies suggest that children with anxiety states do not differ significantly in family background variables from nonanxious children (Rutter et al., 1970; Shaffer et al., 1985). Although anxious parents are more likely to have anxious children (Weissman, Leckman, Merk-kangas, Gammon, & Prusoff, 1984), we do not know what proportion of anxious children are accounted for by anxious families. Other evidence favoring biological mediation come from population genetic studies (Weissman *et al.*, 1984) and studies on twins (Slater & Shields, 1969), which suggest that anxiety is at least partly inherited. In a follow-up study, Shaffer *et al.* (1985) found that neurologic factors determine whether or not anxiety present at age 7 years will persist through childhood and on into adolescence. (These issues are discussed in Chapter 5 of this volume.)

These caveats having been stated, it must be said that learning theory has had heuristic value. It has led to experiment and to the development of effective treatments, based on either the reinforcement of approach behavior or the extinction of avoidance behavior. It is, however, by no means clear that the effective mechanisms of the treatments based on learning theory are those predicted by the learning theory. For example, treatment with reciprocal inhibition is postulated to work by coupling the feared stimulus with a pleasant and reinforcing affect. In their review Mavissakalian and Barlow (1981) suggest that effective behavioral treatment of anxiety requires actual experience with the feared object that may serve purely cognitive ends, that is, increasing a sense of personal efficacy and providing opportunities for reality testing, and that the pairing of exposure to the feared object and relaxation is not necessary.

If the psychological theories seem inadequate to explain pathological states do they suffice to explain normal anxiety? It is not certain that they do. Both psychoanalytic and learning theories posit that it is anxiety that initially triggers the psychological mechanism that leads to the persistent fear. In psychoanalytic theory the mechanism is displacement and repression, and in learning theory it is stimulus generalization and persistent reinforcement. In both, the original affect is accepted as instinctual and beyond theoretical explanation.

In summary, learning theory does not clearly explain the difference between normal and pathological anxiety and it is indeed unclear about which kind of fear it *does* address. Support for learning theory has come mainly from laboratory experiment and from the good results of theoretically based treatment. There has been little support from patient anamnesis or clinical observation. However, given the power of human cognition to modify affect and behavior, laboratory experiments with animals have dubious application in this area, and a condition may respond to treatment through quite different mechanisms than those that led to its original development. For all these caveats, learning theory is undoubtedly interesting. It has had considerable value in generating ideas, observations, experiments, and ultimately, effective treatment.

ACKNOWLEDGMENTS

Preparation of this chapter was supported in part by Grant No. TO1 MH17463-01 and Research Training Grant No. 5 T32 MH16434 from the National Institute of Mental Health.

REFERENCES

Bregman, E. O. An attempt to modify the emotional attitudes of infants by the conditioned response technique. *Journal of Genetic Psychology,* 1934, *45,* 169–198.

Cornwell, D., & Hobbs, S. The strange saga of little Albert. *New Society,* March 18, 1976, pp. 602–604.

Costello, E. J., Edelbrock, C. S., & Costello, A. J. *Validity of the NIMY Diagnostic Interview Schedule for Children: A comparison between psychiatric and pediatric referrals.* Paper presented at the annual meeting of the American Academy of Child Psychiatry, October 1984.

Delprato, D. J. Hereditary determinants of fears and phobias: A critical review. *Behavior Therapy,* 1980, *11,* 79–103.

deSilva, R., Rachman, S., & Seligman, M. E. P. Prepared phobias and obsessions: Therapeutic outcome. *Behaviour Research and Therapy,* 1977, *15,* 65–77.

English, H. B. Three cases of the conditioned fear response. *Journal of Abnormal and Social Psychology,* 1929, *34,* 221–225.

Eysenck, H. J. The learning theory model of enuresis—A new approach. *Behaviour Research and Therapy,* 1976, *14,* 251–267.

Eysenck, H. J. Psychological theories of anxiety. In G. D. Burrows & B. Davies (Eds.), *Handbook of studies on anxiety.* New York: Elsevier/North-Holland Biomedical Press, 1980.

Freud, S. The analysis of a phobia in a five-year-old boy. In J. Strachey (Ed. and Trans.), *Standard edition* (Vol. 3). London: Hogarth Press, 1950. (Originally published 1909)

Garcia, J., & Koelling, R. A. Relation of cue to consequence in avoidance learning. *Psychonomic Science,* 1966, *4,* 123–124.

Grant, D. A. Classical and operant conditioning. In A. W. Melton (Ed.), *Categories of human learning.* New York: Academic Press, 1964.

Harris, B. Whatever happened to little Albert. *American Psychologist*, 1979, *34*(2), 151–160.

Hugdahl, K., Fredrickson, M., & Ohman, A. "Preparedness" and "arousability" as determinants of electrodermal conditioning. *Behaviour Research and Therapy*, 1977, *15*, 345–353.

Lapouse, R., & Monk, M. A. Fears and worries in a representation sample of children. *American Journal of Orthopsychiatry*, 1959, *29*, 803–818.

Marks, I. M. *Fears and phobias*. London: Heinemann, 1969.

McNally, R. J., & Reiss, S. The preparedness theory of phobias and human safety-signal conditioning. *Behaviour Research and Therapy*, 1982, *20*, 153–159.

Mavissakalian, M., & Barlow, N. D. Phobia: An overview. In M. Mavissakalian & D. H. Barlow (Eds.), *Phobia: Psychological and pharmacological treatment*. New York: Guilford, 1981.

Ohman, A., Fredrickson, M., Hugdahl, K., & Rimmo, P. The premise of quipotentiality in human classical conditioning: Conditioned electrodermal responses to potentially phobic stimuli. *Journal of Experimental Psychology*, 1976, *105*, 313–337.

Pavlov, I. *Conditioned reflexes*. New York: Dover, 1927.

Prytula, R. E., Oster, G. D., & Davis, S. F. The "rat rabbit" problem: What did John Wabar really do? *Teaching of Psychology*, 1977, *4*, 44–46.

Rachman, S., & Seligman, M. E. P. Unprepared phobias: "Be prepared." *Behaviour Research Therapy*, 1976, *14*, 333–338.

Rutter, M., Tizard, J., & Whitmore, K. (Eds.). *Education, health, and behavior*. New York: Wiley, 1970.

Seligman, M. E. P. On the generality of the laws of learning. *Psychological Review*, 1970, *77*, 406–418.

Seligman, M. E. P. Phobias and preparedness. *Behavior Therapy*, 1971, *2*, 307–320.

Shaffer, D., Schonfeld, I., O'Connor, P. A., Stokman, C., Trautman, P., Shafer, S., & Ng, S. Neurological soft signs: Their relationship to psychiatric disorder and intelligence in childhood and adolescence. *Archives of General Psychiatry*, 1985, *44*, 342–351.

Slater, E., & Shields, J. Genetical aspects of anxiety. In M. H. Lader (Ed.), Studies of anxiety. *British Journal of Psychiatry*, 1969, Special Edition Number 3.

Valentine, C. W. The innate bases of fear. *Journal of Genetic Psychology*, 1930, *37*, 394–420.

Watson, J. B., & Rayner, R. Conditioned emotional reactions. *Journal of Experimental Psychology*, 1920, *3*, 1–14.

Weissman, M. M., Leckman, J. F., Merikangas, K. R., Gammon, G. D., & Prusoff, B. A. Depression and anxiety disorders in parents and children. *Archives of General Psychiatry*, 1984, *41*, 845–852.

Wolpe, J., & Rachman, S. Psychoanalytic evidence: A critique of Freud's case of Little Hans. *Journal of Nervous and Mental Diseases*, 1960, *130*, 198–230.

‡ 9 ‡

PSYCHODYNAMIC THEORIES OF ANXIETY AND THEIR APPLICATION TO CHILDREN

PAUL D. TRAUTMAN

INTRODUCTION

This chapter reviews several psychoanalytic theories of anxiety, tracing them from their origins in Freud's earliest writings to the present day, and points out some of the gaps in present-day theory. Case examples illustrate current understanding and treatment of phobic anxiety in children. Over a period of more than 30 years, Freud advanced three theories: anxiety as a form of energic discharge, anxiety as a response to danger, and anxiety as a reaction to separation from mother. Although post-Freudian theorists have largely abandoned Freud's energic discharge theory (Compton, 1972b), they continue to use the language of that theory; they have greatly expanded his ideas about separation anxiety and have developed new ideas about the communicative role of anxiety (and other affects) in the interpersonal situation.

Because the roots of Freud's theories are present in his earliest writings and because he rarely abandoned any idea but rather adapted each to later metapsychological formulations, we have chosen to treat each theory separately and to trace its development from its origin to the present day. It should be remembered, however, that Freud's three theories were not serially but simultaneously developed. The chief sources of Freud's ideas about anxiety are "The Neuro-psychoses of Defence" (1894/1962a); "On the Grounds for Detaching a Particular

Paul D. Trautman. New York State Psychiatric Institute, and College of Physicians and Surgeons, Columbia University, New York, New York.

Syndrome from Neurasthenia under the Description 'Anxiety Neurosis'" (1895/1962b); "Analysis of a Phobia in a Five-Year-Old Boy" (1909/1955a); "Anxiety" *(Introductory Lectures on Psychoanalysis)* (1917/1963); and *Inhibitions, Symptoms and Anxiety* (1926/1959).

A word about terms: The language of psychoanalysis is for many of us the first stumbling block to understanding its theory; some definitions will ease the reader's way in this section. Freud distinguished *aktual neurosis* and *psychoneurosis.* The former is a disorder with an organic cause, the latter is caused by unacceptable ideas, wishes, or experiences. Freud identified two *aktual* neuroses: *neurasthenia,* a vaguely defined condition characterized by fatigue and dyspepsia, which he held to be caused by excessive masturbation or spontaneous emissions (Freud, 1896/1962d, p. 108), and *anxiety neurosis,* resulting from the failure of sexual excitation (which he believed was somatically and continuously generated), to be discharged by a "specific or adequate action," that is, copulation with ejaculation (the "spinal reflex") and "all the psychical preparations which have to be made to set off that reflex" (Freud, 1895/1962b, p.108). The *psychoneuroses* include hysteria, conversion, some phobias, obsessive–compulsive reactions, and some anxiety reactions. In psychoneurosis, affect, particularly anxiety, is attached to a "traumatic" memory or unacceptable idea that is kept out of awareness by the process of repression and other mechanisms of defense.

ANXIETY AS ENERGIC DISCHARGE

Freud's earliest theory (1894/1962a, 1895/1962b) defined anxiety as the discharge of a "quota of affect" (or "sum of excitation"). The psyche, he believed, was a kind of electrical system. When it receives a stimulus or input (say, an insulting remark), it becomes charged with affect (anger, for example) and the need arises to discharge that excitation (by punching the fellow in the nose) so as to return to equilibrium. Normally, discharge occurs through motor activity (e.g., the act of punching) and secretory processes (e.g., sweating). When an affect cannot be adequately discharged, it becomes "damned-up" or "strangulated."

Affects, particularly anxiety, which Freud came to consider the central affect, may be generated two different ways: psychically or somatically. In *aktual* neurosis, anxiety is not attached to a repressed idea but is generated by the transformation of unemployable "libidinal tension" ("psychical desire"). Libido is the psychical energy with which sexual ideas are supplied. In normal sexual function somatic sexual excitation is continuously generated and periodically reaches the psyche where libidinal tension is produced. This tension is adequately discharged, in men, by copulation with ejaculation. Freud stated that he was unsure about the analogous process in women. Inadequate discharge, for example, coitus interruptus or abstinence, results in anxiety neurosis.

The mechanism of anxiety neurosis is then stated in mechanical terms. When somatic sexual excitation is not adequately discharged, it is deflected from the psyche and expressed through the physical symptoms of anxiety: tension, tachycardia, dyspnea, vertigo, diarrhea, and so on. "The symptoms of anxiety neurosis are the surrogates of omitted specific action following on sexual excitation. In normal copulation, excitation is expended in increased heart rate, tachypnea, sweating, congestion, etc. In anxiety attacks we see the symptoms of copulation in an isolated and exaggerated form" (Freud, 1895/1962b). Freud added that this deflection of excitation from the psyche may produce symptoms that are more "psychological" in nature, for example, irritability, anxious expectation, hypochondria, "moral anxiety," pavor nocturnus, object phobias, and agoraphobia.

Because anxiety neurosis is internally generated and not linked to a repressed idea, Freud believed it was not amenable to psychotherapy. He made direct suggestions to his patients about intercourse and reported that they improved (Freud, 1895/1962b, p. 104).

In psychoneurosis, a "weak" idea is substituted for a powerful, unacceptable (usually sexual) idea, but the damned-up affect associated with that idea "must be put to another use," either converted into "something somatic," for example, a paralysis, or attached to other ideas, as in obsessional thinking (Freud, 1895/1962b). One can readily see that this explanation is as mechanical as that proposed for anxiety neurosis. The psychoneuroses were considered treatable because of their link to repressed ideas. Initially, Freud advocated abreaction (the discharge of excitation); later, he developed the technique of analysis of free associations to uncover repressed ideas.

Freud's early views on phobias were uncertain (Strachey, 1962). In essence he included hysterical phobias, linked to repressed ideas, among the psychoneuroses, and distinguished these from "typical" phobias, such as object phobias and agoraphobia, which he believed had no psychical basis, and therefore classified with the *aktual* neuroses. He admitted that he was unsure how the anxiety that is linked to the phobic idea is generated (Freud, 1895/1962c). Clearer explication of phobias came with the "Little Hans" case (Freud, 1909/1955a) and with *Inhibitions, Symptoms and Anxiety* (1926/ 1959) (see following discussion).

Freud began by trying to state the data of psychology in neurophysiological terms. In fact, this early theory is not psychological but physiological—excitation and anxiety are equated. An examination of the evolution of the energetic theory of anxiety illustrates how closely Freud adhered to his earliest theoretical formulations. By 1917/1963 *(Introductory Lectures on Psychoanalysis)*, Freud was discussing normal as well as pathological anxiety, but still explaining it in terms of unemployable libidinal energy. As he so cogently put it, with reference to a child's fear of the dark, "a longing [for mother] felt in the dark is transformed into a fear of the dark" (1917/1963, p. 407). Adult neurotic anxiety is explained by the same transformation, via "a regression to the infantile state" (1917/1963, p. 407).

In 1926/1959 Freud significantly revised his theory of anxiety in light of his structural theory (Freud, 1923/1961) and dropped the concept of anxiety as transformed libido. Instead, he argued that anxiety is the response of the ego to the threat of helplessness (the essence of danger). Anxiety mobilizes the ego to react, and this reaction takes the form of repression and the other ego mechanisms of defense (A. Freud, 1936/1966). But where does the ego get its energy? Whereas Freud formerly held that libidinal energy is transformed into anxiety, he now argued that "neutralized" libidinal energy (Freud, 1923/1961) from the id supplies the ego so that it may generate anxiety in situations of helplessness. The new theory, at least in energic terms, seems hardly different from the old.

Many post-Freudian theorists have continued to separate anxiety (and other affects) from ideas as Freud did in the topographic and structural theories and to describe the phenomenology of anxiety in terms of discharge. Arlow (1977) and others have criticized contributions that "tend to define the nature and the quality of affective experience in terms of the rate, rhythm, patterns or quantity of energic discharge" because "they are based on formulations that go beyond what can be derived from observations within the psycho-analytic situation ... [and therefore] cannot be substantiated by reference to clinical experience" (p. 158).

In summary, the energic discharge theory is derived from Freud's earliest efforts to explain psychological phenomena in physiologic terms. Today, these ideas would not be considered truly psychoanalytic, but would be attributed to physiological theories of affect or behavior. While Freud later advanced a more purely "psychological" theory, he never completely abandoned the belief that a physiological basis of mental functioning would be found (Hartmann, Kris, & Loewenstein, 1946). Freud's (1895/1962b) clinical description of anxiety neurosis is not a very satisfactory one, containing as it does a diverse collection of symptoms. Little attention has been paid to *aktual* neurosis since Freud's time. However, Waelder (1976) noted that a close relationship exists between anxiety and sexuality. Even though anxiety may be better understood as a reaction to danger, anxiety/fear may become sexualized and made a source of pleasure, as in "flirting with danger." For a fuller description of the energic theory, see Compton (1972a).

ANXIETY AS A RESPONSE TO DANGER

In his earlier formulations, Freud (1895/1962b, 1917/1963) dis-tinguished two forms of anxiety and linked these to his theory of instinctual drives. He believed that realistic anxiety arises when external, "real" danger (e.g., a mugger with a gun) threatens the self-preservation instinct. Neurotic anxiety arises when internal danger (e.g., unrequited love) gives rise to unpleasure, thereby threatening the second major instinct, the pleasure principle. Initially, Freud (1894/1962a, 1900/1953) equated anxiety and unpleasure. Later (1920/1955b) he acknowledged that there are states of tension that may be experienced as pleasurable or unpleasurable (e.g., sexual tension; see Jacobson, 1953) and that not every unpleasure may be called anxiety (Freud, 1926/1959). In his reformulation (1926/1959) of the theory of anxiety, Freud dropped the distinction between realistic and neurotic anxiety. He stated that the experience of helplessness is the essence of danger and that anxiety is the response of the ego (or serves as a signal to the ego) to the threat of helplessness. He cited five dangers that are liable to precipitate an experience of helplessness: birth, loss of the object (i.e., mother, a significant other who is cathected with libidinal energy), loss of the object's love, loss of penis (castration), and loss of the superego's love. Following is an elaboration of these concepts.

For many years Freud (1895/1962b, 1917/1963) argued that anxiety was a response to danger from outside or from within the organism. Anxiety with external cause was linked to the fight–flight reflex, the instinct of self-preservation, and the reality principle (awareness of and adaptation to environmental demands) (Freud, 1900/1953). These factors were subsumed under the term "ego drive" and were considered to be wholly conscious. In contrast internal or neurotic anxiety was linked to the pleasure principle and "libidinal drive," which he believed was wholly unconscious and concerned with the preservation of the species. Thwarting of instinctual drive was said to lead to tension and unpleasure, and discharge of tension, to pleasure.[1]

Freud (1917/1963) went on to argue that in neurotic anxiety, an internal danger is reacted to as if it were external; that is, the ego makes an attempt at flight from libidinal demands that are experienced as dangerous. Repression (and other mechanisms of defense) were said to represent the flight of ego from libido. The affect that was attached to the libidinal idea is transformed, as a *consequence* of repression, into anxiety. Thus, Freud at first believed that repression causes anxiety (1917/1963). However, he conceded that the analogy to external danger is not an entirely satisfactory one, since it is difficult to explain "how the anxiety which results from the flight of the ego from libido can be derived from that libido" (1917/1963).

As previously noted, Freud's (1926/1959) reformulation of the theory of anxiety dropped the distinction between realistic and neurotic anxiety. Instead, he made the experience or threat of helplessness the critical issue. He argued that helplessness may result from physical or psychic danger. The psychic (internal) danger is that libidinal and aggressive instinctual drives (Freud, 1920/1955b) arising in the id will overwhelm the ego and put the ego in a position of physical (external) danger. For example, "Little Hans" (Freud, 1909/1955a, 1926/1959), the 5-year-old with a fear of horses, de-

1. Note the energic terminology. In fact, a drive is an energic concept; it is defined as a mental representation of an instinct that has a charge of psychic energy (Freud, 1915/1957).

sired his mother and wanted to do away with his father-competitor. But to act on such instinctual wishes would be to put himself in direct conflict with his father in the real world. His father would naturally retaliate, and "Little Hans" would be put in a position of helplessness, unable to defend himself against overwhelming forces.

An experience or threat of helplessness causes anxiety, and anxiety evokes the ego response—flight. When faced with external danger, flight is accomplished through motility (an "ego function"). Flight from internal (instinctual) danger is accomplished through repression. Therefore, *anxiety causes repression,* not vice versa as was previously held (Freud, 1926/1959). It is out of the failure of repression to be completely successful that symptoms arise. A symptom is a condensed, displaced, and symbolic substitute for the instinctual impulse. "Little Hans's" fear of horses is such a substitute. His ambivalence of hostility and passive longing toward his father and consequent fear of castration by father, are condensed and displaced onto the fear that horses might bite him; he is inhibited from going out into the street. An external danger (fear of horses) is substituted for another external danger (castration). The anxiety he experiences in the street is an untransformed fear of castration (Freud, 1926/1959, p. 108).

Melanie Klein (1932) extended Freud's ideas about instinctual dangers by arguing that aggressive (rather than libidinal) wishes are central to anxiety. She believed that a theory of anxiety arising from unacceptable libidinal wishes was insufficient (simply put, why should pleasure give rise to unpleasure?) and that aggressive and sadistic fantasies pose the real danger to the ego. In her view "Little Hans" was afraid not of his sexual attraction to his mother but of his sadistic fantasies about the heterosexual situation and the resultant fear of castration by mother *and* father. Her observations of the fantasies of preschool children (she analyzed children as young as 2¾ years of age) led her to believe that the child populates his or her mental life with representations of libidinal and aggressive wishes toward significant others in the real world. She called these representations "good" and "bad" objects. She believed that aggression originates in the frustration of oral (libidinal) needs and that object relations develop under the dominance of aggression and "frustration–rage." Anxiety and guilt arise out of fear that the aggressive fantasies will destroy the object (e.g., mother) and the self (through the mechanism of projection of aggression onto the object).

Benjamin (1961) took a view similar to Klein's in drawing attention to the aggressive quality of the separation anxiety response, "A necessary condition for anxiety is the organization of aggression into object-directed hostility and anger with resultant marked increase in fear of object loss" (p. 662).

Freud believed birth to be the first experience of helplessness, and he modeled anxiety upon the process of birth: "Birth [is] a prototypic experience of a state of unpleasure" (Freud, 1926/1959, p. 133). A more complete discussion of psychoanalytic ideas about birth will be found in the section entitled "Anxiety and Separation," following.

The second danger situation is loss of the object, that is, the loss of one who satisfies all the infant's needs without delay. Unsatisfied needs lead to an accumulation of tension (again, note the old energic concept), which cannot be disposed or nor mastered psychically; for example, the infant can neither feed himself nor say, "I'm hungry but I'll wait and eat in half an hour." What the child carries with it from birth is a way of indicating the presence of danger (e.g., crying). "When the infant has found out by experience that an external, perceptible object can put an end to the dangerous situation . . . the content of the danger it fears is displaced from the economic situation [e.g., hunger, a need to eat] on to the condition which determines that situation, viz. the loss of object" (Freud, 1926/1959, pp. 137–138). (Here, Freud sounds like a learning theorist. See discussion of ethological theory, following.) The absence of mother becomes the danger. This represents a "great step forward in the provision made by the infant for its self-preservation" (1926/1959, p. 138).

Similarly, castration anxiety represents the fear of being separated from one's genitals. This is connected to the earlier fear (loss of the object) because the "organ is a guarantee that [the child] can be once more united to his mother—i.e., to a substitute for her—in the act of copulation" (Freud, 1926/1959, p. 139). Loss of the object's love was described as a special danger situation for girls in relationship to Father. Freud stated that a girl compensates for her "castration complex" by making a "tender object cathexis" to Father who, in fantasy, could give her a child—a penis-substitute (Freud, 1925/ 1961b). To lose father's love is to endanger this fantasy. Finally, the danger to the ego posed by the superego is that the superego (the internalized parental standards, and more generally, societal standards) should punish it (a further extension of castration anxiety) or cease to love it.

The concept of "signal anxiety" has had great influence on psychoanalytic and nonanalytic writers alike. Freud (1926/1959) said that under most circumstances of danger arising from instinctual impulses, anxiety is not experienced because the ego makes use of the "signal of anxiety" (or of "unpleasure") to accomplish the goal of suppressing (repressing) instinctual wishes, thereby avoiding danger. For example, with reference to the hungry infant and his mother, described above, Freud stated that the ego gives the signal of danger before real danger—nonsatisfaction of needs—arises. That is, anxiety is intentionally reproduced by the ego (via the memory of anxiety associated with previous experience of danger) as a signal of potential danger. Freud called this "non-energic" anxiety because it is produced by the ego and "inhibits . . . the impending cathectic process in the id" (1926/1959, p. 125). (Contemporary theorists prefer to say that the excitatory id process occurs but is prevented from entering the ego organization; Compton, 1972b.)

There are three major objections to Freud's concept of signal anxiety. First, Freud makes signal anxiety an "ego function" (like motor activity or repression); no other affect is given that status. Second, the statement that the ego produces (signal) anxiety is anthropomorphic; man is not the only animal capable of responding in anticipation of danger (Compton, 1972a). Third, a response to danger may occur without conscious awareness of anxiety and the experience of anxiety is not necessarily part of the response to danger (Fisher, 1956, cited in Compton, 1972b; Waelder, 1976). In terms of the structural theory, it is better to say that the ego functions to *recognize* danger (e.g., memory, sensory perceptions) and to *react* to danger (Brenner, 1955), but not to produce anxiety (anxiety is *experienced* by the ego but is *derived* from danger situations). Schur (1953, 1958) held that the ego regulates (tames, neutralizes) anxiety emanating from the id and regulates the anxiety response through delay, inhibition, and anticipation. With maturation the individual is able to respond to danger without conscious awareness of anxiety; this Rado (1956) called "non-reporting fear" and Schur (1953) "thought-like awareness of danger."

In summary, anxiety as a response to present or expected danger, whether of external or internal origin, has proved to be a most useful concept. Anxiety sets in motion the processes of physical and psychological defense, although as noted above, anxiety is not essential to the danger response. Most analysts would no longer accept the idea that the ego produces anxiety as a signal of impending danger. Rather, the ego recognizes and responds to danger and regulates the affect of anxiety.

ANXIETY AND SEPARATION

In his Introductory Lecture of 1917, Freud made his first reference to the primary importance of separation from mother as the origin of anxiety, "A child is first afraid of strange people ... because the stranger's face is not mother's familiar, beloved face" (1917/1963, p. 407). The emergence of anxiety in infancy has been described by Spitz (1950, 1965), Benjamin (1961, 1963), Emde, Gaensbauer, and Harmon (1976), and others. Bowlby's (1969, 1973) ethological theory has emerged as a particularly fruitful one for understanding anxiety in the context mother–infant attachment.

Freud believed that the prototypical separation from mother is birth and that "the affect of anxiety repeats the early impression of the act of birth." This idea is probably borrowed from Darwin (1872/1955) who wrote, "Affects are relics of actions which originally had a meaning" (see editor's discussion in Freud, 1917/1963). Thus, Freud did not mean that the infant is made anxious by birth or experiences anxiety at birth, but that the experience of "restriction in breathing" (from the Greek, *anchien,* to strangle) at birth is later reinstated in the affect of anxiety when the child acquires the cognitive capacity to differentiate mother from strangers.

Rank (1924/1952) carried Freud's idea to an extreme, arguing that birth (the traumatic separation from the intrauterine environment) is the first anxiety experience and that the strength of the anxiety reaction to birth determines later neurosis. All treatment, he argued, involves "abreacting the trauma of birth." Greenacre (1941/1952a, 1945/1952b) revived Rank's theory by proposing that painful stimuli *in utero*, during birth, and in the first weeks of life elicit reflex responses that may be regarded as "pre-anxiety" responses. Greenacre "... further proposed that in certain adults an unusual readiness to develop anxiety which is not analysable may be connected with the experiences of birth and neonatal life" (Compton, 1972b, p. 381). Benjamin (1961), Compton (1972b), and others have objected to this line of thinking, as it tends to attribute the experiences of the older child and adult to the undeveloped infant. While the infant reacts to painful stimuli, both external and internal, there is little evidence that the infant can experience anxiety or any other emotion before the 3rd month of life. Also, too many experiences intervene between birth and adulthood to ever allow proof of a correlation between birth and adult neurosis; "unanalyzable" need not mean "early."

Spitz (1950, 1965), Benjamin (1961), Emde et al. (1976), and others have made careful observations of infants in the first year of life, and have described a gradual transition from neurophysiologic states of "unpleasure" to subjectively experienced psychic states, including anxiety.

Spitz (1950) described the first 2 months of life as limited to states of unpleasure and quiescence only. In the 2nd and 3rd months, the first pleasure responses appear, particularly the social smile in response to the face of any adult seen straight on (Spitz, 1950). The "smiling response," initially elicited by a variety of visual, tactile, auditory, and kinesthetic stimuli, gradually becomes limited to visual stimuli, particularly mother's face (in blind infants, the response is shaped by tactile and auditory stimuli, rather than visual stimuli) (Emde et al., 1976). Benjamin (1961) noted that the smiling response ("a delayed, maturationally-determined innate release mechanism in ethological terms") depends on the infant's prior experience with a mother who has acted as a source of tension reduction (in other words, as a source of undifferentiated positive affect).

From the 4th to 8th months, fearfulness evolves. Initially (4–6 months), the infant shows intense interest in a stranger's face (a "moderately discrepant stimulus," Kagan, 1971), comparing it with mother's face. Later (5–7 months) the infant's facial expression sobers when confronted with a strange face. Finally, at about 8 months (Spitz, 1950) the infant reacts with distress and a facial expression that mothers and other observers recognize as "fearful." At about the same time fearfulness to other stimuli develops, as does distress and inhibition of play when mother leaves the child alone. The strength of the "separation anxiety" response follows an inverted U-shaped course over the period 7–36 months of age (Kagan, 1978).

Separation and stranger anxiety are distinct and independently occurring reactions (Bowlby, 1969). Both depend on the cognitive ability to recognize differences, attachment to a caretaker, and normal maturation. There is little evidence that stranger distress is affected by learning (Emde et al., 1976).

The relationship between separation anxiety in infancy and later psychological adjustment has been examined using the "strange situation" paradigm (Ainsworth, Blehar, Waters, & Wall, 1978). This paradigm is useful for direct observations about separation and stranger anxiety and can reliably indentify "securely attached" and "anxiously attached" 1-year-olds. Sroufe (1983) and Sroufe, Fox, and Pancake (1983) have shown that preschoolers who were "anxiously attached" at 12 months of age are more dependent, less empathic, less socially competent, less flexible in managing impulses and feelings, and have lower self-esteem and seek more (negative) attention than preschoolers who were "securely attached" infants. Similarly, "anxiously attached" 12-month-old boys are more likely to have high behavior problem scores (particularly "internalizing" scores) at age 6 than boys who had been "securely attached" (Lewis, Feiring, McGuffog, & Jaskir, 1983).

Many contemporary writers have noted that the study of the development of anxiety (and affects in general) cannot be separated from the study of the mother–infant pair (e.g., Kestenbaum, 1980). The newborn infant is no longer viewed as passive and helpless, but as dynamically interacting with the care giver. Bowlby (1969, 1973) has argued that the infant comes into the world with a repertoire of behavior patterns that serve as an attachment system and upon which subsequent behavior and affects are organized. Among these behavior patterns are gaze (Stern, 1974), smiling (Spitz, 1965), reciprocal play (Schecter, 1972), and response to mother's high-pitched vocalizations (Lang, 1972) (all cited in Kestenbaum, 1980).

In suggesting that the ego comes to "tame" affect and to produce affect as a signal, Freud implied that affects—of which anxiety is just one—may serve as interpersonal as well as intrapsychic communications (Drellich, 1983). Affects may serve as signals to the individual about himself (Jacobson, 1953, 1954, 1957), as signals to the individual about the outside world (Brierly, 1937, cited in Drellich, 1983), and as signals *to* the outside world (Kestenbaum, 1980). For example, when the 8-month-old cries on the approach of a stranger, his or her anxiety not only serves as an expression of the threat of helplessness, but also signals the infant's preference for mother (Emde *et al.,* 1976). At a later phase when children frequently suffer from nightmares (ages 4–8), the child's anxiety both reflects internal conflict between impulses and new social standards and elicits tender reassurance from parents who are making increasing demands for "prosocial" behavior (Kagan, 1978). Affects (both positive and negative) label or define the quality of relationship between the ego and the object (Szasz, 1957). Affects also motivate or inhibit behavior in the individual and elicit or inhibit behavioral responses in others (Novey, 1959, 1961, 1962). "Affects are not passive discharge channels for drives but dynamic forces with direction which impel toward action" (Novey, quoted in Drellich, 1983, pp. 16–17).

In Sullivan's interpersonal theory (1955a), anxiety is a central response in interpersonal relations that shapes behavior, disciplines attention, and restricts personal awareness. This theory holds that the social pressures of society (the "culture-pattern"), mediated by parents and teachers, mould the character of the developing ego ("self-system"). Sullivan said that impulses, affects, and drives are reactions of individuals to one another in the interpersonal situation, and are not innate, preexiting "biological" entities (as Freud believed). Anxiety is the tool of the "self-system" (or ego) that modifies activity in the interest of biological and security needs. "Not only does anxiety function to discipline attention, but it gradually restricts personal awareness. The facilitations and deprivations by the parents and significant others are the source of the material with is built into the self. . . . The self may be said to be made up of reflected appraisals" (Sullivan, 1955b, quoted in Guntrip, 1961, p. 182).

Similarly, Jacobson (1964) argued that libidinal and aggressive behaviors and feelings are not inborn drives but are "ego-reactions" to real good and bad external objects. "Anxieties, needs and insecurities" experienced by the developing infant promote the differentiation of self and object. "[L]ibido is the . . . urge to object relations . . . and aggressive reactions [are] defensive reactions to fears, anxieties, . . . and especially basic feelings of isolation" (Jacobson, 1964, quoted in Guntrip, 1971, pp. 128–129). Likewise, Bowlby (1973), taking an ethological viewpoint, argued that man and other animals are endowed with inborn behavioral systems that promote withdrawal from the stranger and attachment to the care giver. Fear and anxiety involve both withdrawal from the unfamiliar and potentially dangerous and approach to familiar figures expected to provide protection. Just as Arlow (1977) has argued that anxiety does not exist free of ideas, so Bowlby and object relations theorists have argued that anxiety does not exist free of object relations but arises out of and promotes object relations.

In summary, Freud's observation of separation anxiety in infants has been the source of much fruitful research about the nature of anxiety in infancy and early childhood, particularly Bowlby's ethological theory of infant–mother attachment. This theory takes into account the source of anxiety, flight–fight "instincts," and many of the phenomena of normal anxiety responses. Recent research has shown a relationship between anxious attachment at 1 year of age and a variety of emotional, behavioral, and interpersonal problems in the early school years, but not specifically between anxious attachment and later anxiety disorders. Object relations theorists have emphasized that anxiety is best understood as a form of communication in the mother–infant (object–self) relationship, where it promotes and inhibits behavior by both partners.

CURRENT TREATMENT

Finally, this section illustrates the integration of various theoretical viewpoints in the conceptualization and treatment of anxiety disorders of childhood, specifically the phobic/separation anxious child.

Scharfman (1978) described the case of Nancy, a 5-year-old kindergartener who presented with a 6-month history of increasing fearfulness. She initially was afraid when she saw a friend's parent in a wheelchair, and this fear generalized to anxiety when seeing anyone with an injury, however slight. After her teacher came to school with an arm in a sling, she began to refuse to go to school and would cry and have tantrums if her parents went out at night, even though she was very familiar with the babysitter.

Her phobic symptoms are understood as a regression of libidinal drives from the oedipal to the pre-oedipal phase of development. That is, because she is frustrated in her wish to be the exclusive object of her father's love and affection, she feels resentment and anger toward her mother. Her omnipotent fantasies of doing away with mother, however, remind her of her fears of abandonment (Freud's loss of the object). The phobic symptoms and clinging to both parents represent an avoidance of the oedipal conflict (with mother) and disappointment (by father) and a regression to the earlier developmental issue of separation and individuation from the primary object (mother).

But why does regression occur in this little girl? When she was 3 years old, her mother gave birth to a boy, toward whom Nancy was angry and resentful, believing that her parents must prefer boys or would not have chosen to have another child. Her anger at mother for leaving her to go to the hospital to have this baby was condensed in a memory—which emerged during treatment—of having seen a man, bandaged and in a wheelchair, at the hospital on the day of mother's discharge. Nancy's phobia further expressed her defense against aggressive wishes toward her brother (e.g., by the mechanism of projection, she feared boys at school would beat her) and her feeling of being damaged (no penis, no breasts). Current theorists argue that the feeling of being damaged represents both a "negative" oedipal conflict (without a penis, Nancy feels she is unable to be her mother's chief object of desire) and a pre-oedipal one (Nancy feels weak in comparison to her omnipotent mother, who has a [hidden] penis).

Scharfman approached treatment by telling the child he understood how sad and alone she must feel when seeing injured people, but he intentionally avoided interpretation of Nancy's aggressive wishes toward mother, because bringing these into consciousness would overwhelm an already poorly defended ego and increase Nancy's anxiety (for further discussion of treatment techniques, see Bornstein, 1945; Freud, 1965; Kestenbaum, 1981). He further empathized with her resentment of her brother, her confusion about sexuality, and her wishes to be a boy. Only after months of treatment did he approach her oedipal longings toward her father and her resentment toward her mother for interfering with these longings, and, previously, for "abandoning" her for her baby brother.

Whereas Scharfman (1978) discussed his case purely in terms of intrapsychic conflict, Sperling (1967) presented cases of "school phobia" with more complex interpersonal dynamics. Typically, the child's symptoms also serve a defensive function for the parent, and Sperling therefore refers to "induced" school phobia. For example, Ann, an only child, aged 6, began to refuse school after the 2nd day of first grade, although she had gone to kindergarten without difficulty. Only weeks before she had readily accepted a new babysitter, but vomited the second night the sitter came, and vomited nightly thereafter. Ann would go out with her father only if her mother would promise to stay at home while they were gone. Father insisted that Mother take full responsibility for tending to Ann when she vomited. Mother was chronically depressed and unhappily married; she had become pregnant after 7 years of marriage and disliked the child. Sperling helped Mother to recognize that Ann's symptoms kept

Mother from leaving home (as she unconsciously wanted to do), thereby preserving the marriage and the mother–daughter relationship. Father also contributed to the maintenance of the child's symptoms and to the preservation of the marriage by his refusal to care for Ann himself. Ann readily returned to school when mother told her "I don't need you to stay home anymore." Mother was referred for treatment of her depression and marital difficulties. Sperling's case is more clearly understood in terms of object relations and ethological theories, and illustrates what many have noted, that separation anxiety commonly involves separation issues for parent *and* child (Bowlby, 1960).

CONCLUSIONS

It is often assumed that Freud's last theory of anxiety—the theory of signal anxiety (1926/1959)—is the most comprehensive. That this is not the case has been carefully elucidated by Compton (1972a, 1972b), who has pointed out the deficiencies of Freud's and others' positions. Many post-Freudian theorists have continued to use and mix the language of Freud's energic, drive, instinctual, and structural theories, even when the theories are incompatible (Kardiner, 1956).

I have tried to show that the psychoanalytic theory of anxiety is neither comprehensive nor unitary. Freud never discussed the origins or meaning of anxiety in psychosis (Compton, 1972b). When we talk of anxiety in infancy, we are not necessarily referring to the same phenomena as in older children or adults, nor is there necessarily continuity between anxiety in infancy and later life. Our understanding of anxiety is further complicated by the mixing of developmental and psychopathological issues in the literature. Current interpersonal and ethological views of anxiety are quite different from those of Freud, relying as they do on explanations based on behavioral patterns promoting interpersonal relationships rather than on intrapsychic disequilibrium.

ACKNOWLEDGMENTS

Preparation of this chapter was supported in part by National Institute of Mental Health Grant No. 1 TO1 MH17463-01 and the William T. Grant Foundation. The author thanks David Shaffer, Clarice Kestenbaum, and Kristin Dietz Trautman for their comments.

REFERENCES

Ainsworth, M. D. S., Blehar, M. C., Waters, E., & Wall, S. *Patterns of attachment.* Hillsdale, N.J.: Erlbaum, 1978.

Arlow, J. A. Affects and the psychoanalytic situation. *International Journal of Psycho-Analysis,* 1977, *58,* 157–170.

Benjamin, J. D. Some developmental observations relating to the theory of anxiety. *Journal of the American Psychoanalytic Association,* 1961, *9,* 652–668.

Benjamin, J. D. Further comments on some developmental aspects of anxiety. In H. S. Gaskill (Ed.), *Counterpoint: Libidinal object and subject.* New York: International Universities Press, 1963, pp. 121–153.

Bornstein, B. Clinical notes on child analysis. *Psychoanalytic Study of the Child,* 1945, *1,* 151–166.

Bowlby, J. Separation anxiety: A clinical review of the literature. *Journal of Child Psychology and Psychiatry,* 1960, *1,* 251–262.

Bowlby, J. *Attachment and loss* (Vol. I: *Attachment*). New York: Basic Books, 1969.

Bowlby, J. *Attachment and loss* (Vol. II: *Separation, anxiety and anger*). New York: Basic Books, 1973.

Brenner, C. *An elementary textbook of psychoanalysis.* New York: Doubleday, 1955.

Brierly, M. Affects in theory and practice. *International Journal of Psychoanalysis,* 1937, *18,* 256–269.

Compton, A. A study of the psychoanalytic theory of anxiety. I. The development of Freud's theory of anxiety. *Journal of the American Psychoanalytic Association,* 1972, *20,* 3–44. (a)

Compton, A. A study of the psychoanalytic theory of anxiety. II. Developments in the theory of anxiety since 1926. *Journal of the American Psychoanalytic Association,* 1972, *20,* 341–394. (b)

Darwin, C. *The expression of emotions in man and animal.* New York: Philosophical Library, 1955. (Originally published 1872)

Drellich, M. G. Psychoanalytic theories of affect. In M. B. Cantor & M. L. Glucksman (Eds.), *Affect: Psychoanalytic theory and practice.* New York: Wiley, 1983, pp. 11–25.

Emde, R. N., Gaensbauer, T. J., & Harmon, R. J. *Emotional expression in infancy.* New York: International Universities Press, 1976.

Fisher, C. Dreams, images, and perceptions. *Journal of the American Psychoanalytic Association,* 1956, *4,* 5–48.

Freud, A. The ego and the mechanisms of defense. *The writings of Anna Freud* (Vol. 2). New York: International Universities Press, 1966. (Originally published 1936)

Freud, A. *Normality and pathology in childhood: Assessment of development.* New York: International Universities Press, 1965.

Freud, S. The interpretation of dreams. In J. Strachey (Ed. and Trans.), *Standard edition* (Vol. 4, 5). London: Hogarth Press, 1953. (Originally published 1900).

Freud, S. Analysis of a phobia in a five-year-old boy. In J. Strachey (Ed. and Trans.), *Standard edition* (Vol. 10). London: Hogarth Press, 1955, pp. 3–149. (Originally published 1909) (a)

Freud, S. Beyond the pleasure principle. In J. Strachey (Ed. and Trans.), *Standard edition* (Vol. 18). London: Hogarth Press, 1955, pp. 3–64. (Originally published 1920) (b)

Freud, S. Instincts and their vicissitudes. In J. Strachey (Ed. and Trans.), *Standard edition* (Vol. 14). London: Hogarth Press, 1957, pp. 111–140. (Originally published 1915)

Freud, S. Inhibitions, symptoms and anxiety. In J. Strachey (Ed. and Trans.), *Standard edition* (Vol. 20). London: Hogarth Press, 1959, pp. 75–175. (Originally published 1926)

Freud, S. The ego and the id. In J. Strachey (Ed. and Trans.), *Standard edition* (Vol. 11). London: Hogarth Press, 1961, pp. 3–66. (Originally published 1923) (a)

Freud, S. Some psychical consequences of the anatomical distinction between the sexes. In J. Strachey (Ed. and Trans.), *Standard edition* (Vol. 19). London: Hogarth Press, 1961, pp. 243–258. (Originally published 1925) (b)

Freud, S. The neuro-psychoses of defence. In J. Strachey (Ed. and Trans.), *Standard edition* (Vol. 3). London: Hogarth Press, 1962, pp. 43–61. (Originally published 1894) (a)

Freud, S. On the grounds for detaching a particular syndrome from neurasthenia under the description "anxiety neurosis." In J. Strachey (Ed. and Trans.), *Standard edition* (Vol. 3). London: Hogarth Press, 1962, pp, 87–115. (Originally published 1895) (b)

Freud, S. A reply to criticisms of my paper on anxiety neurosis. In J. Strachey (Ed. and Trans.), *Standard edition* (Vol. 3). London: Hogarth Press, 1962, pp. 121–139. (Originally published 1895) (c)

Freud, S. Heredity and the aetiology of the neuroses. In J. Strachey (Ed. and Trans.), *Standard edition* (Vol. 3). London: Hogarth Press, 1962, pp. 142–156. (Originally published 1896) (d)

Freud, S. Introductory Lectures on Psychoanalysis. Lecture 25: Anxiety. In J. Strachey (Ed. and Trans.), *Standard edition* (Vol. 16). London: Hogarth Press, 1963, pp. 392–411. (Originally published 1917)

Greenacre, P. The predisposition to anxiety. In *Trauma, growth, and personality.* New York: Norton, 1952, pp. 27–82. (Originally published 1941) (a)

Greenacre, P. The biological economy of birth. In *Trauma, growth and personality.* New York: Norton, 1952, pp. 3–26. (Originally published 1945) (b)

Guntrip, H. *Personality structure and human interaction.* New York: International Universities Press, 1961.

Guntrip, H. *Psychoanalytic theory, therapy, and the self.* New York: Basic Books, 1971.

Hartmann, H., Kris, E., & Loewenstein, R. M. Comments on the formation of psychic structure. *Psychoanalytic Study of the Child,* 1946, *2,* 11–38.

Jacobson, E. The affects and their pleasure-unpleasure qualities in relation to the psychic discharge processes. In R. M. Loewenstein (Ed.), *Drives, affects, and behavior.* New York: International Universities Press, 1953, pp. 38–66.

Jacobson, E. The self and the object world: Vicissitudes of their infantile cathexes and their influences on ideational and affective development. *Psychoanalytic Study of the Child,* 1954, *9,* 75–127.

Jacobson, E. Normal and pathological moods: Their nature and function. *Psychoanalytic Study of the Child,* 1947, *12,* 73–113.

Jacobson, E. *The self and the object world.* New York: International Universities Press, 1964.

Kagan, J. *Change and continuity in infancy.* New York: Wiley, 1971.

Kagan, J. On emotion and its development: A working paper. In M. Lewis & L. A. Rosenblum (Eds.), *The development of affect.* New York: Plenum Press, 1978, pp. 15–41.

Kardiner, A. Adaptational theory: The cross cultural point of view. In S. Rado & G. E. Daniels (Eds.), *Changing concepts of psychoanalytic medicine.* New York: Grune & Stratton, 1956, pp. 59–68.

Kestenbaum, C. J. The origins of affect—Normal and pathological. *Journal of the American Academy of Psychoanalysis,* 1980, *8,* 497–520.

Kestenbaum, C. J. Aspects of the therapeutic relationship in child analysis. In S. Klibanow (Ed.), *Changing concepts in psychoanalysis.* New York: Gardner Press, 1981, pp. 129–143.

Klein, M. *The psycho-analysis of children.* New York: Grove Press, 1932.

Lang, R. *Birth book.* Los Angeles: Genesis Press, 1972.

Lewis, M., Feiring, C., McGuffog, C., & Jaskir, J. Predicting psychopathology in six-year-olds from early social relations. *Child Development,* 1983, *55,* 123–136.

Novey, S. A clinical view of affect theory in psychoanalysis. *International Journal of Psycho-Analysis,* 1959, *40,* 94–104.

Novey, S. Further considerations on affect theory in psychoanalysis. *International Journal of Psycho-Analysis,* 1961, *42,* 21–31.

Novey, S. The principle of "working through" in psychoanalysis. *Journal of the American Psychoanalytic Association,* 1962, *10,* 658–676.

Rado, S. On the psychoanalytic exploration of fear and other emotions. In *Collected Papers.* Vol. I: *Psychoanalysis of behavior.* New York: Grune & Stratton, 1956, pp. 243–247.

Rank, O. *The trauma of birth.* New York: Robert Brunner, 1952. (Originally published 1924)

Scharfman, M. A. Psychoanalytic treatment. In B. B. Wolman, J. Egan, & A. O. Ross (Eds.), *Handbook of treatment of mental disorders in childhood and adolescence.* Englewood Cliffs, N.J.: Prentice-Hall, 1978, pp. 47–69.

Schecter, D. On the emergence of human relatedness. In E. G. Witenberg (Ed.), *Interpersonal explorations in psychoanalysis.* New York: Basic Books, 1972.

Schur, M. The ego in anxiety. In R. M. Loewenstein (Ed.), *Drives, affects, and behavior.* New York: International Universities Press, 1953, pp. 67–103.

Schur, M. The ego and the id in anxiety. *Psychoanalytic Study of the Child,* 1958, *13,* 190–220.

Sperling, M. School phobias—Classification, dynamics and treatment. *Psychoanalytic Study of the Child,* 1967, *22,* 375–401.

Spitz, R. A. Anxiety in infancy: A study of its manifestations in the first year of life. *International Journal of Psycho-Analysis,* 1950, *31,* 138–143.

Spitz, R. A. *The first year of life.* New York: International Universities Press, 1965.

Sroufe, L. A. Infant–caregiver attachment and patterns of adaptation in preschool: The roots of maladaption and competence. In M. Perlmutter (Ed.), *Minnesota symposium on child psychology* (Vol. 16). Hillsdale, N.J.: Erlbaum, 1983, pp. 41–83.

Sroufe, L. A., Fox, N. E., & Pancake, V. R. Attachment and dependency in developmental perspective. *Child Development,* 1983, *54,* 1615–1627.

Stern, D. N. Mother and infant at play—The dyadic interaction involving facial, vocal and gaze behavior. In M. Lewis & L. A. Rosenblum (Eds.), *The origins of behavior* (Vol. I: *The effect of the infant on its caregiver*). New York: Wiley, 1974, pp. 187–213.

Strachey, J. Freud's views on phobias. In J. Strachey (Ed. and Trans.), *Standard edition* (Vol. 3). London: Hogarth Press, 1962, pp. 83–84.

Sullivan, H. S. *Conceptions of modern psychiatry.* New York: Norton, 1955. (a)

Sullivan, H. S. *The interpersonal theory and psychiatry.* New York: Norton, 1955. (b)

Szasz, T. S. *Pain and pleasure.* New York: Basic Books, 1957.

Waelder, R. Inhibitions, symptoms and anxiety: Forty years later (1967). In S. A. Guttman (Ed.), *Psychoanalysis: Observations, theory, application.* New York: International Universities Press, 1976, pp. 338–360.

‡ 10 ‡

PHARMACOTHERAPY OF CHILDHOOD ANXIETY DISORDERS

RACHEL GITTELMAN
HAROLD S. KOPLEWICZ

INTRODUCTION

There have been, and continue to be, refinements in the classification of the anxiety disorders of childhood and adulthood. Currently, diagnoses for separation anxiety, overanxious, and avoidant disorders are provided for children (American Psychiatric Association, 1980). In addition, some of the adult anxiety disorders are applicable to children, especially the simple phobia and obsessive–compulsive disorders. A meaningful discussion of pharmacologic management of anxiety disorders necessitates a distinction among the different types of childhood anxiety disorders.

DIAGNOSTIC ISSUES

The nomenclature of childhood anxiety disorders is described in Chapter 4 of this volume and will be noted only briefly here.

Several types of anxiety can be differentiated among children. They frequently overlap, and it is not always clear that they represent discrete pathological processes. Performance anxiety reflects fears of failure and incompetence. Pathological forms of fear of loss or

Rachel Gittelman and Harold S. Koplewicz. New York State Psychiatric Institute, and College of Physicians and Surgeons, Columbia University, New York, New York.

abandonment manifest as separation anxiety disorder. The avoidant disorder refers to children who are shy and severely inhibited in a variety of social situations. Though shyness can be a temperamental variant, it is believed to assume pathological proportions. Avoidant disorder must be distinguished from the schizoid disorder, which includes children who may or may not be anxious in new social situations, but who have little social interest and activity. Schizoid children are isolated and socially inept. In contrast, as defined, children with avoidant disorders want to join social groups; they have adequate social skills when in familiar settings, but they become overwhelmed with anxiety in new social situations. It is important to make this diagnostic differentiation as the prognosis of these two entities is quite different; shy children are believed to have a good prognosis, whereas the outcome for children with a schizoid disorder is probably less benign.

Overanxious disorder is a mixed condition; it includes children who are overconcerned about the quality of their performance, worry excessively about grades, and have excessive fears of doctors, dentists, and other situations. Simple phobias refer to irrational fear of specific objects or situations (excluding social situations). Simple phobias commonly involve animals, and most start in childhood.

Obsessive–compulsive disorder, another anxiety disorder included in the adult nomenclature, frequently has an onset in childhood or adolescence. The essential features consist of persistent, intrusive, unwanted ideas and ego-dystonic repetitive impulses to perform acts that are regarded as unreasonable even by the children performing them. These children experience severe anxiety if they are prevented from carrying out these rituals. The most common obsessions are repetitive thoughts of violence, contamination, and doubt. The most common compulsions involve handwashing, counting, checking, and touching.

The various anxiety disorders can overlap or occur singly. Some reservations about the existence of the avoidant disorder seem in order. In our clinical experience we have not seen any child who presented with it. Of course, any clinician's experience is limited, and cannot be used as a standard for the variety of disorders that exists; in the case of avoidant disorder, however, there are no clinical reports of it in the literature. Therefore, even the minimal criterion of having some recorded observations of a condition for creating a diagnostic category is missing for this childhood anxiety disorder.

It might be argued, and not unreasonbly, that the diagnostic distinctions provided by the DSM-III (American Psychiatric Association, 1980) between the different types of anxiety disorders are premature, since they have not been validated by treatment studies or other means, such as studies of long-term outcome and familial concordance. There is no reason at this time to believe that various childhood anxiety disorders differ with regard to natural course, genetic transmission, etiologic antecedents, or psychophysiology. Thus, there is currently no firm empirical basis upon which to justify the distinctness of the childhood anxiety disorders from one another, as has been done (American Psychiatric Association, 1980). Furthermore, the distinctions may not be diagnosed reliably (Rutter & Shaffer, 1980). By applying diagnostic clinical criteria, however, Werry, Methven, Fitzpatrick, and Dixon (1983) have reported satisfactory reliability for the diagnoses of the separation anxiety and overanxious disorders (interestingly, not for the avoidant disorder). Yet, to combine the disorders together under a procrustean concept such as "emotional disorders" or "neuroses" may be counterproductive, since, by doing so, one would miss the opportunity to discover possibly important distinctions among the childhood anxiety disorders. We then find ourselves in a "Catch-22" dilemma. By improving diagnostic refinements we may be acting prematurely and communicating an unwarranted level of pseudo-precision. By not making diagnostic discriminations we may be missing potentially important clinical differences. Given these options, scientific progress is better served by separating clinical conditions, provided that the nomenclature thus generated is regarded for what it is: A working model that will need reshaping if it does not generate useful information beyond its descriptiveness. The failure to maintain a dispassionate critical eye on the diagnostic schema could lead to diagnostic chaos reminiscent of pre-Kraepelinian nineteenth century psychiatry—a myriad of non-validated diagnoses, whose basis for existence rested mostly on the testimonials of prestigious academicians. The current nomenclature does not escape this shortcoming, since most of its contents are, perforce, a reflection of professional consensus derived from personal convictions rather than systematic clinical research. This shortcoming is likely to continue for a long time to come. At the same time clinical observations and conjectures are indispensable to research strategy of clinical phenomena.

For the most part the treatment literature pertaining to childhood anxiety disorder antedates the appearance of the current nomenclature. Few investigations have specified the exact symptomatology of children treated for anxiety. Therefore, the hope of providing information regarding the pharmacologic treatment of anxiety disorders of childhood as stipulated in the diagnostic manual cannot be met. This lack of precision presents a problem, since the rational approach to chemotherapy is to begin with an accurate, reliable diagnosis. The review of literature here is based on many studies that were vague in their diagnostic content and utilized the concept of anxiety in a general way. Some refer to the problematic term of "neurosis," which poses even more definitional dilemmas than "anxiety," because manifest evidence of anxiety symptoms is not necessary for a neurosis to be diagnosed. Two studies have concluded that neurosis has a better prognosis than many other disorders of childhood and that marked improvement can be observed with various treatment probably because of a high rate of spontaneous remission and/or placebo effects (Cytryn, Gilbert, & Eisenberg, 1960; Eisenberg, Gilbert, Cytryn, & Molling, 1961). If so, the need for well-differentiated diagnoses and double-blind and well-controlled treatment studies in anxiety disorders is critical.

PHARMACOLOGIC STUDIES

A variety of agents have been tried in children with anxiety disorders, not always with a clear rationale; they include neuroleptics, psychostimulants, antihistamines, anxiolytics, and antidepressants. (A new class of compounds, beta-adrenergic blocking agents, have been reported for the management of some adult anxiety disorders, but as of yet these have not been applied to anxiety disorders in children.)

NEUROLEPTICS

When first marketed in the 1950s, and for about two decades thereafter, neuroleptics, such as chlorpromazine (Thorazine), were called major tranquilizers. Tranquilizers such as barbiturates were well known, and the antipsychotic action of neuroleptics was viewed initially as due to their extreme ability to reduce anxiety. Thus, the concepts of major and minor tranquilizers were born. Eventually, it became clear that the antipsychotic effect of neuroleptics had nothing to do with reduction of anxiety (Klein, Gittelman, Quitkin, & Rifkin, 1980). But until then, the use of neuroleptic drugs in anxiety states was not an unusual clinical practice. In an earlier review by Gittelman-Klein (1978), we noted that all the studies of neuroleptics in childhood and adolescent anxiety states were unsatisfactory because of the imprecise nature of the patient groups and the sample inadequacies related to the mixing of children with psychotic as well as behavior disorders, in whom the presence of anxiety was inferred.

Three placebo-controlled studies of neuroleptics have been reported in hospitalized groups. Lucas and Pasley (1969) used heloperidol (Haldol) in unspecified amounts, for 6 weeks, in 10 children (8–15 years old) with mixed diagnoses. No significant differences between the drug and a placebo were obtained on scale ratings of anxiety and tension levels.

Freedman, Effron, and Bender (1955) studied the effectiveness of chlorpromazine (Thorazine, 30–100 mg/day) and reserpine (Serpasil, 0.3–3.0 mg/day) on an array of symptoms in a diagnostically mixed group, aged 7–12. No difference in anxiety level was obtained between the drug-treated and placebo groups. However, the dosage was low, and the number of cases was small (eight and six children in each drug group); it is therefore unlikely that the design allowed for the detection of drug effects should they actually exist.

The third study (Garfield, Helper, Wilcott, & Muffly, 1962) included a more adequate sample size (n = 39) and more appropriate doses of chlorpromazine (75–450 mg/day), but it found no significant change in the children's anxiety as rated by ward personnel.

Several trials with neuroleptics in children attending outpatient clinical settings have also been reported. Cytryn et al. (1960) compared prochlorperazine (Compazine), meprobamate (Miltown), and a placebo in children (aged 5–13 years) described as neurotic, mentally retarded, hyperkinetic, and antisocial. The drug regimen was combined with psychotherapy for 7 weeks. Prochlorperazine, in doses of 20–40 mg/day, was not superior to the placebo on global improvement ratings at home and school. The children who had not responded during the study were further randomized to perphenazine (Trilafon, 1.2–16 mg/day) or to a placebo for 1 month. A significant advantage for the drug over the placebo was obtained in overall outcome. It seemed as if the neurotic children were especially responsive to the medication, but a clear interpretation of a drug–diagnosis relationship was prevented, because the drug group included more neurotic cases than the placebo group. To pursue the possibility that perphenazine was a useful agent in neurotic children, the investigators conducted a placebo-controlled study of perphenazine in neurotic outpatients exclusively (Eisenberg *et al.*, 1961). The results did not bear out the earlier clinical observations.

Because Cytryn *et al.* (1960) had observed a higher rate of improvement among the neurotic children than among those with other disorders across all treatments, they suggested that anxious children improve markedly with any brief intervention, regardless of its specific type.

The neuroleptics are no longer a viable class of drugs for the relief of anxiety disorders, since irreversible serious side effects have been documented and safer competing treatments exist.

PSYCHOSTIMULANTS

There would seem little *a priori* reason to expect psychostimulants to alleviate anxiety symptoms. Some clinicians, however, reported the observation that amphetamines were useful in relieving anxiety and stimulating overly inhibited neurotic children (Bender & Cottingham, 1942; Bender & Nichtern, 1956; Fish, 1960, 1968). In an uncontrolled trial of deaner, an acetycholine analogue stimulant, in children with mixed diagnoses, the drug was reported to alleviate anxiety, moodiness, and sleep difficulties (Bostock & Shakleton, 1962).

In contrast to these reports, Swanson, Kinsbourne, Roberts, and Zucker (1978) observed that hyperactive youngsters who also met diagnostic criteria for overanxious disorder responded adversely on cognitive tests to methylphenidate (average dose 12.5 mg/day). Aman and Werry (1982) reported a similar observation in a 1-week study evaluating the cognitive effect of methylphenidate and diazepam on children with reading disabilities. Specifically, the authors noted that high scores on the Children's Manifest Anxiety Scale were predictive of a poor response to methylphenidate (0.35 mg/kg) on cognitive measures.

We conclude that there is no evidence that stimulants are effective in children whose primary clinical problem is anxiety. There is some clinical evidence that stimulants may be contraindicated in some children with anxiety symptomatology.

ANTIHISTAMINES

Uncontrolled studies of mixed diagnostic groups have claimed that diphenhydramine (Benadryl) and hydroxyzine (Atarax) were helpful in modifying anxiety symptoms (Effron & Freedman, 1953; Fish, 1968). A single double-blind, placebo-controlled study comparing two antihistamines in children with mixed diagnoses has appeared. Diphenhydramine was reported to improve manifest anxiety (Bender & Nichtern, 1956). However, the evidence for the use of anti-histamines as a class of drugs for anxiety disorders in children is clearly wanting.

ANXIOLYTICS (ANTIANXIETY AGENTS)

The anxiolytics, formerly called tranquilizers, were renamed minor tranquilizers when the so-called major tranquilizers appeared. These terms are confusing if not misleading. The tranquilizers may calm some types of patients but not others. They may be helpful in some patients with nonpsychotic anxious feelings, but they are quite useless among anxious manic or schizophrenic patients. Furthermore, other drugs, such as tricyclic antidepressants, are now established as effective agents for adult panic disorders. Because of these and other developments, the term "tranquilizer" is no longer in vogue.

The best-known effect of this class of drugs is its sedative action. The oldest drugs in this group are the barbiturates. In adults they are known to have anxiolytic (antianxiety) properties. They have received very little attention in children, however, perhaps because of their reputation of inducing states of behavioral excitement in young children—exactly the opposite of the hoped-for therapeutic effect.

In one study by Frommer (1967), children suffering from a variety of phobic and affective symptoms received either phenobarbitone, or chlordiazepoxide combined with phenelzine (Librium and Nardil). The children on the barbiturate were less improved than those on the combined antidepressant/antianxiety drugs. Since no placebo group was included, it is not possible to ascertain the value of phenobarbitone. Its effects compared with a placebo could be any of three possible outcomes—inferior, equal, or superior.

For all intents and purposes, barbiturates are no longer part of modern psychopharmacology. They have been replaced by the benzodiazepines, which are similar drugs but are much safer, since sudden overdoses are not lethal and addiction is not a serious consideration, as it is for many of the barbiturates. (This issue is not relevant to the use of phenobarbitol in children with epilepsy, where it continues as a valuable, safe, treatment.) The best-known benzodiazepines are diazepam (Valium) and chlordiazepoxide (Librium). A very large number of such compounds have been synthesized. They differ in length and strength of action and the degree of their sedative effect. There is a huge literature pertaining to the use of benzodiazepines in adult anxiety disorders (for a review, see Klein et al., 1980), however, our understanding of these drugs in children with anxiety disorders is practically nil.

Lucas and Pasley (1969) identified 12 children, in full or part residential care because of severe behavior disorders, as experiencing "neurotic anxiety." They treated the children with diazepam (5–20 mg/day over 1–2 weeks). There was no significant effect for diazepam on ratings of anxiety and tension. The study is limited by the questionable diagnostic characteristics of the children, as well as the very brief treatment period. One to two weeks is insufficient for assessing therapeutic efficacy.

In another study by Cytryn et al. (1960), children judged to be "neurotic" received meprobamate (Miltown) or a placebo for 7 weeks (daily meprobamate dose 800–1000 mg). No difference was found between the two treatments. Given the small number of subjects (the patients in the group given meprobamate numbered only four), it is questionable whether the study can be claimed to be an adequate test of drug efficacy. In addition, in this study, as in others, the concept of neurosis as a diagnostic entity provides little diagnostic information. It merely delineates categorical exclusions such as psychosis or organic mental disorder, but fails to identify the positive clinical phenomena that determine membership in the group. It is therefore difficult to interpret data obtained with "neurotic children" in a way that gives the results general applicability.

The negative results of these controlled trials do not support the clinical reports of positive effects of antianxiety agents.

At present, the benzodiazepines have no documented usefulness in the treatment of anxiety disorders in children. However, this does not rule out their possible efficacy. On the positive side, it is consistently reported that children with uncomplicated anxiety disorders (the ones referred to as neurotic) are the best responders to benzodiazepines. Further, the finding that benzodiazepines are useful preanesthetic compounds in children suggests that these drugs may reduce situational and anticipatory anxiety. In the absence of placebo controlled studies, however, the value of benzodiazepines cannot be assessed.

A new benzodiazepine, alprazolam (Xanax), has been reported to be effective in adults with panic disorders (Sheehan *et al.*, 1984). It has been conjectured that this compound may have clinical properties different from those of other members of the benzodiazepine family. In our clinical experience, which is limited so far to only four youngsters with separation anxiety disorder refractory to psychotherapy, alprazolam was very effective in three patients over a 6-week period in daily doses of 0.5–1.0 mg/day. In the fourth, sedation prevented treatment continuation. It is likely that alprazolam will receive further attention to ascertain whether it has a broad spectrum of clinical efficacy in children and adolescents.

ANTIDEPRESSANTS

Two clinical theories are responsible for the use of antidepressant drugs in childhood anxiety disorders. The first stems from the belief that anxiety disorders in children are really depressive states. According to this view, the depression is demonstrated by the sad affect, weepiness, and misery that the children display. In such situations the diagnostic problem is to distinguish a primary depressive disorder from a dysphoric state secondary to an anxiety disorder. Children with severe anxiety symptoms are inevitably in pain and unhappy. Whether to consider this state a clinical depression is controversial (Puig-Antich & Gittelman, 1982).

The study by Frommer (1967), comparing phenobarbitone to an antidepressant combined with an anxiolytic (penelzine, mean of 30–45 mg/day, and chlordiazepoxide, mean of 20 mg/day), reflects the interpretation that anxiety states are expressed secondarily to a depressive disorder. As we noted previously, the study did not include a placebo-treated group. As a result, the efficacy of the antidepressant cannot be estimated.

The second theory that accounts for the use of antidepressants in childhood anxiety disorders, specifically in separation anxiety disorder, stems from the work done by Klein with adults suffering from agoraphobia (Klein, 1964). Klein observed that a large proportion of these patients had a childhood history of severe separation anxiety and that their response to initial panic in adulthood had been clinging, dependent behavior. Klein (1964) reasoned that these patients suffered from a disruption of the biologic processes that regulate anxiety, triggered by separation. Bowlby subsequently expressed a similar view (Bowlby, 1973). Klein postulated that the panic anxiety was a pathological variant of normal separation anxiety and, since imipramine relieved adult panic anxiety, it might be useful in children with separation anxiety. An initial open clinical trial with imipramine was conducted in children with school phobia, since their phobic disorder is so often the consequence of pathological separation anxiety. In an open clinical trial the drug seemed helpful, since 85% of the children returned to school (Rabiner & Klein, 1969). Gittelman-Klein and Klein (1971) followed with a placebo-controlled 6-week study of imipramine in 7- to 15-year-olds who were unable to attend school regularly (Gittelman-Klein & Klein, 1971, 1973, 1980). Imipramine (mean of 15 mg/day) was significantly superior to placebo, both in inducing school return and in reducing other aspects of anxious sympatomatology, such as separation difficulties and physical symptoms before attending school. Depressive symptoms also improved, but the presence of depression was not necessary for improvement to occur, so that children benefited from the medication regardless of whether depression was present or not.

Berney et al. (1981) investigated the efficacy of clomipramine in doses of 40–75 mg in school phobic children (this drug is not marketed in the United States). The mean daily dose is not indicated. There was no significant difference between the medication and a placebo. Both treatment groups showed little improvement at the end of the 12-week study. For example, over 40% of the children were not attending school on their own, and a large percentage still had significant levels of separation anxiety. These rates of change are similar to those obtained by Gittelman-Klein and Klein (1980) among their children treated with placebo for 6 weeks; of those, 53% were still not attending school independently, and the majority were still suffering from separation anxiety at the end of treatment. Several reasons might account for the different results in the two studies that used tricyclics of similar potency. As Berney *et al.* note, the clomipramine dose used was lower than the imipramine dose used by Gittelman-Klein (1975), who had noted that no child had improved on less than 75 mg/day. Patient characteristics or the type of psychotherapy used could also have contributed to the discrepancies between the two studies. This is improbable, since the placebo effects were very similar in the two trials. Therefore, the clomipramine study cannot be viewed as a failure to replicate the imipramine study.

Noteworthy in the study by Berney *et al.* (1981) is the careful assessment of the pattern of change in the children's symptomatology over the course of the treatment. Before treatment 87% of the children were rated as having moderate to marked separation anxiety, and 44% were felt to have similar levels of depression. After 4 weeks of treatment 68% still had separation anxiety, whereas only 12% were still depressed. These findings argue against the theory that separation anxiety disorders in these children were primarily depressive states. The marked improvement of depression after the first 4 weeks of treatment while separation anxiety continued is consistent with the anxiety disorder being primary in these school phobic children.

Tricyclic antidepressants, including clomipramine, have also been studied in youngsters with obsessive–compulsive disorder, since clomipramine had previously been found to be effective in adults with this disorder (Thoren, Asberg, Cronholm, Jornestedt, & Traskman, 1980).

A preliminary report compared clomipramine, desmethylimipramine, and a placebo given in random order in eight youngsters (mean age, 15.2 years). The maximum daily dose for both active agents was 150 mg/day. The two drugs were not found to differ from the placebo or from each other (Rapoport, Elkins, & Mikkelsen, 1980). The final report of this study included 19 children (mean age, 14.5 years), 7 of whom had been part of the previous trial. In this instance clomipramine and placebo only were used; each condition lasted for a 5-week period in random order, with maximum daily doses of 200 mg (mean, 141 mg). Clomipramine treatment was significantly superior to the placebo on measures of obsessive–compulsive symptomatology. This finding parallels results reported for adult patients. Treatment effectiveness was not associated with the presence of depression. In addition, the blood level of drug metabolites was not related to improvement (Flament *et al.*, 1985).

The two studies that have found significant effects for antidepressants in childhood anxiety have noted that the presence of depression symptomatology did not influence drug efficacy (Gittelman-Klein & Klein, 1980; Flament *et al.,* 1985). In addition, the third study (Berney *et al.,* 1981), in which no drug effect was obtained, reported a marked alleviation of depression without significant alteration of the anxiety symptomatology. Therefore, the weight of the evidence from drug studies and observations of nonspecific treatment response are consistent in supporting the view that, when depression accompanies an anxiety disorder, the anxiety disorder is likely to be a primary disturbance and not an associated feature of an affective disorder.

Tricyclic Side Effects

In any discussion of pharmacotherapy, it is important to discuss side effects. These are only relevant, however, when there are well-established positive central effects. Somewhat of a case can be made for the relevance of the side effects of tricyclics; since no other class of compounds has even suggestive efficacy, no others are mentioned.

This summary presents the highlights of tricyclic side effects. For full information the reader is referred to a more comprehensive text (Klein *et al.,* 1980).

Most studies report a low frequency of clinical side effects with imipramine (Gualtieri, 1977; Klein *et al.,* 1980). However, these studies have used what can be considered low dosages. When found, subjective discomfort associated with the tricyclics is mild and transient. Discomfort most commonly includes drowsiness and dry mouth. A less frequent, but more troublesome effect is dysinhibition consisting of poor frustration tolerance and temper outbursts. It is possible that clomipramine has more side effects than imipramine, since Flament *et al.* (in press) report a relatively larger prevalence of clinical side effects than do imipramine studies.

The greatest concern with tricyclics is myocardial toxicity. Arrhythmias, asystole, ventricular fibrillation, and congestive heart failure have been reported with imipramine acute overdoses. Therefore, sudden high doses are to be avoided at all times. With chronic treatment, changes observed on electrocardiogram (ECG) have been reported in children. These consist of conduction changes. They occur without clinical evidence of heart block. Other side effects reported have been increases in systolic and diastolic blood pressure and increased pulse (Greenberg & Yellin, 1975). Imipramine may lower the convulsive threshold and should be used cautiously in children with a potential for seizures. Barbiturates seem to lower the serum level of imipramine, while stimulants raise it; the concurrent use of stimulants and tricyclics, therefore, requires careful monitoring until a stable dose is achieved.

Because of the potential toxic effects of imipramine, maximum 5-mg/kg daily doses have been recommended by the Food and Drug Administration (FDA) (Hayes, Panitch, & Barker, 1975). Recently, the *Physicians' Desk Reference* (1984) has been modified to indicate 2.5 mg/kg as the FDA approved daily dosage. As far as we know, this change has not resulted from recent findings of tricyclic toxicity. Quite the contrary, recent careful ECG studies of imipramine in children below the age of 12 have documented the safety of doses up to 7 mg/kg using regular ECG monitoring (Puig-Antich, personal communication, 1984).

COMMENT

The bulk of the literature on the pharmacotherapy of anxious children consists of clinical reports. The methodological limitations of these reports are numerous. The length of treatment is extremely variable, and no attempt is made to evaluate treatment outcome at some fixed point. This practice maximizes the likelihood that spontaneous fluctuations in clinical course that are independent of treatment will be interpreted as drug-induced improvement. In addition, in no instance is there any systematic attempt to quantify the children's symptoms before or after treatment (Gittelman-Klein, 1978). Therefore, although the uncontrolled literature is mentioned for the sake of completeness, it even fails to provide an adequate clinical base upon which to justify the undertaking of adequately controlled investigations.

Only three groups have conducted controlled investigations of drug effects of children with uniform conditions who were treated for fixed intervals: (1) the study of school phobic children by Gittelman-Klein and Klein (1980), which supports the efficacy of tricyclic medication; (2) the study by Berney *et al.* (1981), which is limited by the very low tricyclic dose range allowed for treatment; (3) the work of Rapoport and associates (1980), which indicates a role for a tricyclic, clomipramine, in children with obsessive–compulsive disorders. Therefore, if one were to bet on a single horse, the best bet at this point is that tricyclics may have a legitimate role in management of some severe, early anxiety disorders. So far, only two diagnoses, separation anxiety and obsessive–compulsive disorder, have been subjected to systematic scrutiny. One cannot rule out the possibility that adminstration of the benzodiazepines may also be viable treatment. The clinical reports certainly do not seem to preclude the likelihood that benzodiazepines may be effective.

The findings presented by Puig-Antich and Rabinovich in Chapter 7 of this volume are not consistent with the contention that the tricyclic imipramine is useful in separation anxiety, since among depressed children who had failed to respond better to the drug than to a placebo, the depressed children with separation anxiety did not have a better response to drug than those without separation anxiety. One of this study's results stands in marked contrast with other investigations: The placebo response rate is much higher than that reported in other double-blind studies (i.e., 19% in Gittelman-Klein & Klein, 1980; about 30% after 4 weeks in Berney *et al.* 1981; and 68% in Puig-Antich & Rabinovich, Chapter 7, this volume. This important clinical outcome difference indicates that the samples are quite different. The nature of sample differences and the way in which these affect treatment outcomes is unknown.

We believe that there probably is merit to treating separation anxious children with tricyclic drugs, yet, psychotherapeutic interventions are also important (Gittelman-Klein, 1975). Many families have difficulty in understanding how to respond optimally to their anxious child; others may not provide appropriate responses to the child when he or she recovers. The process of treatment can be facilitated by providing guidance to the family and child. At this time, the evidence for antianxiety pharmacologic treatment of children is not firm.

REFERENCES

Aman, M. G., & Werry, J. S. Methylphenidate and diazepam in severe reading retardation. *Journal of the American Academy of Child Psychiatry*, 1982, *21*, 31–37.

American Psychiatric Association. *Diagnostic and statistical manual of mental disorders* (3rd ed.). Washington, D.C.: Author, 1980.

Bender, L., & Cottingham, F. The use of amphetamine sulfate (Benzedrine) in child psychiatry. *American Journal of Psychiatry*, 1942, *99*, 116–121.

Bender, L., & Nichtern, S. Chemotherapy in child psychiatry. *New York State Journal of Medicine*, 1956, *6*, 2791–2795.

Berney, T., Kolvin, I., Bhate, S. R., Garside, R. F., Jeans, J., Kay, B., & Scarth, L. School phobia: A therapeutic trial with clomipramine and short-term outcome. *British Journal of Psychiatry*, 1981, *138*, 110–118.

Bostock, J., & Shakleton, M. The use of DMAE (Deaner) in behavior states. *Medical Journal of Australia*, 1962, *2*, 337–339.

Bowlby, J. *Attachment and loss*. Vol. II: *Separation: Anxiety and anger*. New York: Basic Books, 1973.

Cytryn, L., Gilbert, A., & Eisenberg, L. The effectiveness of tranquilizing drugs plus supportive psychotherapy in treating behavior disorders of children: A double-blind study of eighty out-patients. *American Journal of Orthopsychiatry*, 1960, *30*, 113–129.

Effron, A. S., & Freedman, A. M. The treatment of behavior disorders in children with Benadryl. *Journal of Pediatrics*, 1953, *42*, 261–266.

Eisenberg, L., Gilbert, A., Cytryn, L., & Molling, P. A. The effectiveness of psychotherapy alone and in conjunction with perphenazine or placebo in the treatment of neurotic and hyperkinetic children. *American Journal of Psychiatry*, 1961, *117*, 1088–1093.

Fish, B. Drug therapy in child psychiatry: Psychological aspects. *Comprehensive Psychiatry*, 1960, *1*, 55–61.

Fish, B. Drug use in psychiatric disorders in children. *American Journal of Psychiatry*, 1968, *124* (Suppl.), 31–36.

Flament, M. F., Rapoport, J. L., Berg, C. J., Sceery, W., Kilts, C., Mellstrom, B., & Linnoila, M. Clomipramine treatment of childhood obsessive compulsive disorders: A double-blind controlled study. *Archives of General Psychiatry*, 1985, *42*, 977–983.

Freedman, A. A., Effron, A. S., & Bender, L. Pharmacotherapy in children with psychiatric illness. *Journal of Nervous and Mental Disease*, 1955, *22*, 479–486.

Frommer, E. A. Treatment of childhood depression with antidepressant drugs. *British Medical Journal*, 1967, *1*, 729–732.

Garfield, S. L., Helper, M. M., Wilcott, R. C., & Muffly, R. Effects of chlorpromazine on behavior in emotionally disturbed children. *Journal of Nervous and Mental Disease*, 1962, *135*, 147–154.

Gittelman-Klein, R. Pharmacotherapy and management of pathological separation anxiety. In R. Gittelman (Ed), *Recent advances in child psychopharmacology*. New York: Human Sciences Press, 1975, pp. 255–272.

Gittelman-Klein, R. Psychopharmacological treatment of anxiety disorders, mood disorders and Tourette's disorder in children. In M. A. Lipton, A. DiMascio, & K. F. Killam (Eds.), *Psychopharmacology: A generation of progress*. New York: Raven Press, 1978, pp. 1471–1480.

Gittelman-Klein, R., & Klein, D. F. Controlled imipramine treatment of school phobia. *Archives of General Psychiatry*, 1971, *25*, 204–207.

Gittelman-Klein, R., & Klein, D. F. School phobia: Diagnostic considerations in the light of imipramine effects. *Journal of Nervous and Mental Disease*, 1973, *156*, 199–215.

Gittelman-Klein, R., & Klein, D. F. Separation anxiety in school refusal and its treatment with drugs. In L. Hersov & I. Berg (Eds.), *Out of school.* New York: Wiley, 1980, pp. 321–341.

Greenberg, L. M., & Yellin, A. M. Blood pressure and pulse changes of hyperactive children treated with imipramine and methylphenidate. *American Journal of Psychiatry,* 1975, *132,* 1325–1326.

Gualtieri, C. T. Imipramine and children: A review and some speculations about the mechanism of drug action. *Diseases of the Nervous System,* 1977, *38*(Suppl.), 368–374.

Hayes, T. A., Panitch, M. L., & Barker, E. Imipramine dosage in children: A comment on imipramine and electrocardiographic abnormalities in hyperactive children. *American Journal of Psychiatry,* 1975, *132,* 546–547.

Klein, D. F. Delineation of two drug-responsive anxiety syndromes. *Psychopharmacologia,* 1964, *5,* 397–408.

Klein, D. F., Gittelman, R., Quitkin, F., & Rifkin, A. *Diagnosis and drug treatment of psychiatric disorders: Adults and children* (2nd ed.). Baltimore: Williams & Wilkins, 1980.

Lucas, A. R., & Pasley, F. C. Psychoactive drugs in the treatment of emotionally disturbed children: Haloperidol and diazepam. *Comprehensive Psychiatry,* 1969, *10,* 376–386.

Physicians' Desk Reference (38th ed.). Oradell, N.J.: The Medical Economics Company, 1984.

Puig-Antich, J., & Gittelman, R. Depression in childhood and adolescence. In E. S. Paykel (Ed.), *Handbook of affective disorders.* New York: Churchill Livingstone, 1982, pp. 379–392.

Rabiner, C. J., & Klein, D. F. Imipramine treatment of school phobia. *Comprehensive Psychiatry,* 1969, *10,* 387–390.

Rapoport, J., Elkins, R., & Mikkelsen, E. Clinical controlled trial of clomipramine in adolescents with obsessive–compulsive disorder. *Psychopharmacology Bulletin,* 1980, *16,* 61–63.

Rutter, M., & Shaffer, D. DSM III: A step forward or back in terms of the classification of child psychiatric disorders? *Journal of the American Academy of Child Psychiatry,* 1980, *19,* 371–394.

Sheehan, D. V., Coleman, J. H., Greenblatt, D. J., Jones, K. J., Levine, P. H., Orsulak, P. J., Peterson, M., Schildkraut, J. J., Uzogara, E., & Watkins, D. Some biochemical correlates of panic attacks with agoraphobia and their response to a new treatment. *Journal of Clinical Psychopharmacology,* 1984, *4,* 66–75.

Swanson, J., Kinsbourne, M., Roberts, W., & Zucker, K. Time–response analysis of the effect of stimulant medication on the learning ability of children referred for hyperactivity. *Pediatrics,* 1978, *61,* 21–24.

Thoren, P., Asberg, M., Cronholm, B., Jornestedt, H., & Traskman, L. Clomipramine treatment of obsessive–compulsive disorder. I. A controlled clinical trial. *Archives of General Psychiatry,* 1980, *37,* 1281–1285.

Werry, J. S., Methven, J., Fitzpatrick, J., & Dixon, H. The interrater reliability of DSM-III in children. *Journal of Abnormal Child Psychology,* 1983, *2,* 341–354.

‡ 11 ‡

BEHAVIOR THERAPY FOR CHILDHOOD ANXIETY DISORDERS

CARYN L. CARLSON
ROLANDO G. FIGUEROA
BENJAMIN B. LAHEY

INTRODUCTION

A significant body of research now exists on the use of behavior therapy techniques with children's anxiety disorders. In this chapter we review current research, describe illustrative case histories, and draw some tentative conclusions regarding this area of child behavior therapy. First, some comments should be made concerning the decision to treat anxious children and the meaning of "anxiety disorders" in children.

Any discussion of the treatment of anxious children is hampered by the lack of a widely accepted, empirically based definition of childhood anxiety disorders. We will use the term broadly in this chapter. A variety of behavioral approaches to the treatment of children's *fears* and *phobias* will be reviewed and evaluated, including systematic desensitization, flooding and implosion, modeling procedures, reinforced practice, and cognitive approaches. In addition, the behavioral treatment of the related problems of *obsessive–compulsive* disorders, *somatic complaints,* and *social withdrawal* will be discussed briefly. While this broad use of the term anxiety disorders casts an inclusive net as far as treatment research is concerned, no attempt will be made to defend such a broad and heterogeneous grouping.

Caryn L. Carlson. Department of Psychology, Indiana University, Bloomington, Indiana.
Rolando G. Figueroa. Chief of Psychology, Georgia Retardation Center, Athens, Georgia. Benjamin B. Lahey. Department of Psychology, University of Georgia, Athens, Georgia.

Any discussion of the treatment of anxiety disorders in children must also consider the wisdom of such treatment. Any form of treatment carries with it some risk of negative iatrogenic effects, including treatment of anxiety disorders. At least some research suggests that excessive fears may be transient developmental phenomena in children. Different fears tend to be most prevalent at different ages (Miller, Barrett, & Hampe, 1974), and phobias in prepubertal children tend to dissipate within 2–5 years with or without treatment (Agras, Chapin, & Oliveau, 1972; Hampe, Noble, Miller, & Barrett, 1973). In addition, more broadly defined childhood anxiety disorders have been found to be much less persistent over a 2-year period than conduct disorders (Rutter, 1976). Childhood anxiety disorders have also not been found to create a heightened risk for adult disorders.

These findings suggest that, because anxiety disorders in children may not be long lasting, the benefits of treatment may not outweigh the iatrogenic risks. For example, the results of one well-controlled study found that systematic desensitization led to reductions in the intensity of fear that were statistically significant compared to no treatment, but probably not large enough to be clinically significant. In cases involving mild anxiety problems, these findings may lead clinicians to withold treatment. However, this chapter was written because the decision to treat will undoubtedly be made in many more cases. As has often been stated, the desire to reduce the current suffering of children will be considered by many clinicians to be a strong reason to offer treatment (Graziano, DeGiovanni, & Garcia, 1979; Ollendick, 1979). If treatment is to be offered to these children, it is important that it be the most effective form of treatment to improve the risk–benefit ratio.

MAJOR TREATMENT METHODS FOR ANXIETY AND FEARS

In this section research is described concerning the major treatment methods for anxiety and fears in children. These methods include systematic desensitization, flooding, modeling, operant methods, and cognitive procedures. Excellent reviews of behavioral treatment strategies for excessive fears have recently been published (Kratochwill & Morris, 1985; Morris & Kratochwill, 1983, 1985).

SYSTEMATIC DESENSITIZATION

In Wolpe's (1958) formulation of the method of systematic desensitization, the anxiety response is inhibited by pairing the anxiety-producing stimuli with a response that is incompatible with anxiety. Generally, the incompatible response used with children has been relaxation, but other responses have been used successfully.

Relaxation with graduated imagined stimuli has been used to treat tics, stuttering, fear of ambulances and hospitals, anorexia, school phobia, mathematics phobia, reading anxiety, fear of loud noises, test anxiety, and dog phobia (Hatzenbuehler & Schroeder, 1978). For example, Cavior and Deutsch (1975) reported the use of relaxation and imagery in treating a 16-year-old boy suffering from dream-induced anxiety. The client complained of a recurring dream wherein his father kills his mother. When the dream occurred the client would awake agitated and highly anxious, which prevented him from getting any further sleep. Treatment first consisted of teaching the client a standard relaxation procedure and then constructing a hierarchy of the dream in terms of anxiety-producing steps. The steps were as follows: (1) Hears father coming into the house drunk. (2) Mother yells at father for returning home drunk. (3) Father shouts back at her. (4) Mother and father begin to argue. (5) Father hits mother. (6) Mother hits father back. (7) Both parents are fighting. (8) Subject "hears" father pick up knife from kitchen table. (9) Father shouts, "I'll kill you." (10) Mother begins to scream. (11) Subject runs into living room and actually sees parents fighting. (12) Subject sees father with knife at mother's throat, ready to kill her.

The boy was then presented the hierarchy while in a state of relaxation over three sessions and was told to practice the technique twice a day. He was unable to complete the hierarchy on the first session but met with success thereafter. A 6-month follow-up revealed that although the dream was still recurring, it was no longer anxiety producing.

Relaxation has also been used with graduated external stimuli to treat a dog phobia, school phobias, a bee phobia, a water phobia, and a noise phobia (Hatzenbuehler & Schroeder, 1978). Wish, Hasazi, and Jurgela (1973) treated an 11-year-old noise phobic who also suffered from somatic complaints (e.g., headaches and nausea). Although the study is confounded because the author introduced reinforcement into the treatment procedure, it merits attention for its innovative, economical approach. Wish *et al.* "automated" desensitization to allow self-administration. There were three steps in the treatment process: (1) creation of a fear hierarchy, (2) progressive relaxation for the child (Steven), and (3) taping the deconditioning procedure to allow self-administration. The 40-minute tape consisted of Steven's favorite album, which had the feared noises superimposed in order of least to most feared. Treatment consisted of three sessions a day of increasing length over an 8-day period. Additionally, the tape's volume was increased each day. Steven listened to the tape through headphones in a dark room after having relaxed himself. In the event that he should become anxious, Steven was to turn off the music and relax before proceeding. After each completed session Steven was reinforced with praise and a baseball card. By the last session Steven had no problems listening to the most-feared noises. In order to test for generalization, Steven was then exposed to some of the items on his fear hierarchy and withstood each without any problem. A 9-month follow-up revealed that the treatment remained effective.

Other anxiety-antagonistic responses can be used besides relaxation and can then be paired with either imaginal or external anxiety-producing stimuli. Bentler (1962) used an alternative competing response and graduated external stimuli in treating a young child. Margaret was an 11½-month-old with a water phobia who reacted violently when placed in the bathtub (with or without water), near faucets of water anywhere in the house, or in a wading pool Bentler used "distraction, affective responses towards toys, body-contact and other mother-related stimuli" (1962, p. 187) as the anxiety-antagonistic responses. There were four phases of treatment. First, some toys were placed in the bathtub, and Margaret was allowed to enter and leave at will. At this stage she would remove toys from the bathtub but not stay near it. Second, Margaret was placed on a table with toys that was near the kitchen sink, which was filled with water and contained floating toys. Gradually, she and the toys on the table were moved closer to the sink until all toys were in the sink and she had to move toward the water to play with them. The toys were then placed in the other side of the sink on a ledge, forcing Margaret to walk through the water if she wanted to play with them. Eventually, Margaret hesitantly entered the water, and she was ready for the next phase, which consisted of bathing in the bathroom sink when her diaper needed changing. A mirror over the sink served as an effective distractor, and she was soon playing with the water. The fourth phase consisted of washing Margaret in the tub with the water running. She initially objected loudly, but parental physical restraint and reassurance eliminated the protests, and she was soon bathing comfortably. A follow-up conducted at 18 months of age revealed that the improvements had been maintained and that she no longer exhibited fear of water in or near the house.

Since much of the systematic desensitization literature has involved the use of relaxation techniques, it might be useful to discuss two recent adaptations of the adult procedure for use with children. Ollendick and Cerny (1981) discuss Koeppen's (1974) original adaptation and contrast it to a later revision by Ollendick (1978). An example is provided below of how Koeppen (1974) treats the shoulder and neck muscle group:

> Now pretend you are a turtle. You're sitting out on a rock by a nice, peaceful pond, just relaxing in the warm sun. It feels nice and warm and safe here. Oh-oh! You sense danger. Pull your head into your house. Try to pull your shoulders up to your ears and push your head down into your shoulders. Hold in tight. It isn't easy to be a turtle in a shell. The danger is past now. You can come out into the warm sunshine. Watch out now! More danger. Hurry, pull your head back into your house and hold tight. You have to be closed in tight to protect yourself. Okay, you can relax now. Bring your head out and let your shoulders relax. Notice how much better it feels to be relaxed than to be all tight. One more time, now. Danger! Pull your head in. Push your shoulders way up to your ears and hold tight. Don't let even a tiny piece of your head show outside your shell. Hold it. Feel the tenseness in your neck and shoulders. Okay. You can come out not. It's safe again. Relax and feel comfortable in your safety. There's no more danger. Nothing to worry about. Nothing to be afraid of. You feel good. (p. 524)

Ollendick and his colleagues (Ollendick, 1978; Weissman, Ollendick, & Horne, 1978) observed that this type of procedure tended to distract from the process of relaxation, because children get overly involved in the storyline rather than concentrating on the task. They sought to remedy the situation by constructing a script that avoided such vivid and distracting accounts, but maintained the child's attention at the same time. Following is an example of Ollendick's (1978) revised procedure for the same muscle group:

> Try to pull your shoulders up to your ears and push your head down into your shoulders. Hold in tight. Okay, now relax and feel the warmth.

Again, pull your shoulders up to your ears and push your head down into your shoulders. Do it tightly. Okay, you can relax now. Bring your head out and let your shoulders relax. Notice how much better it feels to be relaxed than to be all tight. One more time now. Push your head down and your shoulders way up to your ears. Hold it. Feel the tenseness in your neck and shoulders. Okay. You can relax now and feel comfortable. You feel good. (Ollendick & Cerny, 1981, p. 71)

Both scripts may be found in their entirety in Ollendick and Cerny (1981). As far as the relative efficacy of these two procedures is concerned, the little research conducted thus far suggests that Ollendick's procedure may be more effective with hyperactive and aggressive 6-, 7-, and 8-year-old children (Ollendick, 1978), but does not differ from Koeppen's (1974) procedure when "normal" 6- and 7-year-old children are used. More research is definitely necessary before any conclusions may be drawn. Both Koeppen (1974) and Ollendick (1978) do agree, however, that the procedures are most effective with children when sessions are limited to teaching two or three muscle groups at one time, lasting no longer than 15–20 minutes and conducted at least twice a week.

FLOODING AND IMPLOSIVE THERAPY

Flooding and implosive therapy are similar to desensitization in that all three involve exposure to anxiety-eliciting stimuli. The difference is in the method of presentation. Desensitization requires that anxiety be kept at a minimum while progressing through a hierarchy of increasingly noxious stimuli. Flooding and implosive therapy, on the other hand, expose clients to stimuli that elicit high levels of anxiety and force clients to remain in the situation until the anxiety response is extinguished (cf. Marks, 1975; Stampfl & Levis, 1967). Implosive therapy, as originally proposed by Stampfl and Levis (1967), is based on learning theory but within a psychodynamic framework. Stampfl and Levis maintain that psychodynamic defense mechanisms are the means through which anxiety-producing stimuli are avoided. Thus, defense mechanisms are reinforced and maintained. Implosive therapy consists of selecting certain cues derived from present behavior and psychodynamic themes such as rejection, aggression, dependency, punishment, sexuality, guilt, bodily injury, orality, and anality (Stampfl & Levis, 1967). The client is then asked by the therapist to react to scenes created from the cues with "genuine emotion and affect" (p. 500). The scenes are presented hierarchically in terms of the degree of associated avoidance, and the process is continued until all anxiety reactions have been extinguished.

Flooding (Marks, 1975) is similar to implosive therapy, except that exposure is only to stimuli directly associated with the fear or anxiety rather than to cues based on psychodynamic theory. Exposure is prolonged or repeated to produce intense levels of anxiety until extinction is complete. Caution should be exercised to assure that treatment is not terminated before extinction occurs. There is evidence suggesting that sensitization may result (Baum, 1970; Rachman, 1969) if flooding is stopped prematurely. Sensitization is an increase in the anxiety aroused in the session, which may make subsequent attempts at extinction more difficult.

Ollendick and Gruen (1972) report a case study of flooding using imaginal stimuli. An 8-year-old boy had developed fears of injurying himself, fear of sleeping in the dark, and fears of certain loud noises, insects, and "monster" movies. It was explained to the parents that once treatment was implemented the condition would initially worsen but their cooperation was crucial for its success. Although reluctant, the parents agreed to the procedure. Ollendick and Gruen used the following images as cues:

1. You are alone walking through a forest going to a lake to fish, and you hear weird noises and see strange things.
2. The wind begins blowing very hard, and you trip and hit your head on a rock.
3. When you get up, blood trickles down your forehead into your eyes, nose, and mouth.
4. You feel dizzy and lost. You cry, and no one is there to help you. You feel all alone, and the blood continues to trickle.
5. You fall down again, and when you open your eyes you see brown hairy rats all around you. There are hundreds of them, and they are coming after you . . . to eat you.
6. They begin nibbling at your feet, biting your toes, and pulling them off. They are scratching and showing their teeth. It is getting very dark now, and it is raining.
7. Now they are over your whole body, running across it and biting you all over. Blood runs from all parts of your body; you hear the thunder, and there is lightning.
8. They pierce your neck. You wish someone would come, even an ambulance; but it doesn't. You scream and a big hairy rat jumps in your mouth. You feel him biting your tongue and scratching you.

9. Finally, the rats that feed on your blood grow and become man-size. They tear off your arms and just keep attacking you. They tear out your eyes, and you can't get away from them. (1972, p. 391)

The script initially resulted in extreme levels of anxiety in the child. He screamed, cried, covered his ears, trembled, and attempted to leave the therapy room. The two sessions (2 hours and 1½ hours in length) resulted in physical and emotional exhaustion for the boy. The boy's fears were greatly reduced after the second session, however, and the parents and therapist reinforced the continued improvements. Six months later the child no longer exhibited the fears. Imaginal flooding was also used by Smith and Sharpe (1970) to treat a 13-year-old school phobic boy.

Sreenivasan, Manocha, and Jain (1979) treated a severely dog phobic 11-year-old girl with flooding utilizing *in vivo* stimuli after desensitization failed to eliminate the fear. No problems arose in learning relaxation procedures during desensitization or in dealing with an imaginal hierarchy as long as live dogs were not introduced. At this stage the parents brought home a puppy, which only worsened the child's condition to the point that hospitalization was required. Flooding consisted of six 1-hour sessions over a 10-day period and was conducted in a trailer (used for play activities) located near the ward. A "passive and friendly" cocker spaniel was used as the flooding stimulus. Sreenivasan *et al.* give the following account of therapy:

> For the first session, Colleen was apprehensive for several hours before. On arrival in the treatment room she was anxiously scanning the area for the dog. When the dog was led in she froze, visibly paled and her pupils were dilated. Staff talked reassuringly to Colleen, but when the dog was freed she jumped on a chair. She cried and pleaded that the dog should be placed on its leash. Gradually she relaxed slightly but stayed on the chair, becoming anxious and retreating if the dog moved towards the chair. Two of the staff played table tennis and tried unsuccessfully to persuade Colleen to join them. In the second session she was equally anxious but would get down from the chair or table she stood on for a few seconds but was never at ease. Prior to the third session Colleen appeared excited, although she expressed fear and dislike of the sessions. She managed to take part in the table tennis game for brief periods, sitting on the table if the dog ambled towards the table. In the fourth session she could pat the dog if it was not facing her. In the sixth session she tolerated the dog in her lap, and then took the dog for a walk holding the leash to the amazement of her parents who happened to arrive. After this, she was able to take the family pet for a walk and then

to go for a drive with the puppy in the car. She spent a weekend at home
without the puppy having to be isolated and was discharged from the
inpatient unit at the end of May, 1977, 7 weeks after admission. (1971,
p. 256)

Follow-up observations at 1, 3, 6, and 14 months after flooding
revealed no further fears of dogs and subsequent improvements in
social relationships and academic performance. Flooding has also been
employed by Yule, Sacks, and Hersov (1974) in the treatment of an 11-
year-old boy who was fearful of loud noises, and Kennedy's (1965)
treatment of school phobia incorporates aspects of flooding.

Before conducting flooding or implosive therapy, great care
should be taken to assure that the welfare of the client is protected.
Toward this end the child and the parents need to be aware of the
procedure and the attendant discomforts involved for both. Full
parental cooperation in treatment is necessary for success, because it is
they who have often maintained the phobia by reinforcing the child's
avoidance behavior (e.g., by allowing the child to sleep with them).
Parents are asked to discontinue this practice to allow the child's fears
to extinguish and are instead instructed to reinforce nonphobic
reactions to the feared stimuli.

It should be additionally noted that, like other methods of
behavior therapy, there has not been an adequate systematic approach
utilizing controlled research, leading investigators like Graziano
(1978), Ollendick (1979), and Ollendick and Cerny (1981) to caution
against indiscriminate use of these procedures. Barrios, Hartmann,
and Shigetomi (1981) address the ethical considerations of such
techniques and the practical difficulties associated with them. At this
stage then, flooding and implosive therapy clearly have not been
convincingly demonstrated to be effective for children and are most
appropriately utilized when other therapy methods have failed to
produce results.

MODELING

Different types of modeling have been distinguished and are most
commonly referred to as symbolic (models on film or videotape), live
(or vicarious) models, and participant modeling (sometimes called
"contact desensitization"). In terms of efficacy of treatment, Ollendick

and Cerny (1981) point out that participant modeling appears most effective, followed by live modeling, and then symbolic modeling. However, the Graziano *et al.* (1979) review of research on the therapeutic effectiveness of modeling suggests that conclusions in this area are still to be regarded as tentative.

Symbolic modeling has the advantage of assuring that the model and phobic object will behave appropriately and consistently (Ross, 1981). The latter is particularly important in research, where it is crucial to minimize method variance. It would also be quite detrimental to the therapeutic process, however, to have the model react adversely to the phobic stimulus (e.g., a child who is serving as a model is startled by a sudden movement of a snake serving as the feared stimulus). The use of film or videotape would eliminate this problem. Unfortunately, not all therapists have access to this kind of equipment, and as has already been mentioned, this appears to be the least effective variant of modeling.

Nevertheless, in a well-controlled study, Melamed and Siegel (1975) used symbolic modeling on 60 children admitted to a pediatric hospital for surgery to reduce fears about the impending surgery. The children were divided into experimental and control groups, having been matched on demographic variables and type of operation. Prior to surgery the experimental group watched a 16-minute film of a 7-year-old who had undergone the same procedure. The control groups were shown a film of a boy on a nature outing. The results indicated that the modeling group displayed significantly less sweat gland activity, self-reported medical fears, and anxiety-related behavior than the control (nature film) group. The same results were obtained immediately postoperation and at a 1-month follow-up.

In live modeling children do not participate in any action associated with the feared stimulus, but rather watch as a "live" model interacts with the feared object. Bandura, Grusec, and Menlove (1967) investigated the effect of live modeling on nursery school children who were afraid of dogs. Forty-eight 3- to 5-year-old children were divided into four equally fearful groups. There were two modeling groups and two control groups. One of the modeling groups consisted of modeling approach behavior within the context of a party (modeling in a positive context); the party was omitted for the other modeling group (modeling in a neutral context). For the control groups there was a party and a dog in one condition but no modeled approach (exposure in a positive context); for the other control group there was a party, but no dog (positive context). Eight treatment sessions lasting 10 minutes each were conducted over a period of 4 days. The models approached the dog in a preestablished graduated sequence (i.e., the extent to which the dog was restrained, proximity and "directness" of the approach, and time spent touching the dog were conducted in graduated sequence). A 1-month follow-up and a generalization test utilizing another dog were conducted, and the results revealed that the two modeling conditions were significantly more effective in reducing the fear of dogs (as measured by the children's willingness to approach the dogs) than the control procedures.

Participant modeling can be viewed as a modeling package (Graziano *et al.,* 1979). First, the child watches a model go through a graded approach sequence. Then, with gentle physical and verbal assistance and reinforcement, the model leads the child through the same response. The last step involves having the child perform the responses without the assistance of the model. The procedure is sometimes referred to as "contact desensitization."

Ritter (1968) compared participant modeling to live modeling in treating 44 children who were fearful of snakes. The children were randomly assigned to either live modeling (children watched five peer and one adult model touching and holding snakes), participant modeling (the children not only watched the five peers and one adult, but also held the snake with the assistance of the model and lastly, held it without assistance), or a control group (that was seen only for assessment pre- and posttreatment). A posttreatment assessment revealed that 80% of the participant modeling group succeeded in performing all items on the avoidance test, whereas only 37% succeeded in the live modeling group and none in the control group. Self-reported fears also decreased for the participant and live modeling groups. Lewis (1974) addressed the issue of which component in participant modeling accounted for the treatment effect by comparing participant modeling (participation plus modeling) with modeling (symbolic) alone, participation alone, and a control (a neutral movie and games with the adults). The participant modeling group showed the greatest improvement, and all three treatment conditions evidenced less fear than the controls.

Before deciding which type of modeling to use, a therapist needs to consider the two currently most suggestive findings relevant to reduction of anxiety in children. First, the effect of modeling is apparently enhanced when it is paired with direct exposure to the phobic stimulus (such as in participant modeling) (Graziano *et al.*, 1979). In addition, the therapist must consider the characteristics of the model. Meichenbaum (1971) has compared the relative effectiveness of coping and mastery models. A coping model is one that displays initial apprehension about the aversive stimulus but gradually learns to "cope" with it until the stimulus is handled fearlessly and confidently. A mastery mode, on the other hand, is fearless and confident from the outset. Meichenbaum found both models more effective than a control group. He also found the coping model to be more effective than the mastery model; others (e.g., Kornhaber & Shroeder, 1975), however, have found the opposite. Still other investigators utilizing coping models have found them to be effective, but have not included a mastery model with which to compare (e.g., Melamed, Hawes, Heiby, & Glick, 1975; Melamed & Siegel, 1975). Additionally, Bandura and Menlove (1968) found evidence suggesting that multiple models are slightly more effective than a single model, at least in symbolic presentation. In the same investigation Bandura and Menlove also contrasted a live and symbolic model and found the live model to be clearly superior.

Two further considerations are necessary for full understanding of the current state of research on modeling. First, most of this research has been conducted on nonclinically referred populations, and the efficacy of these procedures may be impaired if the level of anxiety is so high that the child cannot attend to the models (Bandura & Menlove, 1968; Graziano *et al.*, 1979). Second, Graziano *et al.* (1979) have also pointed out the need for documentation in the areas of generalizability and maintenance of the modeled behavior. Although substantive conclusions are clearly pending, modeling appears to be a reasonably viable alternative in the treatment of fears in children (Ollendick & Cerny, 1981).

REINFORCED PRACTICE

In reinforced practice (Leitenberg & Callahan, 1973; Leitenberg, 1976), the avoidance response exhibited by fearful children is treated through reinforcement of graduated approach responses to the feared object. Leitenberg (1976) distinguishes four components of reinforced practice: (1) graduated *in vivo* practice in approaching the phobic stimulus, (2) reinforcement for improved performance, (3) trial-by-trial feedback on performance, and (4) communication to the client of the therapist's expectations of gradual success. The effectiveness of reinforced practice was evaluated by Leitenberg and Callahan (1973) with seven preschool children displaying fears of the dark. The children, along with seven control children who received no treatment, were recruited from nursery schools and kindergartens on the basis of parent report and the child's willingness to remain alone in a dark room. At pretest the mean time the 14 children were willing to remain alone in a dark room was 22 seconds; children were matched on this pretest time and then randomly assigned to treatment or control conditions.

The children in the treatment group were seen individually twice weekly for a maximum of eight sessions. Treatment was terminated when a child was willing to remain in the dark room for 5 minutes on two consecutive trials. Therapists instructed children in the treatment group to enter the dark room, stay until they felt "the least bit afraid," and then come out. Children were told that for each trial during which they remained in the room longer than they had on the previous trial, they would be able to choose a prize from among a selection of candy. Social reinforcement in the form of praise was also provided by the therapist for improved performances. Feedback was provided to the children in the form of a "thermometer" drawn on a piece of paper which was progressively shaded according to the child's progress.

At posttest the treatment group was willing to remain in the dark room for a mean of 199 seconds, while the control group was willing to remain for a mean of only 28 seconds. Of the seven children in the treatment group, four stayed in the dark room for the maximum of 5 minutes.

As other authors have suggested (Graziano, DeGiovanni, & Garcia, 1979; Ollendick, 1979), the results of the Leitenberg and Callahan (1973) study need to be interpreted cautiously in light of the small number of subjects and the possibility that they were only mildly fearful, the questionable clinical significance of the outcome measure, and the relative ineffectiveness of the treatment for three of the seven children. However, the study does represent a well-designed, systematic attempt at investigating the use of reinforced practice with children.

Several studies have also utilized reinforced practice as one component of a treatment program with fearful children. For example, a 4-year-old child's water phobia was treated with a combination of reinforced practice, *in vivo* desensitization, and participant modeling (Pomerantz, Peterson, Marholin, & Stern, 1977). A hierarchy of items related to taking a bath was constructed, and the child's mother offered a glass of cola to the child upon entering the bathroom and delivered a verbal reinforcement and physical affection upon successful attempts at items on the hierarchy. Prior to treatment the child's fear of water had resulted in the mother's forcefully bathing him once every 10 days. After 11 30-minute sessions, the anxiety associated with bathing was no longer observed, and in a 6-month follow-up evaluation, he was taking four baths per week with no fear of the bath water reported.

Other reinforcement procedures have also been components in the treatment of night fears of sufficient severity to be referred for treatment (Kellerman, 1980), an autistic child with extreme fear of riding a school bus (Luiselli, 1978), a noise phobic child (Tasto, 1969), and a car phobic child (Lazarus, 1960). Despite the apparent promise of reinforcement procedures in treating fearful children, there are surprisingly few published studies existing that adequately assess the usefulness of these procedures in reducing children's fears. Although several researchers treating fearful children have utilized procedures with operant components, it is impossible to separate the effects of these operant components from the effects of other components of the treatment strategies. As several reviewers have indicated (Graziano *et al.*, 1979; Ollendick, 1979), there is presently little research of sufficient experimental rigor to determine the effectiveness of reinforced practice in treating children's fears.

COGNITIVE PROCEDURES

The most frequently cited study supporting the use of cognitive strategies with fearful children was conducted by Kanfer, Karoly, and Newman (1975). Forty-five kindergarten children, selected on the basis of their inability to remain alone in a darkened room for 3 minutes, were assigned to one of two treatment conditions or a control condition. The groups were balanced for sex and scores on the pretreatment dark-tolerance measure. The children rehearsed one of three types of verbal self-statements: (1) competence-related statements (e.g., "I am a brave boy/girl. I can take care of myself in the dark."); (2) stimulus-related statements (e.g., "The dark is a fun place to be. There are many good things about the dark."); or (3) neutral statements (e.g., "Mary had a little lamb. It's fleece was white as snow."). Following mastery of the self-statements, each child remained alone in a lighted room for two trials, during which recorded statements were played elaborating on the content of the sentences the child had learned. The children were instructed to repeat their words following each recorded statement. At posttest both treatment groups significantly outperformed the control group on dark-tolerance measures, with the competence group exhibiting greater tolerance than the stimulus group on some measures.

Ross (1981) discussed several difficulties in interpreting the results of the Kanfer *et al.* (1975) study. Since the children had access to the light source at all times, it is possible that simply having control over the source of one's fear may help one tolerate the situation. In addition, the outcome measure did not assess what effect, if any, the treatment may have had on the child's tolerance of the dark in a more natural setting. Also, the sample was not representative of children exhibiting fears of clinical significance.

Nelson (1981) used a cognitive–behavioral approach in the assessment and treatment of a child's dental phobia. An 11-year-old girl was referred for therapy following a dental appointment in which her crying, screaming, and attempting to leave had prevented the dentist from accomplishing any dental work. An imagery technique was utilized during assessment in which the subject closed her eyes and visualized herself during her recent unsuccessful dental visit. The therapist then asked her to describe her thoughts, feelings, images and behavior during specific intervals, which previous research has found to be critical for dental patients. The results of the assessment, which suggested that the subject's self-statements and images were contributing to the high level of anxiety and avoidant behavior displayed in dental situations, were used to design an individually tailored "stress inoculation" program.

Treatment focused on teaching the client a series of self-statements to help her cope with three specific aspects of the dental visits: (1) preparing for dental visits (e.g., "worrying won't help anything"); (2) confronting a stress and/or pain (e.g., "remember what the dentist said and it will be over a lot quicker"); and, (3) coping with stress and/or pain at critical moments (e.g., "just cool it and relax"). The subject was also taught positive self-statements, such as "I did it" and "Seeing the dentist was a snap!," with which to reinforce herself following the successful completion of the cognitive strategies.

The series of self-statements was taught to the client in a four-step process using procedures similar to those discussed by Meichenbaum (1975) and Meichenbaum and Turk (1976). First, the therapist modeled the appropriate coping statements (cognitive modeling). Second, the subject verbalized the same coping statements under the therapist's guidance (external guidance). Third, the subject verbalized the statements by herself (overt self-guidance). Finally, the subject role played the scenes while verbalizing the statements to herself (covert self-guidance). In addition to rehearsing the self-statements, the subject was instructed to breathe deeply and slowly when she became aware of her typical rapid breathing, and she was taught a distraction technique of counting to 20 while visualizing the numbers when she felt overwhelmed by fear or pain. The treatment program was conducted over two 60-minute treatment sessions and two 15-minute booster sessions.

A series of four dental treatment sessions had been scheduled for the subject. The dentist rated her "in-chair" behavior for each visit as well as for the initial unsuccessful visit, and the subject was administered the State–Trait Anxiety Inventory for Children (STAIC) (Spielberger, Edwards, Lushene, Montouri, & Platzek, 1973) prior to and following each visit. The behavior ratings showed a clear decrease in disruptive behaviors from the initial visit to subsequent visits. Despite some fluctuations the self-report measure also reflected improvements in subjective anxiety levels following treatment. As the author notes, the administration of a mild analgesic during the second visit possibly contributed to the positive therapeutic outcome; nonetheless, the Nelson (1981) report supports the use of cognitive procedures with children displaying phobias of clinical severity. In addition, it illustrates the use of cognitively based assessment procedures to design an individualized treatment package that focuses on the specific self-defeating statements displayed by the client.

Another technique for treating children's fears, which will be discussed here as a cognitive therapy, is emotive imagery (Lazarus & Abramovitz, 1962). Emotive imagery involves teaching children to focus on cognitive images that inhibit anxiety. Typically, fictional characters or events have been employed as the imagery material in emotive imagery. This technique has been used successfully with children to treat fears of the dark, dogs, and school attendance (Lazarus

& Abramovitz, 1962). The use of emotive imagery to treat a 5½-year-old boy's fear of the dark is illustrated in a case study reported by Jackson and King (1981).

Jackson and King (1981) describe the treatment of a child whose home had been broken into by a prowler approximately 1 month prior to his referral for fears of the dark, noises, and shadows that were causing him sleepless nights. In addition to emotive imagery, a "response induction aid" of a flashlight placed by the subject's bedside table at night was utilized. The child was allowed to turn the flashlight on at night briefly if he became afraid, although he was instructed not to leave it on for extended periods of time. For the emotive imagery segment of treatment, which was implemented following the child's inability to relax during systematic desensitization, a 19-item hierarchy of situations related to bedtime was constructed. Batman, a favorite character of the child's, was employed during the procedure as an anxiety-inhibiting agent. The procedure Jackson and King utilized is illustrated by the following excerpt:

> Close your eyes—now I want you to imagine that you are sitting in the lounge room watching TV with your family. You're dressed for bed and the last program before bedtime has finished. Your mother tells you it's time for bed but just then Batman, who you really wish you knew, appears out of nowhere and sits down next to you. Think about it as best you can. Can you see Batman in your head?
> Yes.
> Can you tell me what Batman's wearing? What color are his clothes?
> He's got black and red clothes and big shoes and a gun.
> Oh, you can see him with a gun?
> Yeah, he needs it for the Joker.
> That's terrific M. Now I want you to imagine that Batman tells you he needs you on his missions to catch robbers and other bad people and he's appointed you as his special agent. However, he needs you to get your sleep in your bedroom and he will call on you when he needs you. You're lucky to have been chosen to help him.
> Yes.
> Now, your mother puts you in your bed and leaves both the lights on and leaves the three blinds up. Batman is also there looking as strong as he always does. Think about it as clearly as you can. Can you see it?
> Yes, I can see mummy and Batman in my room and all the lights are on.
> Well, if you're scared raise your finger.... (1981, p. 327)

Although the authors utilized a design consisting of a baseline phase followed by four treatment phases alternating between the flashlight with emotive imagery and emotive imagery alone, it is difficult to separate the effects of the two techniques, since the hierarchy was not completed until the final emotive imagery session. At the completion of treatment, which took place over approximately 1½ months, no fear episodes were reported, and the child slept soundly through the night, as contrasted with the 10-day baseline prior to treatment during which the child experienced fear episodes every night. Follow-up evaluation 18 months after the end of treatment indicated that treatment gains had been maintained.

Graziano and Mooney (1980) published an evaluation of a cognitive procedure that is perhaps the most methodologically adequate experiment on fear reduction in children yet published, but because the treatment also involved muscle relaxation and self-reinforcement, it is not clear how much of the treatment gains can be attributed to the cognitive components. Graziano and Mooney (1980) recruited 17 children with serious fears of going to bed alone in the dark and taught them to relax their muscles in bed, self-reinforce their efforts with praise and tokens, imagine a pleasant scene, and recite brave self-statements. These children were compared on several parent-recorded measures of fear behavior to an untreated control group of 16 children with similar fears. Significant differences between the groups were found after treatment that were of a magnitude that appeared to be clinically significant. These gains were maintained during 2-, 6-, and 12-month follow-up evaluations; a 2½- to 3-year follow-up evaluation (Graziano & Mooney, 1982) of treated children from this and a previous study (Graziano, Mooney, Huber, & Ignasiak, 1979) showed maintenance of gains in 31 out of 34 children.

As other authors have pointed out (Ross, 1981; Graziano et al., 1979), there is not enough evidence at the present time to conclusively determine the effectiveness of cognitive procedures in treating fearful children. Further research in this area seems warranted in light of the promising findings discussed above, however (Graziano & Mooney, 1980).

TREATMENT OF RELATED PROBLEMS

A number of maladaptive patterns of behavior have been associated with anxiety disorders. In this section treatment methods are briefly

described for obsessive thoughts, compulsive behavior, social withdrawal, and somatic complaints.

OBSESSIVE–COMPULSIVE DISORDERS

Although a variety of behavioral interventions have been utilized with
adults displaying obsessive–compulsive disorders, including systematic desensitization, modeling, exposure, punishment, thought-
stopping, and response prevention, there have been few published
reports describing the behavioral treatment of obsessive–compulsive
disorders in children. It seems likely that this lack of research is at least
partially due to the rarity of the disorder in childhood, which has been
found to occur in 2% or less of child psychiatric populations (Judd,
1965; Hollingsworth, Tanquay, Grossman, & Pabst, 1980). Unlike
phobic children, the prognosis for children displaying obsessive–
compulsive disorders is poor, with follow-up studies suggesting that a
majority of these children continue to suffer from obsessive–compulsive problems and report problems with peer relationships over long
periods of time (Hollingsworth *et al.,* 1980).

Response prevention has been among the most successful
behavioral treatments utilized in treating obsessive–compulsive
children. Utilizing a controlled single-case design, Mills, Agras, Barlow
and Mills (1973) describe the treatment of ritualistic behaviors in a
15-year-old boy through response prevention. The subject performed a
set of complex, time-consuming rituals both at bedtime and upon
waking in the morning. The night rituals consisted of behaviors such
as repeatedly checking pillow placement and folding pajamas before
putting them on, and the morning rituals consisted of behaviors such
as laying out clothing in a particular manner and dressing in a rigid
order. Eight elements of each ritual were chosen for observation.

Following a 12-day baseline, response prevention was implemented for the night rituals only. The subject was instructed to stop
performing the night rituals and told that a nurse would remain with
him in the room to ensure that he did. In addition to the immediate
reduction of night rituals to zero, the morning rituals, which were
monitored via a television camera, showed an immediate reduction and
continued to decline throughout the 10-day treatment phase. This
reduction of morning rituals occurred despite the instructions given to
the client that the experimenters did not want to disturb his morning

routine. The possibility of reactive effects due to the presence of the nurse or television camera were controlled by introducing both of these elements during part of the initial baseline phase.

Following treatment the nurse was removed from the subject's room, and he was told that he could perform the rituals if he had the urge to do so. During this return to baseline there were no further occurrences of either night or morning rituals.

The subject was ritual free during the 2 months following his release from the hospital; at this time he developed another set of rituals associated with bathing. Although initial attempts to treat the new set of rituals in the home through the mother only were unsuccessful, a response prevention program in which both parents participated resulted in the elimination of 80% of the target rituals and the reduction of the remaining 20% to an acceptable level.

Stanley (1980) also reported the use of response prevention to treat a complex set of rituals exhibited by an 8-year-old girl. The rituals, which included activities such as fluffing her pillow three times before undressing at night, going to the toilet three times before going to bed, and singing a specific nursery rhyme prior to carrying out the ritual behaviors, had resulted in disruptions of her daily activities. Treatment involved working with the family to ensure that the client engage in the ritual behaviors only once at any given time and then subjecting her to graded situations of increasingly higher "upset" value in which she was prevented from carrying out the rituals. Response prevention resulted in disappearance of the rituals within 2 weeks, with no recurrences reported during a 1-year follow-up.

Several researchers have also reported case studies in which operant procedures were utilized in treatment of obsessive–compulsive behaviors in children. Phillips and Wolpe (1981) treated a 12-year-old boy who displayed severe separation anxiety in addition to obsessive–compulsive behaviors. Baseline counts showed that the subject engaged in a high frequency of ritualistic behavior daily, including kicking objects as he passed them, waving his head, waving his arms, repeating behaviors in sets of threes, and making multiple phone calls to his father in a repetitive fashion. The subject was told to use muscle relaxation, which he had been taught earlier in treatment during the *in vivo* desensitization of fears related to leaving his parents, as a substitute for performing the rituals. He was also asked to self-monitor the occurrence of rituals each day and was able to earn rewards contingent upon gradual reductions in ritual performance. After 2 months of treatment, the frequency of head waving had been reduced to zero. Although the authors do not report the time required to treat the total repertoire of rituals, all rituals had ceased by the end of treatment. In a 2-year follow-up evaluation, it was reported that the subject had maintained treatment gains, although no specific mention was made of the ritual behaviors.

In addition to providing positive reinforcement for the absence of ritualistic behaviors, some researchers have used extinction, response cost (Hallam, 1974), or punishment (Harbin, 1979) to treat obsessive–compulsive behaviors in children. Hallam (1974) describes the inpatient treatment of a 15-year-old girl displaying a variety of maladaptive behaviors including social skills deficits, excessive ruminations, washing rituals, and persistent questioning concerning her personal appearance, the truth of factual statements, the implications of supposedly unkind remarks, and so on. Following a social skills training phase, treatment was implemented to extinguish the subject's questioning through withdrawal of reassurances. Since a high degree of environmental control was required, the subject was isolated in her room, and personnel were instructed to respond to her questions by saying, "I can't answer that," or "That is a ritual question."

After 2 weeks of treatment it was decided that changes in the program were needed, since the subject could not be kept voluntarily in her room and responded to the personnel's handling of her questions by asking whether they would answer her next question or whether her question was a ritual question. The subject was transferred to a locked section of the ward and personnel were instructed to say nothing, look away, and attempt to redirect the conversation when the subject began questioning. In the first session of the revised treatment program, the subject displayed extreme agitation, demanding answers to her questions, tugging at the therapist's arm, and threatening to cut her wrists if the questions were not answered. Hallam (1974) reports that subsequently her distress lessened, although she still displayed intense anxiety during the first few days. No baseline data were reported, and daily frequency counts of ritual questions were not recorded until the 2nd day of the revised treatment program. Nonetheless, following 1 week of treatment, questioning had been substantially reduced from an estimated frequency of between 50 and 100 on the 1st day to 17 on the 7th day.

As a means of speeding the subject's progress, a response-cost procedure was implemented whereby her free time (the subject received 1 hour of time each evening to socialize and watch television) was reduced by 1 minute for each ritualistic question asked. From the 14th day of treatment to the end of data recording on day 37, the frequency of ritual questioning ranged from 1 to 5 questions per day. The author reports improved general functioning in the subject, who was discharged 5 months following treatment. In a 14-month follow-up assessment, questioning was no longer present, although some ruminations and washing rituals persisted. Hallam (1974) hypothesized that obsessive questioning was reinforced by tension reduction, and the author thus attributed the success of the program to the withdrawal of reassurances, which functioned to extinguish the negatively reinforced habit. It is difficult to evaluate the relative effectiveness of the response-cost procedure, since a downward trend in the frequency of questioning could have resulted simply from the extinction procedure.

It is obvious that more research is needed before any empirically based recommendations for treating obsessive–compulsive children can be made. In a thorough review of the literature regarding the treatment of obsessive–compulsive disorders in adults, Rachman and Hodgson (1980) conclude that a treatment program combining the elements of exposure to the provoking stimuli along with response prevention offers the most powerful and reliable method of achieving success. Since response prevention has also been effective in case studies involving obsessive–compulsive children (Mills *et al.*, 1973; Stanley, 1980), this procedure would seem to be the treatment of choice at the present time.

SOMATIC COMPLAINTS

Although there appear to be a number of psychologically based somatic disorders in children (Finch, 1972; Verville, 1967) this discussion is limited to the minor complaints such as headaches and stomachaches that are common in anxious children. The anxiety and somatic complaints often appear to be functionally related, at least in response to treatment. In some cases it has been found that successful treatment of fear also eliminated somatic complaints. For example, the child mentioned in the Wish *et al.* (1973) case study of noise phobia complained of severe headaches, nausea, and other somatic symptoms whenever he became frightened. These complaints disappeared after treatment for a noise phobia was successfully completed.

In other cases the somatic complaints will need to be the direct focus of treatment. Yen and McIntire (1971) report treating a 14-year-old girl whose headaches resulted in immediate attention from her foster mother (possible positive reinforcement or secondary gain). A medical evaluation had revealed no organic cause, thus a behavioral intervention was implemented. The authors simply required that an "inconvenient consequence" accompany the headache complaints. This was accomplished by having the girl maintain a journal. Entries were to be recorded as soon as she had a headache and consisted of (1) noting the time of the occurrence and (2) what she did as a consequence. She was later asked to write down (3) what she thought caused it and (4) what activities she might engage in it if were not for the headache. The mother was asked not to provide any attention or medication until the child complied with the record-keeping requirements. Headache complaints were dramatically reduced when treatment was implemented and maintained. Follow-up evaluations revealed virtually no headaches.

In many cases the somatic complaints may be accompanied by a vague generalized anxiety that is difficult to treat. In our clinic cases are often referred by physicians because of prominent somatic complaints that are accompanied by ill-defined ancillary characteristics of anxiety disorders. In these cases treatment consists of attempting to identify and eliminate sources of stress (e.g., parental conflict, threats from bullies, etc.), to eliminate positive reinforcement for the complaints, and to provide relaxation training to reduce general arousal. For example, an 11-year-old boy was referred by a physician for recurrent headaches. Relaxation training was moderately successful in eliminating the frequency of headaches, but they were completely eliminated when a possible source of stress was removed (a teacher changed his rule of paddling children for not turning in homework), and the parents no longer allowed the boy to change his routine (e.g., miss school or scout meetings) because of headaches. The reduction of headaches was accompanied by a reduction in general anxiety.

SOCIAL WITHDRAWAL

Social withdrawal, characterized by shyness and disrupted peer relationships, is classified by some authors as a subset of children's anxiety disorders. The DSM-III (American Psychiatric Association,

1980) includes social withdrawal, labeled "Avoidant Disorders of Childhood or Adolescence," as one of three categories of the subclass "Anxiety Disorders of Childhood or Adolescence." Researchers have typically incorporated modeling and operant reinforcement techniques in social skills training programs for treating socially withdrawn children. A number of researchers have conducted well-controlled research in the area of social skills training with children, but a review of the extensive literature on these techniques is beyond the scope of this chapter. For a discussion of behavioral interventions with socially withdrawn children, the reader is referred to Ollendick and Cerny (1981) and Asher and Renshaw (1981).

CONCLUSION

Researchers utilizing a variety of behavioral techniques have apparently successfully treated childhood fears and phobias. Nonetheless, the lack of controlled experimentation, particularly with children exhibiting phobias of clinical significance, prohibits any empirically based conclusions regarding the effectiveness of behavioral interventions or the superiority of one treatment over another. Drawing inferences from case studies or group studies that do not employ a control group seems particularly dangerous in research regarding children's phobias, in light of findings suggesting that many childhood fears are transient (e.g., Hampe et al., 1973; Hagman, 1932).

Ollendick (1979) notes that many of the techniques used to treat children's phobias, such as desensitization, modeling, and reinforced practice, contain the common element of graduated exposure to the feared object to promote maximal fear reduction. He recommends a comprehensive treatment program for treating children's fears that involves graduated exposure along with the following elements: (1) counter-conditioning, (2) participant modeling, and (3) reinforcement for approach behaviors. While acknowledging the possible over-inclusivity of his proposed treatment program, Ollendick (1979) suggests that it is necessary to first demonstrate conclusively that behavior therapy with childhood phobias *works*. Later research efforts could then be directed at isolating the active components of the treatment "packages" and developing the most *efficient* treatment strategies.

Given the current state of knowledge, Ollendick's conservative strategy is probably the correct one. After reviewing the behavioral literature addressing the treatment of children's fears and phobias, it is apparent that we still cannot answer the crucial questions for clinical research: "What treatment, by whom, is most effective for a particular individual with a specific problem, under what set of circumstances, and how does it come about?" (Paul, 1969, p. 44). Even less is known about the treatment of obsessions, compulsions and somatic complaints, and virtually nothing is known about the treatment of generalized anxiety in children. Much is needed in the way of clinical research in this entire area of child behavior therapy.

REFERENCES

Agras, W. S., Chapin, H. N., & Oliveau, D. C. The natural history of phobias: Course and prognosis. *Archives of General Psychiatry*, 1972, *26*, 315–317.

American Psychiatric Association. *Diagnostic and statistical manual of mental disorders* (3rd ed.). Washington, D.C.: Author, 1980.

Asher, S. R., & Renshaw, P. D. Children without friends: Social knowledge and social skill training. In S. R. Asher & J. M. Gottman (Eds.), *The development of children's friendships*. New York: Cambridge University Press, 1981.

Bandura, A., Grusec, J. E., & Menlove, F. L. Vicarious extinction of avoidance behavior. *Journal of Personality and Social Psychology*, 1967, *5*, 16–23.

Bandura, A., & Menlove, F. Factors determining vicarious extinction of avoidance behavior through symbolic modeling. *Journal of Personality and Social Psychology*, 1968, *8*, 99–108.

Barrios, B. A., Hartmann, D. P., & Shigetomi, C. Fears and anxieties in children. In E. J. Mash & L. G. Terdal (Eds.), *Behavioral assessment of childhood disorders*. New York: Guilford, 1981.

Baum, M. Extinction of avoidance responding through response prevention (flooding). *Psychological Bulletin*, 1970, *74*, 276–284.

Bentler, P. M. An infant's phobia treated with reciprocal inhibition therapy. *Journal of Child Psychology and Psychiatry*, 1962, *3*, 185–189.

Cavior, N., & Deutsch, A. Systematic desensitization to reduce dream-induced anxiety. *Journal of Nervous and Mental Disease*, 1975, *161*, 433–435.

Finch, S. M. Psychophysiological disorders of children. In A. M. Freedman & H. I. Kaplan (Eds.), *The child: His psychological and cultural development* (Vol. 2). New York: Atheneum, 1972.

Graziano, A. M. Reduction of children's fears. In A. M. Graziano (Ed.), *Behavior therapy with children* (Vol. 2). Chicago: Aldine, 1975.

Graziano, A. M. Behavior therapy. In B. B. Wolman, J. Egan, & A. O. Ross (Eds.), *Handbook of treatment of mental disorders in childhood and adolescence*. Englewood Cliffs, N.J.: Prentice-Hall, 1978.

Graziano, A. M., DeGiovanni, I., & Garcia, K. Behavioral treatment of child's fear. *Psychological Bulletin*, 1979, *56*, 804–830.

Graziano, A. M., & Mooney, K. C. Family self-control instruction for children's nighttime fear reduction. *Journal of Consulting and Clinical Psychology*, 1980, *48*, 206–213.

Graziano, A. M., & Mooney, K. C. Behavioral treatment of "nightfears" in children: Maintenance of improvement at 2½- to 3-year follow-up. *Journal of Consulting and Clinical Psychology*, 1982, *50*, 598–599.

Graziano, A. M., Mooney, K. C., Huber, C., & Ignasiak, D. Self-control instruction. *Behavior Therapy and Experimental Psychiatry*, 1979, *10*, 221–227.

Hagman, E. A study of fears of children of preschool age. *Journal of Experimental Psychology*, 1932, *1*, 110–130.

Hallam, R. S. Extinction of ruminations: A case study. *Behavior Therapy*, 1974, *5*, 565–568.

Hampe, E., Noble, H., Miller, L. C., & Barrett, C. L. Phobic children one and two years posttreatment. *Journal of Abnormal Psychology*, 1973, *82*, 446–453.

Harbin, H. T. Cure by ordeal: Treatment of an obsessive–compulsive neurotic. *International Journal of Family Therapy*, 1979, *4*, 324–332.

Hatzenbuehler, L. C., & Schroeder, H. E. Desensitization procedures in the treatment of childhood disorders. *Psychology Bulletin*, 1978, *85*, 331–844.

Hollingsworth, C. E., Tanquay, P. E., Grossman, L., & Pabst, P. Long-term outcome of obsessive–compulsive disorder in childhood. *Journal of the American Academy of Child Psychiatry*, 1980, *19*, 134–144.

Jackson, H. J., & King, N. J. The emotive imagery treatment of a child's trauma-induced phobia. *Journal of Behavior Therapy and Experimental Psychiatry*, 1981, *12*, 325–328.

Judd, L. L. Obsessive–compulsive neurosis in children. *Archives of General Psychiatry*, 1965, *12*, 136–143.

Kanfer, F. H., Karoly, P., & Newman, A. Reduction of children's fear of the dark by competence-related and situation threat-related verbal cues. *Journal of Consulting and Clinical Psychology*, 1975, *43*, 251–258.

Kellerman, J. Rapid treatment of nocturnal anxiety in children. *Journal of Behavior Therapy and Experimental Psychiatry*, 1980, *11*, 9–11.

Kennedy, W. A. School phobia: Rapid treatment of 50 cases. *Journal of Abnormal Psychology*, 1965, *70*, 285–289.

Koeppen, A. S. Relaxation training for children. *Elementary School Guidance and Counseling*, 1974, *9*, 521–528.

Kornhaber, R. C., & Shroeder, H. E. Importance of model similarity on the extinction of avoidance behavior in children. *Journal of Counseling and Clinical Psychology*, 1975, *43*, 601–607.

Kratochwill, T. R., & Morris, R. J. Conceptual and methodological issues in the behavioral assessment and treatment of children's fears and phobias. *School Psychology Review*, 1985, *14*, 94–107.

Lazarus, A. A. The elimination of children's phobias by deconditioning. In H. J. Eysenck (Ed.), *Behavior therapy and the neuroses*. New York: Pergamon, 1960.

Lazarus, A. A., & Abramovitz, A. The use of "emotive imagery" in the treatment of children's phobias. *Journal of Mental Science,* 1962, *108,* 191–195.

Leitenberg, H. Behavioral approaches to treatment of neuroses. In H. Leitenberg (Ed.), *Handbook of behavior modification and behavior therapy.* Englewood Cliffs, N.J.: Prentice-Hall, 1976.

Leitenberg, H., & Callahan, E. J. Reinforced practice and reduction of different kinds of fears in adults and children. *Behaviour Research and Therapy,* 1973, *11,* 19–30.

Lewis, S. A. A comparison of behavior therapy techniques in the reduction of fearful avoidance behavior. *Behavior Therapy,* 1974, *5,* 648–655.

Luiselli, J. K. Treatment of an autistic child's fear of riding a school bus through exposure and reinforcement. *Journal of Behavior Therapy and Experimental Psychiatry,* 1978, *9,* 169–172.

Marks, I. M. Behavioral treatments of phobic and obsessive–compulsive disorders: A critical appraisal. In M. Hersen, R. M. Eisler, & P. M. Miller (Eds), *Progress in behavior modification* (Vol. 1). New York: Academic Press, 1975.

Meichenbaum, D. Examination of model characteristics in reducing avoidance behavior. *Journal of Personality and Social Psychology,* 1971, *17,* 298–307.

Meichenbaum, D. A self-instructional approach to stress management: A proposal for stress inoculation training. In C. D. Spielberger & I. Sarason (Eds.), *Stress and anxiety* (Vol. 2). New York: Wiley, 1975.

Meichenbaum, D., & Turk, D. The cognitive–behavioral management of anxiety, anger, and pain. In P. O. Davidson (Ed.), *The behavioral management of anxiety, depression, and pain.* New York: Brunner/Mazel, 1976.

Melamed, B. G., Hawes, R. R., Heiby, E., & Glick, J. The use of filmed modeling to reduce uncooperative behavior of children during dental treatment. *Journal of Dental Research,* 1975, *54,* 797–801.

Melamed, B. G., & Siegel, L. J. Reduction of anxiety in children facing hospitalization and surgery by use of filmed modeling. *Journal of Consulting and Clinical Psychology,* 1975, *43,* 511–521.

Miller, L. C., Barrett, C. L., & Hampe, E. Phobias of childhood in a prescientific era. In A. Davids (Ed.), *Child personality and psychopathology: Current topics* (Vol. 1). New York: Wiley, 1974.

Mills, H. L., Agras, W. S., Barlow, D. H., & Mills, J. R. Compulsive rituals treated by response prevention: An experimental analysis. *Archives of General Psychiatry,* 1973, *38,* 524–529.

Morris, R. J., & Kratochwill, T. R. *Treating children's fears and phobias: A behavioral approach.* New York: Pergamon, 1983.

Morris, R. J., & Kratochwill, T. R. Behavioral treatment of children's fears and phobias. *School Psychology Review,* 1985, *14,* 84–93.

Nelson, W. M., III. A cognitive–behavioral treatment for disproportionate dental anxiety and pain: A case study. *Journal of Clinical Child Psychology,* 1981, *10,* 79–82.

Ollendick, T. H. *Relaxation techniques with hyperactive, aggressive children.* Unpublished manuscript, Indiana State University, 1978.

Ollendick, T. H. Fear reduction techniques with children. In M. Hersen, R. M. Eisler, & P. M. Miller (Eds.), *Progress in behavior modification* (Vol. 8). New York: Academic Press, 1979.

Ollendick, T. H., & Cerny, J. A. *Clinical behavior therapy with children.* New York: Plenum Press, 1981.

Ollendick, T. H., & Gruen, G. E. Treatment of a bodily injury phobia with implosive therapy. *Journal of Consulting and Clinical Psychology,* 1972, *38,* 389–393.

Paul, G. L. Behavior modification research design and tactics. In C. M. Franks (Ed.), *Behavior therapy: Appraisal and status.* New York: McGraw-Hill, 1969.

Phillips, D., & Wolpe, S. Multiple behavior techniques in severe separation anxiety of a twelve-year-old. *Journal of Behavior Therapy and Experimental Psychiatry,* 1981, *12,* 329–332.

Pomerantz, P. B., Peterson, N. J., Marholin, D., II, & Stern, S. The *in vivo* elimination of a childhood phobia by a paraprofessional interventionist at home. *Journal of Behavior Therapy and Experimental Psychiatry,* 1977, *8,* 417–421.

Rachman, S. J. Treatment of prolonged exposure to high intensity stimulation. *Behaviour Research and Therapy,* 1969, *7,* 295–302.

Rachman, S. J., & Hodgson, R. J. *Obsessions and compulsions.* Englewood Cliffs, N.J.: Prentice-Hall, 1980.

Ritter, B. The group desensitization of children's snake phobias using vicarious and contact desensitization procedures. *Behaviour Research and Therapy,* 1968, *6,* 1–6.

Ross, A. O. *Child behavior therapy: Principles, procedures, and empirical basis.* New York: Wiley, 1981.

Rutter, M. *Helping troubled children.* New York: Plenum Press, 1976.

Smith, R. E., & Sharpe, T. M. Treatment of school phobia with implosive therapy. *Journal of Consulting and Clinical Psychology,* 1970, *35,* 239–243.

Spielberger, C. D., Edwards, C. D., Lushene, R. E., Montouri, J., & Platzek, D. *Preliminary manual for the State–Trait Anxiety Inventory for Children.* Palo Alto, Calif.: Counseling Psychologists Press, 1973.

Sreenivasan, V., Manocha, S. N., & Jain, V. K. Treatment of severe dog phobia in childhood by flooding: A case report. *Journal of Child Psychology and Psychiatry,* 1979, *20,* 255–256.

Stampfl, T. G., & Levis, D. J. Essentials of implosive therapy: A learning-theory-based psychodynamic behavioral therapy. *Journal of Abnormal Psychology,* 1967, *72,* 496–503.

Stanley, L. Treatment of ritualistic behavior in an eight-year-old girl by response prevention: A case report. *Journal of Child Psychology and Psychiatry,* 1980, *21,* 85–90.

Tasto, D. L. Systematic desensitization, muscle relaxation and visual imagery in the counterconditioning of a four-year-old phobic child. *Behaviour Research and Therapy,* 1969, *7,* 409–411.

Verville, E. *Behavior problems of children.* Phildelphia: Saunders, 1967.

Weisman, D., Ollendick, T. H., & Horne, A. M. *A comparison of muscle relaxation techniques with children.* Unpublished manuscript, Indiana State University, 1978.

Wish, P. A., Hasazi, J. E., & Jurgela, A. R. Automated direct deconditioning of a childhood phobia. *Journal of Behavior Therapy and Experimental Psychiatry,* 1973, *4,* 279–283.

Wolpe, J. *Psychotherapy by reciprocal inhibition.* Stanford: Stanford University Press, 1958.

Yen, S., & McIntire, W. Operant therapy for constant headache complaints: A simple response-cost approach. *Psychological Reports,* 1971, *28,* 267–270.

Yule, W., Sacks, B., & Hersov, L. Successful flooding treatment of a noise phobia in an eleven-year-old. *Journal of Behavior Therapy and Experimental Psychiatry,* 1974, *5,* 209–211.

‡12‡

PRINCIPLES OF INTENSIVE INDIVIDUAL PSYCHOANALYTIC PSYCHOTHERAPY FOR CHILDHOOD ANXIETY DISORDERS

MELVIN LEWIS

INTRODUCTION

The general goal of intensive individual psychotherapy is the same in children and adolescents as it is in adults: "to make the best of him [or her] that his [or her] inherited capacities will allow and so to make him [or her] as efficient and as capable of enjoyment as is possible" (Freud, 1928/1955, p. 251). Specific aims may include reduction of anxiety, improvement in self-esteem, increased frustration tolerance, disappearance of symptoms, better coping strategies, appropriate independence, good relationships with peers and adults, satisfactory and satisfying schoolwork, feelings of pleasure and joy, and a sense of resumption of development. The method essentially similarly involves a trusting, confidential, real relationship between a trained, motivated, caring, and accepting person who offers help and a person who needs that help. Usually there is agreement between therapist and patient about the type of theory used. Generally, opportunities are provided for the verbal expression of feelings, increasing self-knowledge, and improving self-mastery (Karasu, 1977; Langs, 1982; Paolino, 1981). The therapy is usually divided into periods of 30–50 minutes given

Melvin Lewis. Child Study Center, Yale University, New Haven, Connecticut.

from one to four times a week in a suitable office setting. Although numerous methods, techniques, and theories have been categorized (London & Klerman, 1982) and described (Varma, 1974), un- equivocable superiority of any one method has not been established (Luborsky, Singer, & Luborsky, 1975; McDermott & Harrison, 1979; Schaefer & Millman, 1977; Wolman, Egan, & Ross, 1978).

How does one become a child therapist? First, it has to be said that neither the amount nor the kind of training are very reliable guides to the eventual effectiveness of a therapist; indeed, highly trained psychotherapists often achieve no more with their patients than do those with much less experience (Strupp & Hadley, 1979). Victor Raimy once observed that "psychotherapy is an undefined technique applied to unspecified cases with unpredictable results. For this technique, rigorous training is required" (quoted in London, 1964, p. 155). Supervison and continuous case conferences with acknowl- edged experts seem to be the generally accepted methods of acquiring psychotherapy skills. The amount required varies with the endowment and needs of the individual psychotherapist. Buckley, Conte, Plutchik, Karasu, and Wild (1982) in a brief (8-month) longitudinal study of 12 beginning psychiatric residents, found that appropriate use of clarification, confrontation, management of resistance, and the ability to deal with negative transference could be learned with supervision and experience, while the capacity for empathy and awareness of countertransference did not change during the period of the study. There is some evidence that ordinary communication skills and empathic understanding can be taught very quickly (Bird, 1980; Ivey, 1980; Matarazzo, 1978; MacGuire, 1980) and that the rest is experience. There is no evidence that a personal analysis must be a part of psychotherapeutic training (Marks, 1982).

The question of when intensive individual psychoanalytic psychotherapy in childhood is the treatment of choice nowadays often resolves into the question of what other forms of therapy are available and indicated for a particular child with a particular diagnosis. Diagnosis is thus an essential prerequisite and for this purpose must go beyond DSM-III (American Psychiatric Association, 1980) to an assessment of the personality structure (A. Freud, 1968). Rarely does a single form of treatment for the child suffice. In most instances, various combinations of treatment are necessary, including pharmaco- therapy, behavior therapy, family therapy, educational remedies, environmental changes, and concomitant work with the parents. For example, multimodality treatment including various combinations of individual therapy, group therapy, parent training, and medication have been found to bring about significant improvement in children with attention deficit disorder (Satterfield, Satterfield, & Cantwell, 1980). A useful account of the steps in the process by planning treatment for children and adolescents is given by Looney (1984).

Anxiety is present in almost all psychiatric conditions of childhood, and to the extent that anxiety is either unrecognized or evokes earlier infantile anxieties, psychoanalytic psychotherapeutic treatment for that anxiety may be indicated. Anxiety disorders in childhood by definition may require a special focus or emphasis. The principles of treatment for anxiety as defined previously are still operative, however, no matter what other treatments are required for diagnosis in which the other, primarily biologic, causes are present.

Pure, intensive, individual psychoanalytic psychotherapy alone is thus rarely indicated, and only with confidence when the child's problem is internal, confined to the so-called infantile neurosis of the past, and there is no other known factor amenable to treatment of any other kind. Such is rarely the case. Conversely, when the child's problems are more external than internal or internalized, and other etiologic factors are recognized, one becomes less confident in the solitary use of intensive individual psychotherapy. Thus, there may also be present various current conflicts and frustrations, losses, physical illness and other stresses, as well as other psychiatric diagnoses, that may require the addition of one or more of the previously mentioned measures.

Yet, no matter what accompanying treatments are necessary, when individual psychotherapy is used, the same essential elements of the process unfold, albeit modified by the age, diagnosis, and presence of these other factors, with or without the other forms of treatment. The basic requirements for psychotherapy for children, together with a broad description of the stages and various components of the ongoing clinical work, have been described by McDermott and Chan (1984). Brief psychotherapy with children, adolescents, and their families has been described by Dulcan (1984). This chapter focuses on the particular essential elements of intensive individual psychoanalytic psychotherapy.

Intensive individual psychoanalytic psychotherapy specifically places great importance on interpretation (making the unconscious or preconscious conscious), particularly interpretation of the transference, as the principal therapeutic agent (Lewis, 1974). This holds true whether one is treating a preschool child (Neubauer, 1972), school-age child (A. Freud, 1946/1950, 1968), or an adolescent (Blos, 1962) and across a wide range of diagnoses (Witmer, 1946).

For purposes of discussion intensive individual psychoanalytic psychotherapy can be approached as a process with three major phases: initial phase, middle phase, and termination phase.

INITIAL PHASE

The major goal of the initial phase is to foster the therapeutic alliance between therapist and child. This general goal is usually achieved by enabling the child to experience a nonjudgmental, understanding response to his or her behavior. The actual relationship itself is, in fact, a therapeutic agent in its own right, as well as the soil upon which the seed of an interpretation may flourish. A positive actual relationship therefore is encouraged.

The child must first be given some understanding by the parents of why he or she is being brought to a therapist and what therapy is like. Essentially, the child can be told that, in addition to himself or herself, others such as parents or teachers are concerned about how the child is feeling and/or behaving and that the child's parents believe the child may be troubled or upset, possibly by something he or she is not aware of.

Next, the parents may tell the child that talking with someone who understands children may help them and the child understand what may be troubling the child. The child can be told that the parents know of such a person, and the parents can describe the person, the setting, and the arrangements to the child. The child should then be encouraged to ask any questions, and the parents should be prepared to answer truthfully and accurately.

The child will feel understood if he or she is offered an interpretation that provides the child with some insight, yet does not arouse undue anxiety. The therapist can do this by using a range of preliminiary interpretative statements (Lewis, 1974), culminating in the interpretation of the transference, which is discussed shortly. Such preliminary interpretations include setting statements, attention statements, reductive statements, and situational statements.

SETTING STATEMENTS

A child may first be told in language appropriate to the child's developmental level that this is a time set aside for the child so that he or she can allow himself or herself to think freely and begin to understand why he or she sometimes feels troubled. The child should also be told that sometimes the therapist will intervene but with the understanding that it will always be in the interest of helping the child understand himself or herself better.

ATTENTION STATEMENTS

Next, the child's attention can be directed to the content of his or her actions or verbalizations. Sometimes attention is drawn to a coincidence that the child has perceived but has not, or professes not to have, registered; more frequently, attention is drawn to certain paradoxes. The immediate aim is to free the child to produce new material and to consolidate existing gains (Devereux, 1951). In the course of the child's play, the therapist may, for example, provide a verbal counterpart to the action being portrayed, to an affect that might be present, or to the conspicuous absence of certain persons, actions, or affects.

An 8-year-old boy with a severe school phobia repeatedly enacted a war scene in which the general was attacked and almost killed. Many fantasies were contained in this play, but one prominent feature was the absence of any female, not only in this play item but in any other play. After attention was drawn to this "fact," the child recognized his fear of attack from his mother, his wish to attack her, his resentment that his father was often attacked and offered him no protection, the displacement of his aggression toward his mother to his father, and his anxiety about even mentioning his mother.

This is quite different from any kind of direct translation of possible symbolic representation in the play. The play characteristic to which attention is drawn is in bold relief, and capable of being understood by the child. This is emphasized to draw the distinction from more subtle paradoxes, which are not readily perceived, at least not by the younger child.

REDUCTIVE STATEMENTS

Certain statements reduce apparently disparate behavioral patterns to a common form that has hitherto not been noticed by the child. Thus, a child may manifest certain kinds of behavior whenever he or she is, say, angry. The child may not have been aware of this anger.

In the course of the treatment of a 10-year-old boy, it was noticed that there were recurring episodes of mocking, insulting, or denigrating behavior toward the therapist. Each of these episodes was related in time to one of the frequent trips away from home that the boy's mother would take. His resentment at being left behind, together with his anxiety at being left alone with his father, led to the behavior just described. This type of behavior could be reduced to a single behavioral reaction to underlying rage and anxiety precipitated by the temporary loss of his mother. When the child was told of this relationship, he reacted first of all by an intensification of the behavior pattern, but subsequently was able to recognize for the first time his underlying feelings when he stated, "My parents are always nice to me when we do fun things, but they don't help me with the serious things when I'm unhappy."

The child here was manifesting a more or less fixed defense, which, in the example given, was brought into sharper relief. A certain level of cognitive development, including some capacity to take distance from and observe affects, must be available to the child for this to occur.

SITUATIONAL STATEMENTS

Situational statements naturally follow from those previously described. For example, the child now aware of his or her anger can be shown the situations that give rise to this anger and how in certain instances he or she has repeatedly brought about such situations, either in current relationships or in the transference. However, the degree of directness with which such situational statements may be made varies with the cognitive and developmental levels of the child. Children who are at the stage of concrete operations and in latency can usually be approached directly. Children who are at the preoperational stage of cognitive development or in oedipal or preoedipal phases probably need to have these statements made to them in the context of the play, either through dolls and puppets, or indirectly through some other hypothetical child or children.

MIDDLE PHASE

The essence of the middle phase of psychotherapy is the interpretation of the transference and "working through." Notwithstanding the difficulties of the initial phase, a child soon understands one of the goals of psychotherapy: the attempt to gain an understanding of the way he or she feels and behaves. After the initial phase of treatment, the child realizes that everything he or she says and does is subject to use by the therapist. Consequently, the child's play that follows is part of the associative process in the context of therapy. In certain respects, however, the developmental difference between the child and the adult influences the form of these associations. The child is much more susceptible to current reality, which exerts a powerful influence on his or her play. The play is often goal directed and not freely associative. Again, the child has a tendency to act rather than think, giving at least the impression of an overemphasized aggressive transference (A. Freud, 1965, p. 36). Further, in school-age children especially, the play is often characterized by organization, reflecting a developmental shift. Lastly, the child may become totally absorbed in his or her play and may then be unable to exercise an observing function.

At the same time, in addition to play, a child also communicates through most of the other elements that constitute "free association." That is, the child talks, pauses, shows affects, exhibits mannerisms, and portrays attitudes. It is this total picture, viewed as a whole over the course of several hours, that enables the therapist to discern an associative thread. And it is this overall connection that can often be grasped by the child.

TRANSFERENCE

In the course of discerning this total picture, a true transference neurosis—that is, those previously fixed conflicts and neurotic symptoms of the child that are now being experienced currently by the child in relation to the therapist (Harley, 1967)—can usually be observed. Again, the developmental differences between child and adult modify, but do not eradicate, this emerging transference neurosis in three ways: (1) To the extent that the child is normally dependent, the parents with whom the original conflict was concerned are still with the child and continue to exert their influence on the child. (2) The child is not an equal with the therapist: He or she is still a child relating to an adult as well as a patient relating to a therapist. Thus, besides the mutual respect that should exist between patient and therapist, the child also has certain expectations of the adult, such as appropriate birthday and holiday greetings. (3) The continuing development of the child continues to modify the transference, especially during shifts from the oedipal period to the so-called latency and from latency to adolescence. In addition, fixations that occurred earlier may be modified with the increased range, flexibility, and shifts of defenses that occur with the development of the child.

For all these reasons, the transference neurosis in child psychotherapy is incomplete and more unstable than the transference neurosis in the therapy of an adult. Nevertheless, to the extent that there is a transference neurosis, however modified, it is available for interpretation. The more common situation in work with children is one in which a relatively simple current displacement from parent to therapist is recognized and interpreted. Even within such apparently simple displacements, however, elements of a transference neurosis can be found, and when they are interpreted, they throw light on the child's current behavior.

RECONSTRUCTION

At any rate, an etiologic link between the complexities of the child's current behavior and his or her earlier fantasies may be offered to the child. Such earlier material is derived from the personal myth of the child or from reconstruction. The striking aspect of a reconstruction is that it helps the child "make sense" out of what was previously discomforting and/or perplexing. Further, it occasionally helps a child by confirming what was probably an essentially correct perception by the child at the time, but which has since undergone distortion. The conceptual abilities of the child are such that he or she often attributes affects he or she thinks he or she perceives in his or her parents as resulting from thoughts or wishes of his or her own. Further, the child frequently projects his or her own fantasies and affects onto his or her parents, and subsequently acts against the parents whom the child now regards as, say, dangerous or angry. The preoperational child also has difficulty in distinguishing fantasies from reality (Piaget, 1929).

PROCESS OF INTERPRETATION

Some further general points on the process of making an interpretation may now be considered. Loewenstein (1951), whose account would be more complete had he placed greater emphasis on the interpretation of unconscious, or at least preconscious, material, described the following steps: (1) Show the patient that certain common elements exist in a series of events. (2) Point out the similar behavior of the patient in each of these situations. (3) Demonstrate that such behavior was manifested in circumstances that all involved, for example, competitive elements and where rivalry might have been expected. (4) Point out that rivalry does exist unconsciously, but is replaced by another kind of behavior, such as avoiding competition. (5) Show that this behavior originates in certain critical events of the patient's life and encompasses reactions and tendencies that can be grouped together.

In the stages just outlined, the interpretation of mechanism, as opposed to that of content or affect, is significant. Further, it can also be seen that there is a gradual transition from preparatory intervention, through confrontation, to an interpretation containing a genetic component. Ferenczi once described his own experiences as he proceeded in the steps just outlined:

> One allows oneself to be influenced by the free associations of the patient; simultaneously one permits one's own imagination to play on these associations; intermittently one compares new connections that appear with previous products . . . without, for a moment, losing sight of, regard for, and criticism of one's own biases.
>
> Essentially, one might speak of an endless process of oscillation between empathy, self-observation, and judgment. This last, wholly spontaneously, declares itself intermittently as a signal that one naturally immediately evaluates for what it is; only on the basis of further evidence may one ultimately decide to make an interpretation. (quoted in Kris, 1951, p. 29)

The description given by Erikson (1940) is remarkably similar. Speculations are first derived from the observer's impressions, associations, and recollections; for example, "It was as if. . . ." The observer also associates past impressions in the same child, from other children, or from data derived from the parents. The therapist reflects on the latent possibilities, that the associations may possibly correspond to a genetic or associative connection in the child's mind, and pictures what the child is doing under the observer's eyes and what the child is said to have done in other situations. This all leads up to the interpretation. Erikson then describes three steps in making the interpretation. First, there are observations, feelings, and reflections that lead to interpretational hints. For example, a symbolic equation or metaphor may make it possible to recognize a play act as alluding to and standing for an otherwise manifestly avoided item (a person, an object, an idea). Or a play arrangement may prove to represent a special effort on the part of the child to rearrange in effigy his or her psychological position in an experienced or expected danger situation. Such an arrangement usually corresponds to the child's defense mechanisms. Second, these hints are then subject to further observations and reflections and emerge as a conviction in the observer's mind in the form of the reconstruction of a genetic sequence or of a dynamic configuration pertaining to the patient's inner or outer history. Finally, the therapist may proceed to convey part of these reconstructions to the child whenever the therapist feels the time has come to do so. Erikson considers the last step to be the therapeutic interpretation.

The significant point here is the step-by-step progression in working with children implied in Erikson's statement that "The observe may proceed to convey parts of these reconstructions to the child whenever he feels the time has come to do so" (1940, p. 589). However, it is important to keep in mind here the developmental level of the child, since massive interpretations given to a young child are more likely to be heard as interfering noises than helpful statements, with a consequent heightening of resistance and play disruption or, worse, a play inhibition.

In short, the therapist, while still engaging with the child, takes mental distance from the immediate transaction and tries to place the immediate observations into the context of what has previously taken place. The therapist does this by means of a kind of mental "play back." Material from previous sessions is not only "played back" mentally, but is also translated to a higher level of abstraction, which enables the therapist to formulate to himself or herself "what is going on" as a basis for formulating an interpretation. The therapist then mentally translates this back to the level of the child and the immediate situation and makes his or her interpretation at that level.

GENERAL GUIDELINES FOR INTERPRETATION

Multiple Appeal

As a general rule, interpretations are probably more effective when they have "multiple appeal" (Hartmann, 1951). The therapist also describes clinically when to interpret the past, current reality, the transference—or all three.

Sequence

A number of other guidelines for the order of interpretation have been suggested. Resistances or defenses should be interpreted before the instinctual derivatives (Loewenstein, 1951). One should avoid interpreting an important neurotic symptom at the beginning, and one should start with interpretation of still-mobile defense traits in preference to rigid, characterologic defenses.

An 8-year-old boy wanted to take along some tracing paper belonging to his therapist on the eve of his going on a car trip with his mother and father, the anticipation of which had already aroused considerable anxiety. What were the possibilities here for interpretation?

1. The therapist could simply have confronted the child with his wish to take something along. At the particular stage in the therapy of this child, however, this would have been redundant.

2. The therapist could have shown the child how anxious he was about the trip with his parents, but doing so might have forced the child to face abruptly his anxiety without the therapist's support.

3. The therapist might conceivably have tried to link this wish with the boy's reactions in other similar situations in which he had become anxious, but this could not be done without the previous steps.

4. The therapist might also have interpreted the patient's wishes toward the therapist for protection, but in this patient such a move might have left the patient feeling stripped and defenseless.

5. The therapist might have made the connection for the child between this coming event and earlier events in his life, but this intervention might have had little use for this particular patient, since he did not yet have a clear idea of his feelings about the coming event.

6. It might then be asked whether anything should be said at all. Something should be said, but something that would temporarily buttress the child and offer support, at the same time that both the defense and the fear were being interpreted. For example, the therapist could say to the child: "How nice it will be to have something to take along, especially if you are worried about the trip." There would be no need to interpret the positive transference aspect at this point, since the movement is in a forward direction; or the therapist might also decide to include an aspect of the transference, but in a supportive way. The therapist might say, for example, "I think you would like to have something of mine with you on this trip." He might then allow the child to keep the paper and reserve for a later date any further exploration of the act: "Why don't you take the paper with you? When you come back we can talk again about how you feel when you have to take a trip with your mother and father."

These examples are not meant to be recommendations of specific things to say, but rather illustrations of underlying principles. The choice of level and wording depends on such factors as the diagnosis, the stage of the therapy, and the developmental level of the child. A 6-year-old child at the beginning of psychotherapy might experience his or her anxiety on the eve of such a trip as ego syntonic and fail to understand an interpretation of the anxiety. On the other hand, a 10-year-old who was more advanced in therapy might well experience such anxiety as inappropriate and ego alien, and might find such an interpretation useful.

Timing

An interpretation is probably well timed when the therapist thinks that the statement at that moment will help to consolidate existing gains and elicit new material (Devereux, 1951). Devereux described an interpretation as being "timely" when it is capable of being utilized by the patient, and this in turn can occur only if the patient understands it.

Focus of Interpretation

When should an interpretation be made in the play, and when should it be taken out of the play? When attention statements are made, the interpretations are clearly made "in the play." Reductive statements imply that the child is receptive to statements about himself, that is, "out of the play," while transference interpretations in their most effective form are made quite distinctly "out of the play," given the earlier steps of preparation. The use of play in psychotherapy with children has been extensively described previously (Beiser, 1979; Buxbaum, 1954; Haworth, 1964; McDermott & Harrison, 1977; Winnicott, 1971).

Tact

Tact is required when significant developmental differences are considered. A young child may have great difficulty in tolerating ambivalence and may find it especially difficult to accept a hostile or aggressive wish or fantasy. This reluctance may be overcome by placing within a fuller context the anger, say, that is to be interpreted. For example, one might more tactfully say to a child: "It is very hard to be angry at someone you love."

Glover (1930) tried to be more specific with regard to tact, stating that the interpretation should be delivered as a plain statement in terms devoid of active emotional stress. The purpose appeared to be to prevent an immediate, overwhelming conscious conviction on the patient's part that his or her therapist was in a state of counter-transference.

Glover also cautioned about the use of wit, the exploitation of the comic, and the shelter provided by technical expressions. It is usually preferable to refer to the child's parents as "mother" or "father." Only with a very young child would one use such terms as "mommy" and "daddy," and then only because they are developmentally and age appropriate.

Wording

Wording should be specific and concrete; the interpretation should also be worded to fit the individual situation. Again, the therapist is cautioned to avoid the same defense mechanism as the patient, for example, laughing things off and minimizing them. Interpretations appear to gain when they contain an element of time, for example, "now," "before," "at the age of," "after this happened."

Wording becomes particularly critical with children, not only from the point of view of the level of cognitive development, but also from the point of view of what the child can accept in his or her dependent position with respect to the parents and of the child's own struggle against regressive pulls or progressive pushes. The child attaches greater meaning to certain words than does the adult, and it becomes necessary for the therapist to understand these special meanings.

Inexact and Incomplete Interpretation

Glover (1930) distinguished between inexact and incomplete interpretations. An incomplete interpretation was termed by Glover a "preliminary interpretation." For example, one would interpret a genital fantasy before an anal fantasy. He contrasted this with an inexact interpretation when one might never interpret the anal fantasy at all. That is to say, if the interpretation of the genital fantasy was regarded as the complete interpretation, then the interpretation was *ipso facto* inexact.

An interpretation is never complete until the immediat defensive reactions following on the interpretations are subjected to investigation. The complete interpretation is really the complete treatment: ". . . every construction is an incomplete one. . . . As a rule he [the patient] will not give his assent until he has learnt the whole truth—which often covers a very great deal of ground" (Freud, 1937/1964, pp. 263, 265ff.).

In the case of the child, one rarely achieves a state of completion, and neither is it necessary. Often, all that is necessary is to bring about a reduction of anxiety sufficient to enable development to proceed.

COUNTERTRANSFERENCE

In work with children the therapist is particularly prone to countertransference phenomena. For example, there is a much greater "regressive pull" (Bornstein, 1948). The therapist must learn to recognize the feelings aroused in himself or herself so that he or she can deal with the child in a way that is helpful. Feelings are a vital instrument for understanding. At the same time if the therapist is not aware of, or not clear about, the nature of his or her aroused feelings and their sources (both external and internal), he or she may be hampered in working effectively with the child. Indications that countertransference feelings may be at work include the following:

1. The therapist may fail to recognize where a child is in his or her development. Expectations will then not be commensurate with the child's maturational and developmental capacities. Unrealistic goals, alternating with despair, may then be experienced by the therapist.

2. The regressive pull experienced by the therapist playing and working with a child may give rise to the temptation to identify and/or act out with the child, or infantilization of the child may occur.

3. A misreading of the child's relationship to the therapist may occur, in which the relationship is seen as realistic when in fact it may be a transference from the child's feelings toward his or her parents. Therapists are usually well aware of a child's aggressive feelings, but may be less aware of a child's seductiveness toward an adult (parent).

4. Remnants of the therapist's own childhood relations with his or her brothers and sisters may be an important source of the therapist's ambivalence to the child. For example, excessive concern— or lack of concern—for a child climbing a chair or approaching a tall column of heavy building blocks may mask an underlying wish that the child will hurt himself or herself and may be associated with guilt feelings when the child does stumble or fall. This feeling of guilt may come about because of the partial unsuspected fulfillment of the unacceptable wish.

5. The stirring up of old conflicts within the therapist, when exposed to certain behavior in the child, may cause anxiety in the therapist. For example, uncontrolled aggression, sex play, or masturbation may be upsetting to the therapist.

6. Sometimes the therapist may himself or herself transfer old feelings from his or her own childhood onto the parents of the child. One may thus identify with the child in his or her struggle with his or her parents. Rescue fantasies may then occur. Conversely, the therapist may erroneously identify with the parents (perhaps through an identification with the aggressor mechanism) and consequently exercise unnecessary, even punitive, controls against the child who is acting too aggressively or sexually for the therapist's comfort.

7. Sometimes the therapist simply cannot understand the meaning of certain behavior in a child. Of course there are times when all of us find some item or other of behavior inexplicable. However, the persistent drawing of a blank in understanding a repeated item of behavior should lead to the suspicion of an interference by one's own conflicts—an emotional blind spot, so to speak.

8. A therapist may find himself or herself feeling depressed or uneasy during his or her work with children. Assuming the therapist is not suffering from a true depression, the possibility exists that emotions from old conflicts have been aroused and are interfering with the therapist's functioning. Occasionally, a therapist may find himself or herself aroused and experiencing great affection for a child. This too may interfere with his or her work with the child.

9. It sometimes happens that a therapist will permit, or even encourage, acting out in the child. For example, a therapist may suggest to a child that he or she must stand up for himself or herself and hit back. On occasion a therapist may even feel the impulse to act out with a child.

10. A therapist may need the admiration obtained by having the child like him or her. This too may represent a need of the therapist and may not be in the best interests of the child.

11. Conversely, repeated arguing with a child may suggest that the therapist has not only become involved but has become enmeshed with the child.

12. Recurring countertransference problems commonly arise in relation to specific characteristics of a child. For example, a retarded child may evoke guilt and defenses against such guilt with the therapist, or omnipotent rescue fantasies, which are acted out. Passive, hostile children may arouse anger in a therapist. Aggressive children may evoke counteraggression. Sexually attractive children may evoke counteraggression. Sexually attractive children and adolescents of the same or opposite sex as the therapist may threaten the therapist, leading to either vicarious and excessive "exploitation" of sexual issues or denial and avoidance.

WORKING THROUGH

It is clear that working through is necessary to sustain any therapeutic effect (Greenacre, 1956). The defensive conflicts remain somewhat structured unless they are dealt with repetitively in relation to various behaviors, events, and feelings. Historically, working through was first stressed from the point of view of being of educative value and compared with mourning and the progressive detachment of the individual libido from the organized tensions and aims that permeated the later life.

The concept of the corrective emotional experience is really an aspect of working through, at least in its more modern construction. Originally, the idea involved replenishment of earlier deficiencies through the current relationship. This appealing idea unfortunately proved to be soo simplistic. Among other things, it failed to take into account the power of the unconscious repetition compulsion. The concept has some merit, however, if it is modified to provide the child in the here-and-now with a reaction different from his or her previous experiences, a reaction that is now more appropriate and does not perpetuate the malignant interactions to which he or she has become accustomed. The concept then is also a different idea, however, and one that is more in keeping with the concept of working through. With the rise of ego psychology, the recognition of the need for consistent work with the patterns of defense and the affects related to them once more becomes paramount (Bornstein, 1948).

From a developmental point of view, working through with children poses a special problem. The chief difficulty lies in the fact that the live parents are usually present and may continue to exert a reinforcing influence upon the child's original conflicts. Sometimes this interference can be alleviated by concomitant work with the parents, through some form of psychotherapy, or through regular meetings between the parents and the child's therapist. Occasionally, it becomes clear that the child cannot work through a conflict while in the home, and an alternative plan may become necessary, such as boarding school in the case of an older child. Sometimes the difficulty is insuperable at the time, and the therapy must be interrupted until the child is in a more advantageous situation for therapy. Occasionally, it is possible to hold the child in therapy until such a situation occurs. In some instances the child can be helped to understand the repetitive and reinforcing behavior of the parents and his or her involvement in precipitating or responding to their behavior. If the influence of the parents is not too strong, the child can be helped to modify his or her own behavior in this regard and interrupt the vicious cycle.

TERMINATION PHASE

The criteria for termination ideally include some actual achievement (as opposed to a "flight into health"; Train, 1953) of the goals of therapy: reduced anxiety, improved self-esteem, increased frustration tolerance, disappearance of symptoms, better coping strategies, relative independence, good relationships with peers and adults, satisfying schoolwork, feelings of pleasure and joy, and a sense of resumed developmental progress.

In almost every instance these achievements are judged clinically rather than measured scientifically. Clinically, there is no such thing as a perfect therapy (or for that matter, a perfect patient or therapist). Every therapy eventually stops, and when it does the child should be more or less along the road toward these laudable goals. A child may even have gained a better understanding of himself or herself and may no longer need to act out so much of his or her infantile longings, frustrations, and feelings, and may have learned instead more adaptive ways, say, to love and be loved. But in some cases the therapy simply stops because there is a sense of diminishing returns, the resistances are too great, the treatment is inappropriate, or for various other reasons the treatment is a failure. In one survey of terminated analytic cases (n = 49), only 14% terminated by mutual agreement among parent, therapist, and child (A. Freud, 1971).

The actual phase of termination is a useful period to explore issues of separation, reactions to loss, dependency versus independence, and anxiety about progressive developmental movements. Some children undergo a temporary regression, manifested by a reappearance of their presenting symptoms, in the face of leaving the therapist and returning, as it were, to the family. Others are able to "reconstruct" and recall the beginning of their treatment rather than reenact it through regressive behavior. Depending on the frequency, duration, and intensity of the psychotherapy, a reasonable period of time is required to deal with these issues. Thus, when the question of whether to terminate has been decided, preferably by mutual agreement, a termination date is set that will allow a suitable amount of time for the termination phase. This period may vary from 6 weeks to 3 months or so.

Follow-up communication is often helpful in consolidating the work of the termination phase.

THERAPEUTIC ACTION AND THEORY

Many attempts have been made to describe the therapeutic effects of interpretation in terms of the insight achieved. The particular type of interpretation that will produce a therapeutic insight, that is, a structural change, has been given different names, as has the actual therapeutic insight. For example, "transference" (Fenichel, 1945) or "mutative" (Strachey, 1934) interpretations may produce "emotional," "psychological," "ostensive" (Richfield, 1954), or "dynamic" insights as opposed to "intellectual," "descriptive,"or "neutral" (Reid & Finesinger, 1952) insights. The significant point is that shifts in cathexis from the unconscious to conscious awareness are thought to occur only after derivatives of the original feeling are recognized with an experiential sense of conviction and worked through. Bergler (1945) considered that the whole process of working through is centered chiefly in the correct handling and mobilization of the feeling of guilt. Devereux (1951) felt that an interpretation (which consists of supplying an unconscious closure element) is effective when practically all conscious and preconscious material pertaining to the neurotic gestalt has been produced. Loewenstein (1951) believed that the therapeutic effect is due to a psychic process in which each of the following parts has its respective place: (1) the overcoming of resistances, (2) the working through, (3) the remembering and reliving of repressed material, and (4) the effect of the reconstruction.

Anticipated changes resulting from psychotherapy are also to some extent a function of normal development. Therefore, all of the factors that facilitate normal development will also facilitate the desired changes in psychotherapy.

The experience with the psychotherapist is not only a corrective one, but also represents an oasis phenomenon for the child who now finds himself or herself, at least temporarily, in a relatively protected, facilitating environment that enables development to proceed by reducing the impact of trauma and the acting-out tendencies in the child. Another way of putting this is to say that the child in psychotherapy finds himself or herself at least momentarily at a distance from the acute upset of the current developmental turmoil, whether it be a too exciting, sexualized relationship with a parent, a sadomasochistic relationship with a parent, a grief reaction at the birth of a sibling, or frightening fantasies of bodily harm.

The child is also afforded an opportunity for confirmation of his or her essentially correct perception of his parents, leading to a strengthening of reality testing and an increase in self-esteem. The play of the child, as well as the use of words, inasmuch as they represent an intermediate stage between action and thought, provide a handle by which the child grasps affects and is enabled to delay. Most important, the play itself undergoes a development that carries with it a significant shift from primary process to secondary process. The dyadic therapeutic relationship provides an introspective opportunity for the child, and also serves to foster an identification with an appropriate adult model. Indeed, the child may "borrow" from the psychotherapist as the child struggles to deal with an acute developmental crisis. Concomitant work with other family members also leads to shifts in the dynamic equilibrium within the family, release the child and parents from their locked-in, fixed positions and allowing development to proceed. A further significant therapeutic force is the change from despair to hope, leading to a therapeutic optimism. Lastly, the extended moment of time, the opportunity to examine in detail, itself contributes to clearer, more direct communications.

EVALUATION OF OUTCOME OF PSYCHOTHERAPY

Evaluation of the effectiveness of psychotherapy is in general a complex phenomenon (Strupp & Hadley, 1977), and research is plagued by methodological problems (Hine, Werman, & Simpson, 1982). Parloff (1982) recently reviewed nearly 500 rigorous controlled studies providing research evidence on outcome. Parloff concluded that all forms of psychological treatment are comparably effective in producing therapeutic benefits and such benefits are reliably superior to those found in controls. Ultimately, outcome in psychotherapy is a value judgment, requiring that we recognize the multiple values, criteria, and factors that go into such judgments. Research on psychotherapy with children in particular is especially sparse (Levitt, 1971; Shaffer, 1984). More research is needed in all of the areas discussed in this chapter.

ACKNOWLEDGMENT

This chapter is drawn in part from an earlier publication (Lewis, 1974).

REFERENCES

American Psychiatric Association. *Diagnostic and statistical manual of mental disorders* (3rd ed.). Washington, D.C.: Author, 1980.

Beiser, H. R. Formal games in diagnosis and therapy. *Journal of the American Academy of Child Psychiatry,* 1979, *18,* 480–491.

Bergler, E. "Working through," in psychoanalysis. *Psychoanalytic Review,* 1945, *32,* 449–480.

Bird, J. Teaching medical interviewing skills: A comparison of medical and non-medical tutors. In *Research in medical education: Proceedings of the Association of American Medical Colleges.* Washington, D.C.: Association of American Medical Colleges, 1980.

Blos, P. *On adolescence: A psychoanalytic interpretation.* New York: Free Press, 1962.

Bornstein, B. Emotional barriers in the understanding and treatment of young children. *American Journal of Orthopsychiatry,* 1948, *18,* 691–697.

Buckley, P., Conte, H. R., Plutchik, R., Karasu, T. B., & Wild, K. V. Learning dynamic psychotherapy: A longitudinal study. *American Journal of Psychiatry,* 1982, *139,* 1607–1610.

Buxbaum, E. Technique of child therapy. *Psychoanalytic Study of the Child,* 1954, *9,* 297–333.

Devereux, G. Some criteria for the timing of confrontations and interpretations. *International Journal of Psycho-Analysis,* 1951, *32,* 19–24.

Dulcan, M. K. Brief psychotherapy with children and their families: The state of the art. *Journal of the American Academy of Child Psychiatry,* 1984, *23,* 544–551.

Erikson, E. H. Studies in the interpretation of play. *Genetic Psychology Monographs,* 1940, *22,* 557–671.

Fenichel, O. *The psychoanalytic theory of neurosis.* New York: Norton, 1945.

Freud, A. *The psycho-analytic treatment of children.* New York: International Universities Press, 1950. (Originally published 1946)

Freud, A. *Normality and pathology in childhood,* International Universities Press, New York, 1965.

Freud, A. Indications and contraindications of child analysis. *Psychoanalytic Study of the Child,* 1968, *23,* 37–46.

Freud, A. Termination of child analysis. In *The writings of Anna Freud* (Vol. 7). New York: International Universities Press, 1971, pp. 3–21.

Freud, S. Two encyclopedia articles. In J. Strachey (Ed. and Trans.), *The standard edition of the complete psychological works of Sigmund Freud* (Vol. 18). London: Hogarth Press, 1955, pp. 235–263. (Originally published 1928)

Freud, S. Constructions in analysis. In J. Strachey (Ed. and Trans.), *Standard edition* (Vol. 23). London: Hogarth Press, 1964, pp. 257–269. (Originally published 1937)

Glover, E. The "vehicle" of interpretations. *International Journal of Psycho-Analysis,* 1930, *11,* 340–344.

Greenacre, P. Re-evaluation of the process of working through. *International Journal of Psycho-Analysis,* 1956, *37,* 439–444.

Harley, M. Transference developments in a five-year-old child. In E. R. Geleerd (Ed.), *The child analyst at work.* New York: International Universities Press, 1967, pp. 115–141.

Hartmann, H. Technical implications of ego psychology. *Psychoanalytic Quarterly,* 1951, *20,* 31–43.

Haworth, M. R. (Ed.). *Child psychotherapy.* New York: Basic Books, 1964.

Hine, F. R., Werman, D. S., & Simpson, D. M. Effectiveness of psychotherapy: Problems of research on complex phenomena. *American Journal of Psychiatry,* 1982, *139,* 204–208.

Ivey, A. E. *Counselling and psychotherapy: Skills, theories and practice.* Englewood Cliffs, N.J.: Prentice-Hall, 1980.

Karasu, T. B. Psychotherapies: An overview. *American Journal of Psychiatry,* 1977, *134,* 851–863.

Kris, E. Ego psychology and interpretation in psychoanalytic therapy. *Psychoanalytic Quarterly,* 1951, *20,* 15–30.

Langs, R. *Psychotherapy.* New York: Jason Aronson, 1982.

Levitt, E. E. Research on psychotherapy with children. In A. E. Bergin & S. L. Garfield (Eds.), *Handbook of psychotherapy and behavior change.* New York: Wiley-Interscience, 1971, pp. 474–494.

Lewis, M. Interpretation in child analysis: Developmental considerations. *Journal of the American Academy of Child Psychiatry,* 1974, *13,* 32.

Loewenstein, R. M. The problem of interpretation. *Psychoanalytic Quarterly,* 1951, *20,* 1–14.

London, P. *The modes and morals of psychotherapy.* New York: Holt, Rinehart & Winston, 1964.

London, P., & Klerman, G. L. Evaluating psychotherapy. *American Journal of Psychiatry,* 1982, *139,* 709–717.

Looney, J. G. Treatment planning in child psychiatry. *Journal of the American Academy of Child Psychiatry,* 1984, *23,* 529–536.

Luborsky, L., Singer, B., & Luborsky, L. Comparative studies of psychotherapies: Is it true that "Everyone has won and all must have prizes"? *Archives of General Psychiatry,* 1975, *32,* 995–1008.

MacGuire, P. Teaching medical students to interview psychiatric patients. *Bulletin of the Royal College of Psychiatry,* 1980, *4,* 188–190.

Marks, I. Personal psychotherapy in the training of a psychiatrist? *Bulletin of Royal College Psychiatry,* 1982, *6,* 39–40.

Matarazzo, R. Research on the teaching and learning of psychotherapeutic skills. In S. Garfield & A. R. Bergin (Eds.), *Handbook of psychotherapy and behavior modification* (2nd ed.). New York: Wiley, 1978, pp. 941–966.

McDermott, J. F., & Chan, W. F. Stage-related models of psychotherapy with children. *Journal of the American Academy of Child Psychiatry,* 1984, *23,* 537–543.

McDermott, J. F., & Harrison, S. I. (Eds.). *Psychiatric treatment of children.* New York: Jason Aronson, 1977.

Neubauer, P. B. Psychoanalysis of the preschool child. In B. B. Wolman, (Ed.), *Handbook of child psychoanalysis.* New York: Van Nostrand Reinhold, 1972, pp. 221–252.

Paolino, T. J. *Psychoanalytic psychotherapy.* New York: Brunner/Mazel, 1981.

Parloff, M. B. Psychotherapy research evidence and reimbursement decisions: Bambi meets Godzilla. *American Journal of Psychiatry,* 1982, *139,* 718–727.

Piaget, J. *The child's conception of the world.* New York: Harcourt Brace, 1929.

Reid, J. R., & Finesinger, J. E. The role of insight in psychotherapy. *American Journal of Psychiatry*, 1952, *108*, 726–734.

Richfield, J. An analysis of the concept of insight. *Psychoanalytic Quarterly*, 1954, *23*, 390–408.

Satterfield, J., Satterfield, B., & Cantwell, D. Multimodal treatment: A two-year evaluation of 61 hyperactive boys. *Archives of General Psychiatry*, 1980, *37*, 915–919.

Schaefer, C. E., & Millman, H. L. *Therapies for children*. San Francisco: Jossey-Bass, 1977.

Shaffer, D. Notes on psychotherapy research among children and adolescents. *Journal of the American Academy of Child Psychiatry*, 1984, *23*, 552–561.

Strachey, J. The nature of the therapeutic action of psycho-analysis. *International Journal of Psycho-Analysis*, 1934, *15*, 127–159.

Strupp, H. H., & Hadley, S. W. A tripartite model of mental health and therapeutic outcomes. *American Psychologist*, 1977, *32*, 187–196.

Strupp, H., & Hadley, S. Specific vs. nonspecific factors in psychotherapy. *Archives of General Psychiatry*, 1979, *36*, 1125–1136.

Train, G. F. Flight into health. *American Journal of Psychotherapy*, 1953, *7*, 463–486.

Varma, V. (Ed.). *Psychotherapy today*. London: Constable, 1974.

Winnicott, D. W. *Therapeutic consultations in child psychiatry*. New York: Basic Books, 1971.

Witmer, H. L. (Ed.). *Psychiatric interviews with children*. Cambridge: Harvard University Press, 1946.

Wolman, B. B., Egan, J., & Ross, A. O. (Eds.). *Handbook of treatment of mental disorders in childhood and adolescence*. Englewood Cliffs, N.J.: Prentice-Hall, 1978.

AUTHOR INDEX

257

SUBJECT INDEX

265

ANXIETY DISORDERS OF CHILDHOOD